WOMEN AND KINSHIP

Comparative Perspectives on Gender in Asia

WOMEN AND KINSHIP

Comparative Perspectives on Gender in Asia

Ramakant Tiwari

MD PUBLICATIONS PVT LTD
NEW DELHI
www.mdppl.com

Published by :

MD Publications Pvt Ltd
"MD House", 11, Darya Ganj,
New Delhi-110 002
Phone : +91-11-45355555
E-mail : contact@mdppl.com
Website : www.mdppl.com

ISBN : 978-81-7533-251-5

Published and Printed by Mr. Pranav Gupta on behalf of **MD Publications Pvt Ltd** at Printext, New Delhi.

PREFACE

Kinship may be broadly defined as a system of special relationships among a certain people. This definition, of course, is far from being satisfactory, for individuals may relate to each other and not be relatives. For decades, anthropologists believed that biology is the determinant factor of kinship: two individuals are relatives inasmuch as they share a biological nexus. But, it became increasingly evident that many of the so called 'relatives' do not necessarily have a biological connection. Virtually all cultures have instituted strong parent-child relationships, husband-wife bonds, man-woman division, and special relationships, cultural roles, and statuses, according to one's biological connection with other individuals. In a word, all cultures know of some form of kinship relationship, for the incest taboo is universal, regulating sexual relationships and establishing differences among people according to their kinship status.

Kinship is one of the most basic principles for organizing individuals into social groups. A group can be defined as two or more humans that interact with one another, accept expectations and obligations as members of the group, and share a common identity. By this definition, society can be viewed as a large group, though most social groups are considerably smaller, roles, categories, and genealogy. Family relations can be represented concretely (mother, brother, grandfather) or abstractly after degrees of relationship. A relationship may have relative purchase (e.g., father is one regarding a child), or reflect an absolute (e.g., status difference between a mother and a childless woman). Degrees of relationship are not identical to heirship or legal succession.

The incest taboo may be considered the core of kinship systems. Inasmuch as restrictions on sexual partners come up, culture creates a system of differentiated relationships that assigns a specific place to each individual, according to his position in the larger system. The incest taboo gives rise to the first great kinship differentiation among individuals: there is a group of people one is forbidden to have intercourse with (relatives), and a group of people one is permitted to have intercourse with (non-relatives).

A worthy kinship vision will reclaim living from the realm of habit and necessity to make it an art form we are all capable of practicing and refining. But there is no pretense that all this can be achieved over night. Nor is there reason to think a single kind of partner-parenting institution is best for all. While the contemporary nuclear family, particularly if it is the overwhelmingly present living pattern or at least the most admired, has proven all too compatible with patriarchal norms, a different kind of nuclear family will no doubt evolve along with a host of other kinship forms as people experiment with how to achieve the goals of feminism.

I am very grateful to Mr. Pranav Gupta, Director of MD Publications Pvt Ltd, New Delhi, for his kind cooperation and support for this book.

Ramakant Tiwari

CONTENTS

1

Kinship and Family Organization

WOMEN IN PRE-MODERN SOUTHEAST ASIA

The eleven countries of Southeast Asia include over 550 million people. Despite great linguistic and cultural diversity, the region is characterized by the relatively favorable position of women in comparison with neighboring East or South Asia. This has been explained by several factors: traditionally, kinship was traced though both maternal and paternal lines; a daughter was not a financial burden because of the widespread practice of bride price; a married couple often lived with or near the wife's parents; women had prominent roles in indigenous ritual; their labor was essential in agricultural, and they dominated local markets. Over time, however, the rise of centralized states and the spread of imported philosophies and religions (Confucianism, Daoism, Buddhism, Islam, and Christianity) increasingly privileged males and stressed female subordination.

Although such influences were most noticeable among the elite, the strength of local traditions was always a moderating force. In the nineteenth century Southeast Asia's economic resources and strategic position between India and China led to increasing European involvement. By the 1890s the entire region except for Siam (Thailand) was under European control. In some areas women were recruited as cheap wage labor on plantations (tea, sugar, tobacco, rubber) and in processing factories. At the village level colonial regimes strengthened the male position as head of the household and "reformed" customary laws that had given women considerable autonomy. Similar trends can be found in Siam, the only non-colonized country, where legal codification strengthened patrilineality. These developments encouraged a preference for sons rather than daughters.

Nonetheless, women were still influential in community life, at times even leading anti-colonial rebellions. Increasing female literacy (especially in the Philippines) and exposure to Western feminism encouraged elite women to confront issues of gender inequality. From the late nineteenth century nationalist movements developed across Southeast Asia. Male leaders focused on political independence, but educated women were equally concerned with polygamy, divorce, domestic abuse and the financial responsibilities of fathers.

For the most part, however, politicized women accepted the male argument that attention to "female" concerns should be delayed until after independence was attained. Yet despite active involvement in anti-colonial movements, sometimes as fighters, but more often as strike organizers, journalists, couriers and clandestine agents, women were viewed as auxiliaries rather than partners. Such attitudes were still evident in the independence movements that exploded after the surrender of the Japanese, who occupied most of Southeast Asia between 1942 and 1945.

WOMEN IN CONTEMPORARY SOUTHEAST ASIA

The end of World War II signaled the demise of European colonialism in Southeast Asia. Theoretically, the independent states that emerged over the next fifteen years were committed to gender equality, but this has rarely been translated into reality. In recent years the number of women holding public office has increased, especially in local government, but only in the Philippines has female representation in national government risen above 10 per cent. When women do manage to enter the political arena, they often find themselves marginalized in a male-dominated culture, with real power remaining in men's hands.

The few individuals who have attained the highest political offices (such as President in the Philippines and Indonesia) have done so because they are the daughter or wife of a famous man. They have not become advocates of women's issues, for this would risk alienating their male colleagues or the male electorate. Greater female involvement in politics is impeded by the way candidates are recruited as well as entrenched attitudes that see women's primary role as that of wife and mother. Gender stereotypes that favor males over females are often reinforced in school textbooks and are sometimes encouraged by religious teachings.

For example, Buddhists still believe that rebirth as a woman rather than a man indicates that less merit was accrued in past lives. Southeast Asian Islam has traditionally been very tolerant, but over the last twenty years there has been greater stress on "correct" dress (notably head covering) and public behavior. Although all Southeast Asian countries except Laos and Vietnam have signed the Convention on the Elimination of All Forms of Discrimination Against Women and have made advances promoting gender equality, it is difficult to change the preference for sons, especially in Vietnam with its strong Confucian heritage. It is not easy to generalize about the economic position of Southeast Asian women because of the gap in development between Timor Lorosae, Cambodia and Laos (among the poorest countries in the world), and prosperous Singapore and Brunei Darussalam.

Nonetheless, the continuing acceptance of the idea that a woman can generate and control her own income is still evident, although women receive less pay than men for the same work and the options for unskilled workers are limited. In poorer countries and impoverished regions this is apparent in the prevalence of prostitution and the disturbing trafficking of women. From the mid 1960s, however, as Southeast Asian countries gradually shifted to export-oriented economies, lower-paid women have become essential to factory work. In consequence, women have been more active in labor movements. As overseas domestic workers, they have also been increasingly important to national economies, remitting large amounts of money to their families. Because of world-wide shortages, qualified women can find employment abroad in skilled occupations such as nursing.

Obtaining vocational skills and academic qualifications is far more possible than hitherto as Southeast Asian women gain greater access to education. With the exception of Cambodia and Laos, the numbers of women progressing to post-secondary training is also rising, and in Brunei, Malaysia, Thailand and the Philippines there are more female graduates than males; the rates for Vietnam and Indonesia are almost equal. The expansion in education has contributed to the blossoming of female-oriented Non-Governmental Organizations (NGOs) since the 1980s, which have given the knowledge and organization skills that equip them to argue for issues. Despite the region's economic, political and cultural diversity, Southeast Asian countries generally fare well in measures of human development. The heritage of relatively favorable gender relations and the resilience and pragmatism of local societies indicate that Southeast Asian women can look towards a promising future.

INCREASING CONTRIBUTIONS AND PERSISTING DRUDGERY

Rural women throughout Asia and the Pacific region make critical contributions to household production and consequently to household and national food security. Although the specific nature of their contribution varies among the various Asian and Pacific countries, clearly the majority of rural women take on an increasing share of household labour and their lives are characterized by mounting drudgery. Various studies produced in different countries in the region provide important findings on gender roles to guide policies and programme interventions that will improve the productivity of rural households. The lack of a systematic synthesis of the findings hinders efforts to build a realistic scenario of rural women's roles in household food security.

However, a general pattern of gender roles emerges from these studies indicating that both rural men and rural women in Asia and the Pacific contribute to farm and home production. Gender roles vary within and between countries determined by agro-ecological systems and crops grown, farming systems adopted, linkages with livestock and fish production and opportunities for off-farm occupations in the rural economy. This analysis of rural women's situation in household production synthesizes information from diverse sources into a framework portraying the diversity and complexity of rural women's contributions.

The framework presents linkages among gender specific contributions, drudgery and resource access constraints within the household and community setting. Rural women's role in household production is considered in terms of farm production, home production, off-farm production and community production. The foundations of rural women's contributions can be seen in terms of labour and managerial inputs, as well as local and traditional knowledge and expertise.

In the context of economic, political, sociocultural and ethnic diversity in Asia and the Pacific region, the factors shaping rural women's work and their economic and social contributions can be grouped in two broad categories, namely those imbedded in the community and those embedded within the household. In the nexus of a community, the economic production base determines rural women's work in the various segments of production. In most countries, rural women actively contribute to community production thus improving social linkages and kinship relationships and facilitating resource exchange in times of need.

In the household nexus, the traditional gender role ideology, founded on culture and religious tenets, determines rural women's participation in household production. Contributions made by women within the household increasingly are affected by changes external to the household. For instance, rural poverty has acted as a push factor whereas new economic opportunities outside the household have emerged as pull factors encouraging rural women to cross customary gender role boundaries and to participate in the economy outside the household, often in farm production and off-farm production.

Yet although recent trends in agricultural diversification accompanied by commercialisation and marketisation have generated opportunities for off-farm paid work, rural women's poor educational attainment, inadequate training and social immobility often have prevented them from responding to these opportunities. Even though short-term internal migration induced by subsistence economies and seasonal dimensions of agriculture production sometimes bring new work patterns for rural women, certain gender roles in household production tend to remain inexorably fixed. Across the region, work inside the home space that involves family care giving is almost always seen as women's work. The women are primary care givers and domestic workers within the household space in every stage of the life cycle and this responsibility of care giving is expanded to serve the community's needs too.

RURAL WOMEN'S INCREASING ECONOMIC CONTRIBUTIONS

In general, rural women's work patterns are marked by change and continuity as well as flexibility and rigidity. Change and flexibility are characterized by women taking on new roles in farm production, off-farm production and community production to ensure the family's access to food and household resources. Continuity and rigidity relate to social norms that define gender roles and dictate that rural women and girls should assume home production responsibilities in rural households.

The intrahousehold decisions on allocation of labour often are biased and relegate domestic tasks to women and girls. In the region, tradition driven socialization defines the tasks and taboos in the economic and social spheres among rural women. Increasingly, faced with economic pressures, gender roles may become flexible to enable women to engage in work traditionally regarded as belonging in the male domain. However, the rigid gender role definitions dictate that men should not perform household tasks. A pattern of gender roles marked by diversity in flexibility and change as well as convergence in rigidity and continuity is described with illustrations from various countries.

SOUTH ASIAN RURAL WOMEN

In Bangladesh, participation in economic activities varies considerably according to gender, the type of activity and the place of residence. Rural women traditionally have played an important role in a wide range of income-generating activities. These rural production activities include post-harvesting, cow fattening and milking, goat farming, backyard poultry rearing, pisciculture, agriculture, horticulture, food processing, cane and bamboo works, silk reeling, handloom weaving, garment making, fishnet making, coir production and handicrafts. A significant number of rural women, particularly from extremely poor landless households, also engage in paid labour in construction, earthwork and field-based agricultural work, activities that traditionally have fallen within the male domain.

The tradition of female seclusion is overlooked to provide for the economic needs of the family. Unpaid family workers, among whom women are disproportionately represented, are a major source of labour in the agriculture sector in Bangladesh. One study of intrahousehold organization of rice production (based on a relatively small sample) found that the extent to which male and female household members are involved in irrigated agriculture and irrigation management is related to the amount of land owned by the household and to religion. It suggests that female family labour plays a more important role in rice production than male family labour, and points to differences among households in different economic categories.

For instance, a higher per cent age of female labourers from middle class households are involved in rice production (mostly transplanting and crop processing tasks) compared to marginal farmer households. In the middle strata, women in Hindu male-headed households contribute 54 per cent of all labour in rice production, compared to 31 per cent in Muslim male-headed households. When a comparison is made of labour allocation based on tasks, a modified labour pattern emerges. Apart from the traditional crop processing tasks, female family labour also is used for making seedbeds, uprooting seedlings and transplanting, fertilising, weeding and harvesting, all traditional male activities. Women, almost equal to the contribution of male family labour, carry out some 40 to 50 per cent of field irrigation and non-farm water management.

In Bhutan agriculture is the primary economic activity in rural areas; other dominant activities are kitchen garden and livestock. Rural women engage in main economic activities and are main workers of supplementary activities with some differences among the locations. Certain regions have more women main agricultural workers than men with distinct divisions of labour on gender lines.

In India, the national rural female work participation rate is 22 per cent according to the National Sample Survey Organization (1996). However, this national average masks significant regional variations among states as a result of diversity among population groups, agro-ecological systems and the social and economic organization of production. The level of mechanization in the agriculture sector also helps to explain the variations in women's participation in the rural labour force. For instance, in Punjab where the Green Revolution ushered in prosperity and where agriculture is highly mechanized the rural female work participation rate is the lowest. By comparison, Andra Pradesh, which depends on women for labour-intensive crops like cotton and groundnut that are grown in dry conditions, shows the highest level of rural female work participation.

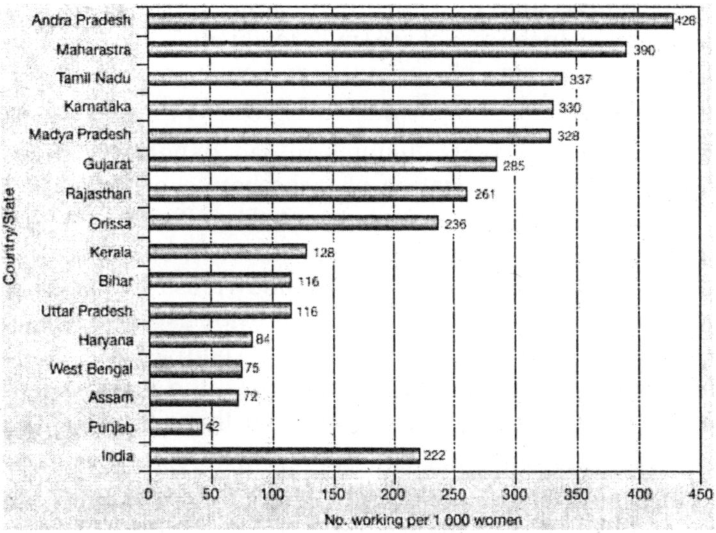

Fig: *India: Participation of rural women in India in the labour force*

Social customs, traditions and cultural considerations as well as cropping patterns and cultivation practices affect the type of work performed by men and women in India. A study by IFAD in the tribal areas of Madya Pradesh in 1997 recognized male-female sharing of domestic and productive work. It found that both women and men work in agriculture, collect and sell non-timber forest products during certain months of the year, and engage in wage labour. However, this equality in work activities was not reflected in decision-making concerning income allocation in which men played a dominant role.

Another study that covered three ecologically distinct and fragile regions in India concluded that while agriculture is a household enterprise, social norms demarcate the division of labour based on sex and age. In general, land preparation and ploughing are seen as the responsibility of men, and activities like transplanting and weeding are regarded as women's jobs, whereas both men and women perform activities like harvesting and post-harvesting. However, in certain areas, at times of heavy demand for labour, women also undertake some of the heavier traditional male activities like land preparation. In the case of little millet cultivation in the Kolli Hills, women are responsible for most agronomic practices and post-harvest operations including seed storage, supply and exchange.

In the Maldives, changes in the fishery sector have reinforced the segregation of tasks between the sexes and exacerbated the inequalities between them. Traditionally, men were engaged in fishing and women in small-scale fish processing. The resulting product, known as "Maldives fish", was recognized as a delicacy in countries like Sri Lanka and exported widely. At the time when "Maldives fish" formed the country's main merchandise export, the participation of women in the labour force was greater than 50 per cent.

This was one of the highest rates in the developing world at the time. Since then, modernization of the fishing industry has enhanced opportunities for fishermen, enabling them to increase their catch and sell it directly to collection vessels, which subsequently export it in frozen form or give it to canning factories for processing. Consequently, opportunities for women to engage in fish processing were seriously curtailed, causing the female labour force participation rate to drop to 21 per cent in 1985, and 19 per cent in 1996. At the same time, women became more heavily involved in subsistence agriculture, practiced as home gardens in small plots, and seed selection.

A substantial proportion of Nepalese women (40 per cent) are economically active. Most of these women are employed in the agriculture sector, the majority working as unpaid family labourers in subsistence agriculture characterized by low technology and primitive farming practices. Indeed, with as men increasingly move out of farming, agriculture is becoming increasingly feminized. In addition to a culturally based division of labour, women's work load has increased because of:

i. Geographic and infrastructure factors;
ii. Out-migration, and
iii. New activities promoted under development projects (IFAD, 1997).

Important changes in the traditional agropastoral economy and increases in non-agricultural activity have created formal and non-formal employment opportunities in the export-led industrial market which relies heavily on low wage female labour. This new phenomenon has arisen in response to a mix of basic survival needs and new desires generated by increased exposure to the world beyond the village. A nationwide study has identified three resource development strategies - the family farm economy, the local market economy and short term migration - adopted by rural families. About 67 per cent of women participate in the family farm economy and 59 per cent in the local market economy, whereas 75 per cent engage in short term migration. It should be further noted that the strategy adopted by women varies according to busy and slack agriculture periods.

"In Nepal, in addition to a culturally based division of labour, women's work load has increased because of i) geographic and infrastructure factors; ii) out-migration, and iii) new activities promoted under development projects."

In Pakistan, women are key players in the agriculture sector which employs almost 12 million women in the production of crops, vegetables and livestock. The cotton crop, accounting for half of national export earnings, depends heavily on female labour. Women have the exclusive responsibility for cotton picking, exposing themselves in the process to health hazards emanating from the intensive use of pesticides. One study on gender in Pakistan found overwhelming evidence of a division of labour based on gender and family status in which men are responsible for "market" work (such as farming, herding and other income generating activities) and women are responsible for "home production" activities.

"South Asian rural women contribute to agriculture and rural production as unpaid family labour in the farm and in the home as well as increasingly as agriculture wage labourers and producers of crafts and processed products. By comparison, in many parts of South Asia (notably Bangladesh and India), purdah and other cultural norms traditionally have restricted women's movement and limited their participation in fish harvesting."

Since the days when women from southern India were recruited to fulfil the labour demands of colonial plantations in Sri Lanka and thus become the first wage earners in the country, women have played an important role in the agriculture sector. In 1997, about 42 per cent of the female labour force in Sri Lanka was engaged in agricultural activities. Gender roles in *Chena* (slash and burn cultivation), rice paddies and home gardens vary according to the cultivation practiced in these systems of production. Whereas men participate extensively in land preparation, sowing, the application of chemical fertilisers and pesticides and marketing, women take on activities related to transplanting, post-harvesting and household level processing of home garden produce.

Yet despite the contribution of women to the sector, their role has tended to be seen as secondary to that of men. Consequently, women farmers in Sri Lanka are normally seen as "farmers' wives" rather than as economic producers in their own right. The failure to develop local industries in the rural sector has further limited women's access to off-farm employment opportunities.

"Women farmers in Sri Lanka are normally seen as "farmers' wives" rather than economic producers in their own right."

SOUTHEAST ASIAN RURAL WOMEN

According to the Cambodia Human Development Report, 55 per cent of the labour force in the agriculture, forestry and fishery sectors is made up of women. Another report finds that nearly 80 per cent of workers in the agriculture labour force are engaged primarily in subsistence agriculture; women comprise 56 per cent of the primary workforce in subsistence agriculture and 54 per cent of the workforce in market oriented agriculture. Most of these women are unpaid family workers. The organization of labour appears to be centred on household availability of labour, exchange labour and hired labour. As such, men and women share many farm activities (such as carrying water and fuel wood and tending livestock) within the wide variety of tasks carried out by household members.

In Indonesia, women represent the mainstay of rural households, providing family as well as farm labour. Agriculture accounts for the highest share of rural employment, with some 63 women working in agriculture per 100 men. Since most rural households control small amounts of land or have no land at all, rural women often seek to supplement household income and food security through off-farm employment in small and medium enterprises, some of which have links to agricultural production. In Bali, women are active in fish marketing, but in South Sulawesi men completely control marketing.

In Lao PDR, studies have recorded that women and girls perform 50 to 70 per cent of agriculture and productive tasks in addition to household activities. Women farmers produce mostly for household consumption, and rural women obtain as much as 30 per cent of the family diet and household needs from foraging (UNICEF, 1996). Gender roles and the involvement of women in household decision-making processes related to agriculture and aquac ulture vary by region and ethnic group.

Malaysia, one of the East Asian success stories, experienced a fundamental shift in employment patterns over the last 15 years. Though previously major sources of Malaysian women's employment was agriculture, forestry, livestock and fishing, these sectors in 1995 employed just 15.9 per cent of female workers and 20.3 per cent of male workers. Malaysian women have taken advantage of the economic transformation to move into relatively better paid opportunities in other sectors. At present, the manufacturing sector is the single largest employer of women, followed by community work, the public sector, social services, trade and agriculture. Agriculture sector data from various studies show different participation levels of women according to different crops.

Women are most extensively involved in field crops (working on estates and smallholdings) such as rubber, cocoa, coconut, coffee, tea and other diversified short term cash crops cultivation and mixed farming. Very few are directly involved in oil palms, except to work as labourers for weeding. In irrigated rice cultivation areas, mechanization has displaced female labour to a large extent. A study conducted by Kumi *et al.*, (1996) shows that despite mechanization, male farmers still depend on family labour for certain farm activities. Women's participation in rice production areas has declined. In other sub sectors of agriculture, however, (apart from oil palm and irrigated, mechanized rice production), the per cent age and extent of women's involvement is still high.

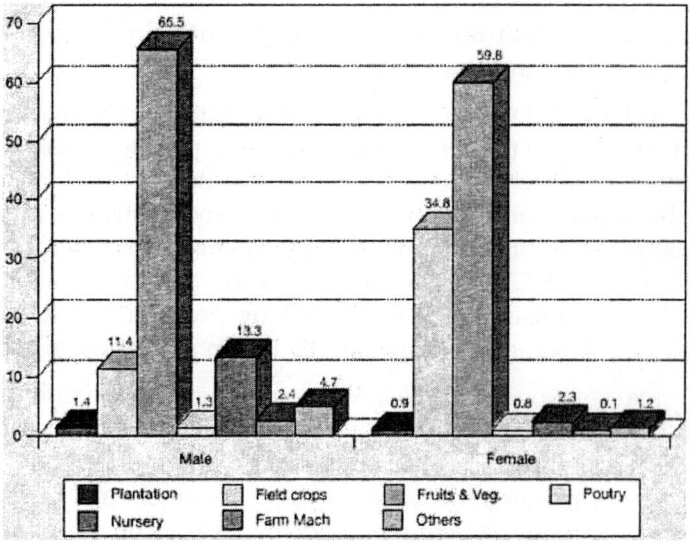

Fig: *Malaysia: Percentage distribution of employed persons in selected agriculture occupations by sex, 1995*

Findings from a study completed by FAO in Myanmar, record rural women's key contributions to household food security marked by diversity in work patterns in agriculture and food production, but there is evidence of gender role flexibility as occasion demands. Traditionally, men's agriculture activities include land preparation, ploughing and levelling fields, whereas sowing, transplanting, weeding and reaping are women's work. Post-harvest activities of threshing, winnowing, seed management and transporting grains from field to home is the work of both men and women. Women from poorer households are more involved in agriculture fieldwork than those from less poor families.

Poorer women are also heavily involved as family farm workers and agricultural labourers to contribute to family income and food security. Women also participate in the cultivation of secondary crops and work as waged agricultural labourers in cash crop production. Home garden cultivation is the responsibility of women. The majority of working women in the Philippines - more than 50 per cent in 1997 - continues to work in the agricultural sector. Women also dominate the rural informal employment market. Data from five rice-growing villages indicate that women tend to work as much as men in both farm and non-farm activities. It is now documented and recognized that the contributions of female family members are higher in rainfed and upland rice farming environments whereas the contributions of hired female labourers are higher in irrigated rice environments.

The contribution of women to livelihood appears to be evident in the sweet potato-based livelihood systems of the Philippines. They have been known to contribute a more significant part of the labour force in sweet potato production than in any other crop. They also are active traders of sweet potato in local markets. In Thailand, women play a major role in rural production systems and income generation; in 1995 about 40 per cent of women worked in agriculture. All members of smallholder households, regardless of age and sex, participate in agricultural production. Yet the participation of rural women in the labour force is highest - approximately 80 per cent - among older age groups (30-34, 35-39, and 40-49 years).

As opportunities for wage and self-employment outside rural households have increased along with economic transformation, the participation of rural women in the economy has begun to resemble that of urban women. A study in one neighbourhood of Bangkok confirmed the importance of women in marketing agriculture produce. A survey of ten agricultural produce markets indicated that about 80 per cent of fruit and vegetables stalls were owned by women. In a study of gender roles and technology needs in six villages of Thailand it was found that rural women in all of the villages played a major role in all aspects of paddy production, including seed preparation, transplanting, weeding, fertilizer application, harvesting and seed preparation.

Given the lack of appropriate technologies for most paddy farming activities, women perform labour-intensive tasks with the use of simple and traditional technologies. By comparison, men are responsible for those aspects of paddy production that are mechanized such as use of the tractor for ploughing. Similarly, in orchard (such as guava and mango) and cash crop production (such as peanuts and mung beans), women engage in labour-intensive, simple and low prestige tasks, whereas men are responsible for mechanized tasks. For instance, in cassava production women are responsible for weeding, hoeing and digging at harvest time.

"In Southeast Asia countries like Malaysia, Thailand and Vietnam, women normally play an important role in processing and marketing fish."

In Vietnam, data from the recent Vietnam Living Standards Survey have demonstrated the extensive participation of women in the agriculture sector. The data show that the contribution of rural women exceeds that of rural men in livestock production, and equals that of men in crop production. The survey data further revealed that in the five-year period between 1992/93 and 1997/98, wage employment increased from 26 per cent to 32 per cent among male and female adults in the 18 to 64 year age group. Moreover, in the case of women, most of this increase occurred in rural areas; there was no change in urban areas. Another recent study corroborates these findings regarding women's contributions to rural production systems and reiterates the major role of women in livestock rearing. It found that women's labour accounts for an average of 69 per cent of a household's total labour.

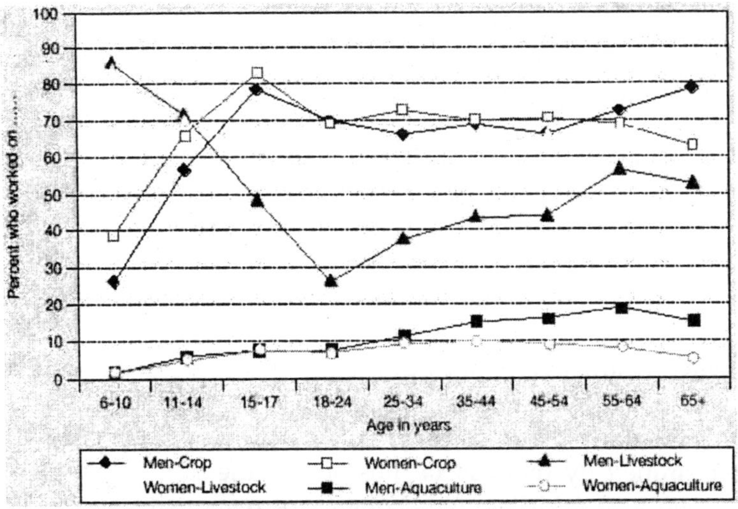

Fig: *Participation of the Labour Force in Crop Production, Livestock Maintenance and Aquaculture in Vietnam*

EAST ASIAN RURAL WOMEN

In China, large variations in agroecological characteristics, crops grown and livelihood options result in wide differences in the situation of rural women. The pace of economic growth and the move towards a market-based economy has quickened during recent years, bringing a number of changes that have had both positive and negative influences on the lives of rural women throughout the country. Although some rural women have benefited from emerging economic opportunities in the expanding economy, others have encountered threats to their rural livelihoods and a greater struggle in their daily lives. An IFAD study found that rural women in China spend more time in their reproductive role (56.7 per cent) than in their productive role (43.3 per cent).

It is important to note, though, that there were considerable variations in time allocations among the provinces studied, and that time use patterns varied significantly by age and education. For instance, women over the age of 50 spend most of their day on housework, as physical labour in the fields is considered too taxing. Middle-aged women play a key role in the home and share crop and livestock activities with men. As in many places, younger women often prefer alternatives to farming whenever possible. The study also recognized seasonal differences in time use patterns in rural areas. For example, women might work from 8 to 10 hours in the fields during the busiest agricultural season, and they engage in green house production and other income generating activities during less busy periods.

A case study in the mountainous Yunnan Province found that women perform 80 per cent of agricultural work and engage in all activities (including cultivation, crop management, harvesting and marketing) with the exception of ploughing. The involvement of women in agriculture appeared to be determined by their social position in the family. Younger women and middle-aged women are responsible for most agriculture and forestry activities (such as collecting fuel wood, non-timber products and pine leaves for barn yard manure) during the slacker farming season from November to January. Women older than 60 years do not perform any agricultural activities, while girl children help with household chores and look after their younger sisters or brothers. The efforts of boy children are relatively less structured.

"In China, large variations in agro-ecological characteristics, crops grown and livelihood options result in wide differences in the situation of rural women. The pace of economic growth and the move towards a market-based economy has quickened during recent years, bringing with it a number of changes that have had both positive and negative influences on the lives of rural women. Although a segment of rural women has benefited from emerging economic opportunities in the expanding economy, others have encountered threats to their rural livelihoods and a greater struggle in their daily lives."

A study from a different province in China found that women are not uniformly excluded from off-farm employment opportunities and that economic development does not uniformly increase gender inequalities within Chinese households. It observed that although men are more likely than women to obtain off-farm employment, women's opportunities for off-farm work improve significantly when the coexistence of local and regional marketisation creates a shortage of male workers and compels employers to hire women. It further noted that the relative size of contributions to household income for male and female non-farm workers narrows incrementally with increased marketisation. At the same time, women who are left to perform agricultural work are more likely to become heads of household, a position that brings greater household decision-making power to female family members.

Nomadic households in Mongolia play a part in the productive and reproductive economies; rights and responsibilities within households are differentiated by gender. Although traditional nomadic herding maintained clear distinctions between men's and women's work marked by a mix of cooperation and specialization, the emergence of privatization has blurred some of the role distinctions with more women and boys taking on work that traditionally was perceived to be in the male domain. Privatization also provided opportunities to increase herd size and expand milk processing, traditionally the work of women in the *ger,* which in turn has resulted in more work for women. Although the volume of paid and unpaid productive work that is regarded as women's responsibility has increased, some traditional work divisions are strictly maintained. As a result of this flexibility in some work activities (where women and boys take on men's work) and continuing rigidity in others (where women's tasks remain theirs alone despite an increase in workload), the overall work load has intensified for women.

CENTRAL ASIAN RURAL WOMEN

In 1998, Kazakhstan's rural areas incomes predominantly depends on the agricultural sector which employs approximately half of the female rural labour force. In 1998, women accounted for about 3513 million of the agricultural population (total of 7107 million) which accounted for 46.2 per cent of the entire female population. The wages for agricultural workers is the lowest among all sectors of employment. Economic difficulties complicate the lives of rural women.

Economic reforms in Kyrgyzstan affect the economic conditions of rural women. In 1997, female employment in the agriculture sector was 37.5 per cent which had decreased slightly since 1991. Home farming helps to ease economic hardship. The self-employment trend shows that women work in home farms, take the produce to market and sell their home garden produce. Most women also take up dairy and animal farming.

In Tajikistan, provisional official statistics show that women's relative share of agriculture, forestry and fishing increased from 18.8 per cent in 1991 to 29.3 per cent in 1998, and that women earned an average monthly wage of just $6 in 1998. The agriculture sector employs 54.1 per cent women and 46.2 per cent men. Women make up about 8.5 per cent of collective farmers. Employment status compared by type of enterprise and ownership shows that under the collective farmer category 29.9 per cent men and 40.6 per cent women are represented; under the private farm category, 2.2 per cent men and 2.4 per cent women are included. Women's low wages are a function of women's occupational segregation into low paid occupations such as education and health and low skilled occupations such as agriculture.

Women in the rural areas of Turkmenistan make up 22.2 per cent of the employed labour force. The main areas of employment for rural women are farmer associations, farms and the informal sector. Women account for 64 per cent of home farm workers and almost 71 per cent of household workers. Hence, widespread home farming and lease of agricultural land result in the use of women and children as unpaid labour.

In the Republic of Uzbekistan, in 1998, most of the employment was still found in the rural areas with 39 per cent employed in agriculture; men accounted for 60.3 per cent and women for 39.7 per cent of the total agriculture and forestry workforce. In agriculture, men work as highly qualified machine operators whereas women remain unqualified, seasonal labourers. Female employment in agriculture was high. Privatization has not provided rural income and employment opportunities due to the interplay of complex factors. Women, however, have taken advantage of other opportunities such as food processing and the sale of agriculture products from their home gardening.

In the countries of the Pacific Islands, smallholders represent the largest production unit, producing goods for use in the home, for exchange, and for sale in domestic and export markets. Traditionally, women and girls assumed primary responsibility for food production and family food security by growing crops in homestead gardens, rearing small livestock, producing handicrafts and engaging in other value added activities (such as copra making, fish drying, weaving, coconut oil production, preparation of traditional medicines, planting materials and seeds). Men, on the other hand, engaged in cash cropping. Over time, as cash cropping acquired a higher status for its economic value and contribution to national development, the various kinds of agricultural work performed by women remained associated with food security and were regarded as somewhat lesser in importance in the emerging economic model.

Although some reports indicate that agricultural production may be declining in the Pacific, the limited data available show that women's role in agriculture is increasing throughout the entire production and post production chain. The most current data on women and men's work in the family smallholder system comes from the 1999 Samoa Agricultural Survey, which indicates that women of all ages are engaged in farm management, production and marketing. According to the survey, the overwhelming majority of farm operators are male (17, 993) as opposed to female; two out of every five farm labourers are female; women are responsible for almost half of agricultural trading and women outnumber men in handicraft production by a ratio of nine to one. Given the similarities with neighbouring countries, this data set reinforces the view that sharing tasks by gender is the norm in family systems throughout the Pacific Islands.

The findings of the Samoa Agricultural Census further reflect the role of women in waged agricultural employment and point to new trends for women to become involved in part-time farming. Women in part-time employment spend an average of 58 hours per month in agriculture, which is close to the amount of time recorded for agricultural workers (63 hours) and more than that of male part-time workers (53 hours). Women in full-time waged employment spend roughly 8 hours per week working in agriculture in addition to their full-time jobs. These trends, which also have been observed in neighbouring Pacific Island nations, may reflect a loss of confidence in agriculture, the desire to spread risks, the need to supplement incomes because of the increased cost of living and/or the low degree of regular or specialized input required. High levels of female participation in part-time agricultural work also reflect unique local factors. For instance, in Samoa those factors probably are tied to the shortage of agricultural labour caused by migration, whereas in Tuvalu they point to the absence of men because of employment on seagoing vessels.

"In the countries of the Pacific islands, smallholders represent the largest production unit, producing goods for use in the home, for exchange, and for sale in domestic and export markets. Traditionally, women and girls assumed primary responsibility for food production and family food security by growing crops in homestead gardens, rearing small livestock, producing handicrafts and engaging in other value-added activities. Sharing tasks by gender is the norm in family systems throughout the Pacific Islands."

Studies indicate that women in Fiji and Samoa play a significant role in the dairy industry, and that women in Vanuatu are involved alongside men in pasture establishment, weeding and fencing on 73 per cent of cattle smallholdings. Studies from Fiji show that among inhabitants of the same village, women recognize and use more plants, which can be explained by their multiple family and community responsibilities.

Worsening economic conditions in Fiji, the Solomon Islands, Vanuatu and Samoa have stimulated a marked increase by women in informal trading, particularly in agricultural goods (such as crops, marine goods, livestock, handicrafts and cooked foods), which augurs well for family food security. A random sample from the Solomon Islands shows that some 66 per cent of women engage in informal trade, compared to 70 per cent in Samoa. The survey also underlined the importance of income from informal trading in these countries where it represents the single source of income for as much as 70 per cent of families in the Fiji sample, 33 per cent in the Solomon Islands and 24 per cent in Samoa.

Cook Islands' women's significant involvement in agriculture is reflected in their extensive role as market gardeners to meet local consumer demand that serves the tourism industry. Women also tend livestock, do subsistence fishing, process fish, make copra and do pearl farming. These women's role in agricultural activities changed from that of traditional domestic input to small commercial producers within the last 20 years. Many women continue as unpaid workers for family and community endeavours.

Deep-sea fishing, an essential part of local economies in the Pacific Islands, traditionally was the domain of men; women and girls traditionally gleaned the reef and inshore lagoons for marine foods. Recently, increasing global demand for marine products, new technology (for instance in the aquaculture and seaweed industries), depleting fish stocks and the need to earn cash have initiated changes in the traditional gender divisions of labour. Consequently, women now are more involved in fishing than previously, particularly in atoll communities like Kiribati where marine products have become key export goods.

The above review examined the working lives of rural women in various Asian and Pacific Island countries and presents evidence of the crucial contribution by women of all ages to food production and food security across the region. The extensive and diverse responsibilities taken up by rural women in local agricultural and non-farm production systems are established in the community and household nexus in which they function, and are influenced by national and global factors beyond their control.

PERSISTING HOUSEHOLD DRUDGERY

Rural women throughout Asia and the Pacific region work long hours and confront drudgery as a reality of their daily existence. Poor women pursue a number of survival strategies to earn enough cash to feed and maintain their families; one indisputable facet of these strategies is the frequent and inordinate extension of working hours inside and outside the home. A review of case studies provides evidence suggesting that poor access to basic services such as water and sanitation, coupled with the need to search for fuel and food supplements, extends and intensifies the typical day of a rural woman, while adding innumerable difficulties.

A case study of mountain women in Darjeeling, India recorded their increased difficulty to find fuelwood in the forest following deforestation, and the consequent addition to women's workload and the toll on their health. Similarly, women in Nepal take on the double burden of working for the family and on the farm (Acharya, Acharya, and Sharma, 1999). A recent IFAD study found that women in Nepalese hill districts had heavy workloads and high levels of physical vulnerability, albeit with differences between classes and castes, working for about 16 hours per day compared to only 9-10 hours for men. In addition to being overworked, the study found that many of these women also were hungry (IFAD, 1999).

In Pakistan, the plight of many rural women and girls is little different. Not only are their responsibilities for water fetching, food preparation, agricultural and other household duties physically demanding, but they also rob girls of the opportunity to attend school. At the same time, the "invisibility" of women as farmers means that little attention is paid to perilous aspects of their work such as the detrimental health effects of pesticides on Pakistani cotton pickers who are exclusively female.

In China, a village study in Yunnan Province found that women are responsible for fetching fuel wood and typically spend two to three hours per day carrying 70-80 kg of fuel wood from far mountainous areas to their homes. According to a study from the Philippines, rural women work up to 16 hours per day, much longer than men (APEC North-South Institute, 1999). In Mongolia, where the move toward privatization has increased the workload of female herders, lengthening their (already long) working day, women's labour appears to be over utilized, though no reliable time use data based on systematic study are currently available.

In Central Asian countries in transition, the economic reforms have created economic uncertainly and hardship. To provide for their family's needs, rural women take up additional work in home farms, dairy and livestock sectors. Rural families are characterized by large family size demanding time for care giving tasks. The service sector to assist rural households is yet to evolve adequately. These factors contribute to women's work load and drudgery (ESCAP, 1999). Vietnamese men and women spend nearly the same amount of time on income-generating activities, but women spend almost twice as much time as men on household work. Consequently, the total number of hours worked by women is consistently greater than that of men at each point in the life cycle.

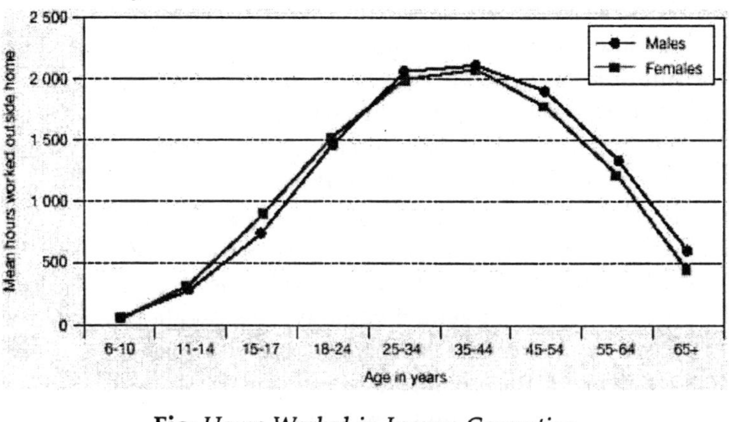

Fig: *Hours Worked in Income-Generation in the Past Year in Vietnam*

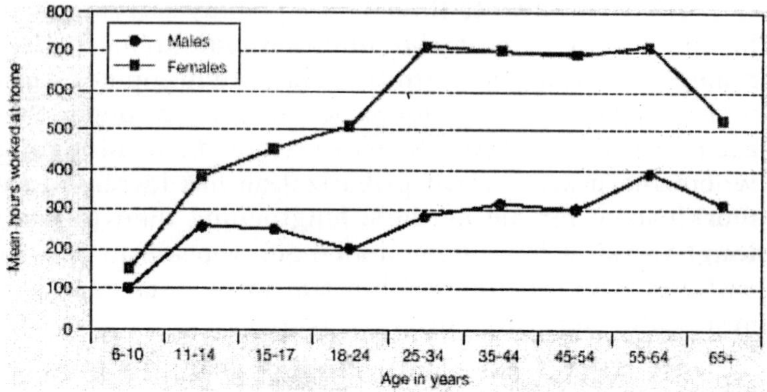

Fig: *Hours Worked in Past Year in Household Maintenance Activities in Vietnam*

In Pacific Island countries, households balance the amount of time spent on subsistence farming and cash cropping with social obligations, domestic duties, and off-farm business and employment commitments. A comparison of women's and men's domestic work in Samoa reveals that young men (between the ages of 10 and 24 years) appear to spend more time cooking than women. It is important to keep in view that ceremonial cooking is a male domain task. Because women continue to play a predominant role in child care and washing, both traditional female domains, it is likely that they continue to face drudgery.

Women in the Cook Islands continue to carry the work load for multiple tasks comprising food production, domestic work, family care giving, health care, social agents, community and kinship obligations and commercial and religious responsibilities. As economic opportunities expand for women to take up wage work outside the home to help meet family needs, most of the home responsibilities continue to rest with women, thus their work load has significantly increased. The drudgery of rural women's work raises gender equality considerations concerning rural women and their efforts to improve household food security. Time is the key resource in women's strategies to access food and livelihood commodities, yet most rural women in Asia and the Pacific region have insufficient time.

A heavy work burden leaves women little time to participate in capacity improvement interventions even if opportunities are available. According to an assessment by the World Bank, women in developing countries generally work longer hours than men and bear a disproportionate share of the responsibilities and time for household maintenance and care activities. The amount of time devoted to such responsibilities frequently means that women have fewer opportunities than men to participate in market-based work or to earn income independently, which in turn affects their bargaining and decision-making power within the household and means they have less time free for rest and personal care. In recognition of these challenges, the World Bank and others have proposed a range of gender-responsive actions to reduce the burden on women's time.

In Cambodia, for example, interventions have been proposed to improve physical infrastructure that will reduce women's travel time, and to develop users' groups to reduce the time spent by women on gathering water and fuel and on water resource management. As agricultural diversification continues to shift labour-intensive activities into the domain of rural women, it is even more important to understand the effects of women's increased work burden on the well-being of rural households, and to ensure that interventions to empower women also focus on providing for their practical needs to reduce household drudgery. The work burden of rural women also should be reviewed in the context of work intensity and its gendered effects on well-being which affect intrahousehold "bargaining" and the gender division of labour.

Given women's situation, addressing rural neglect manifested in working women's inadequate access to water, fuel wood, sanitation and health resources should be an important priority in the gender equality manifesto.

ENDURING INDIFFERENCE TO RURAL WOMEN'S WORK AND INEQUITY IN RESOURCE ACCESS

An analytical review of rural women throughout Asia and the Pacific region identifies two common determinants of their situation, namely the persisting under valuation of rural women's work by the community and the household and the inequity in access to resources.

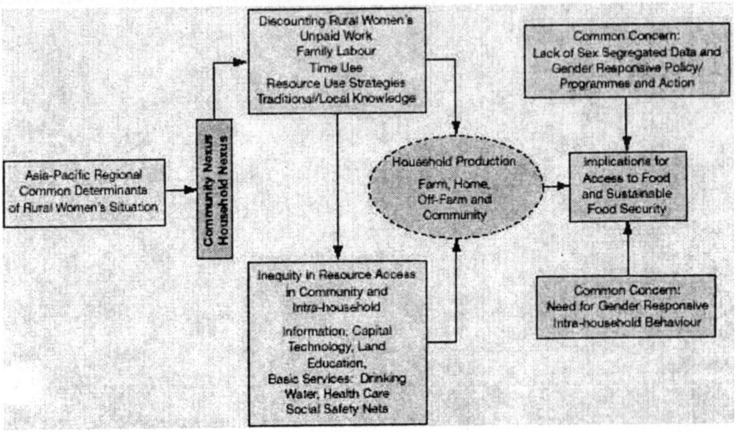

Fig: *Common Determinants of the Situation of Rural Women in Asia and the Pacific*

An outcome of the inexorable indifference to rural women's work at both the household and community level is that women's contributions to agricultural and household production routinely are discounted and/or ignored. The combined forces of social ignorance and economic indifference lead to explicit and implicit inequity in women's access to various resources that are necessary to support and improve their contributions to a wide range of activities. Deep-rooted attitudes further undervalue the worth of women within the household, resulting in gender biases that affect community interactions and the policy arena.

The limited availability of data on rural women's work, coupled with a lack of attention to and value for unpaid work in the agriculture and rural development sector, further perpetuates women's inequitable situation. Official underestimation of rural women's contributions, based on inadequate information about the agricultural sector's human capital potential and constraints, results in policy and programme initiatives that do not reflect the true status of the human resources available for agriculture productivity and rural economic vitality. Indeed, the persisting underestimation of rural women's contributions results in sector policies and development strategies that ignore rural women and ultimately that undermine national efforts to promote agricultural development and sustainable food security.

PERSISTING SOCIAL IGNORANCE AND ECONOMIC INDIFFERENCE

One of the most persistent challenges hampering a comprehensive understanding of rural women's situation in Asia and the Pacific region relates to the general lack of reliable, systematically gathered and objectively analysed data. Stephens observes that problems arising from the scarcity of data on rural women often are exacerbated by misleading information on women's role in agriculture. Thus, women farmers seldom are reflected in development policy and plans and they reap commensurately few rewards for their increasing hours working on the family farm. In particular, the undercounting of women's participation in agriculture and income-generation production within the rural economy is a common weakness of available macrostatistics in the region. In the case of South Asia, it is stated:

Despite the critical involvement and contribution of women in agriculture, their presence is officially invisible with few statistics reflecting their actual contributions to agricultural output and rural employment, and thereby to the Gross Domestic Product. The data surveys are male focused with little acceptance and understanding of the role women play. The process of measurement itself has numerous flaws.

As a result of the prevailing, erroneous social perception of what constitutes work, the majority of rural women workers are invisible to national statistics, which fail to recognize unpaid work in the household, on family land or in family enterprises (such as cooking, cleaning, care of children and the elderly, the collection of water, fuel and fodder).

"Work "refers to the participation of individuals in productive activities for which they either receive remuneration (in cash or in kind) for their participation or are unpaid because they are contributors to a family business enterprise. It also includes subsistence production of goods for their own households and non-economic activities such as domestic work, family and elderly care, construction or repair of owner occupied buildings, and volunteer work for which individuals receive no remuneration."

In Bangladesh, women account for 83.2 per cent of the 42.5 per cent of unpaid family helpers in rural areas (Bangladesh Bureau of Statistics, 1996). In Cambodia, women account for 66 per cent of unpaid family workers in the labour force over 15 years of age. In India, national statistics classified just 22 per cent of rural women as workers in 1997. However, national data collection agencies recognized the serious under-counting of women's contribution as workers, and the National Sample Survey estimated that as much as 17 per cent of rural women and nearly 6 per cent of urban women were incorrectly recorded as "non-workers".

One Report Explained,

In South Asia, female employment rates recorded by official sources are usually low because of arbitrary definitions. If definitions are revised and all activities for which women are traditionally responsible incorporated, a huge difference in activity rates is noted. An undercounting of women's work is demonstrated in Pakistan, Bangladesh and Sri Lanka.

This phenomenon of statistical invisibility is illustrated in Pakistan where only 15 per cent of women are registered in the Labour Force Survey, even though the 1980 Agricultural Census estimated that 73 per cent of women in agricultural households were economically active. The 1990/91 Labour Force Survey reported a female economic activity rate of just 7 per cent using the conventional questionnaire. However, this rate increased to 31 per cent when respondents were also asked questions about specific activities like transplanting rice, picking cotton, grinding, drying seeds and tending livestock. In countries with cultural norms like Pakistan's, where women's waged work is considered a threat to the male ego and identity, women are insufficiently remunerated for their considerable contributions to multiple home-based economic activities.

In the Philippines, excessive undercounting of women in the rural workforce largely results from confusion and ambiguity in the definitions of "productive work", "housework" and "the worker". However, the main reason that women's work is excluded in the calculation of the gross national product is that much of it is of subsistence nature and done within the family setting. In some other countries, changes in the rural economy have had a fundamental shift in the type of work performed by women, which is reflected in national employment statistics. For instance, in the Maldives, the development of an export-oriented fishing industry deprived women of opportunities to work for a cash income, thus causing them to become invisible unpaid family labourers.

Although statistics indicate that women play a vital role in the economies of Pacific Island countries, women in several of these countries struggle to have a say in community fisheries management because their informal day-to-day fishing activities are not recognized as work by governments, industry and banks. As a result, they are less able to receive loans to develop small businesses, less likely to receive skills training in manufacturing positions and less likely to be reached with valuable information about conservation practices. Summarizing the findings of studies completed among mountain women in the Hindu-Kush area of the Himalayas, Gurung (1999) asserts that "suffering from the myopia of labelling women's subsistence work 'domestic' and therefore trivial, development planners have not, until recently, recognized the critical contribution of women's work to agriculture production and the very survival of the family."

As a result of this short sightedness, the incalculable role and contribution of rural women in the unpaid work sector throughout Asia and the Pacific region continue to be ignored in economic analyses and are undervalued by the society. Since women's contribution to agriculture and food security is held in such low esteem, few if any supportive measures are available locally to improve women's situation and to reduce hardships resulting from discrimination in resource access. At the same time, the general lack of national economic analyses that consider the demonstrable contribution of working rural women results in gender-blind policies and programmes that have negative effects on national productivity.

In this context, ambiguities in definitions of work must be clarified so that the contributions of currently invisible women workers are no longer concealed. Indeed, the case of home-based workers demonstrates the need for improved informal sector statistics, as well as a better understanding of the effect of policies on the informal sector and the contribution of the informal sector to national economies. It is important to acknowledge that "all work is productive work. All work is economic work. All people who perform work, either paid or unpaid, are economically active".

FACETS OF INEQUITY IN RURAL WOMEN'S ACCESS TO RESOURCES

A recent World Bank study highlighted the double disadvantage poor women confront in access to resources and opportunity for articulation - they are poor and women. It is easy to present illustrations of women's current realties in rural areas of Asia and the Pacific region where inequity in access to resources is intensified by persistent neglect in provisioning of services and infrastructure facilities in rural areas. These persisting inequities are further reinforced by traditional perceptions and attitudes that perpetuate gender biases and discriminate against rural women's access to community and household resources.

At the same time, degradation of the natural resource base is threatening women's access to subsistence livelihood resources in rural areas. Another growing concern is that the forces of globalization could further marginalize rural women and result in greater inequity in access to resources. New and emerging technologies in both the agriculture and information sectors may well bypass poorly educated rural women and widen their knowledge gaps. The following review highlights the resource access inequities experienced by rural women in the region.

LAND ASSETS

Many countries still lack adequate provision for women to hold land rights independently of their husbands or male relatives. Statutory laws often do not ensure independent land rights for women. In traditional or under "customary" practices, women's direct ownership access to land may be limited, yet they may have greater management and use rights than men. Land ownership in rural areas determines the asset for production as well as access to credit and agriculture support services and the social power to negotiate for resources and membership in decision-making agencies.

Rural women's access to land - as owners and users - presents a mixed picture of conflict between legal rights and customary laws, as well as inheritance of property directed by family priorities and personal practices. In Sumatra the inheritance system is evolving from a strictly matrilineal system to a more egalitarian system in which sons and daughters inherit the type of land that is more relevant to their respective work. Although gender bias is non-existent or small in land inheritance, daughters tend to be disadvantaged with respect to schooling.

In South Asia, according to Agarwal (1994), "land defines social status and political power in the village, and it structures relationships within and outside the household. Yet for most women, effective rights in land remain elusive, even as their marital and kin support erodes and female-headed households multiply. In legal terms, women have struggled for and won fairly extensive rights to inherit and control land in much of South Asia, but in practice most stand disinherited. Few own land; even fewer can exercise effective control over it." In India, women's land rights are seen as particularly important in the context of demographic changes in occupational patterns, with more and more men migrating to urban areas or looking for non-farm work in rural areas.

Given that the relative share of women in the agricultural labour force is higher than that of men, the lack of women's land rights is seen as a major bottleneck in improving agricultural production. Although an egalitarian trade in resources may prevail in certain societies, most often land laws or their implementation are biased against women. In the rural context, lack of ownership or direct lease rights to land may further prevent women from accessing other resources such as irrigation and credit. For instance, throughout the Pacific Islands family members hold most land in customary tenure under the protection of the family head.

Although rights to land may be passed on through patrilineal or matrilineal lines, women tend to have difficulty activating their rights for a number of reasons. Specifically, customary beliefs dictate that women do not need land because agriculture is male work and women are protected by the family support systems. There is also a fear that land given to women is lost land since women marry out of the family. Recently, these and other social customs have been formalized into legal rights, which discriminate against women. The codification of customary laws into statutory laws in Kiribati in the Lands Code stipulates that in the distribution of an estate between sons and daughters, the shares of the eldest son should exceed that of his brothers, and the shares of sons should exceed the shares of daughters.

NATURAL RESOURCE ASSETS

Women are rural agriculture producers, and rural production depends on natural resources as primary assets to produce crops, home garden, fishing, food processing and crafts. Women also collect non-wood forest products for food and production. The forests also offer fuel wood, shelter materials and medicinal plants. Hence, food security and the economic vitality of the local communities are affected by the availability of and access to natural resources. Natural resource degradation has direct consequences for rural women's productivity and access to livelihood alternatives. "In rural areas the depletion of natural resources by environmental degradation has a significant effect on the daily life of a woman and the well-being of her family".

Most studies to date have focused on the effect of forest and coastal resource degradation on women's access to resources, but information on the impact of soil and water resource degradation on female work patterns is very limited. One study has illustrated how the livelihoods of indigenous communities in Northern Sarawak, Malaysia that traditionally have been based on hunting, gathering and shifting agriculture, are being threatened by logging, deforestation and changes in government policies regarding native land. The consequences are severe soil erosion, deterioration in the quality of river water, a reduction in biodiversity and a decline in fish and wildlife populations. The subsequent search for alternative livelihoods induced male migration, leaving women behind to cope with a declining resource base.

Gender inequalities in access to environmental resources, command over labour, capacity to diversify livelihood strategies and decision-making processes contribute to significant differences in how men and women experience poverty and environmental changes. Analyzing regional variations and temporal shifts in rural India over a 30-year period, Agarwal (1997) concluded that natural resource degradation, privatization and the appropriation of natural resources by the state have tended to result in particularly adverse implications for female members of rural households. In Northern Pakistan, forest cover has been reduced dramatically in recent years at the same time that agricultural productivity has risen significantly with an increase in livestock farming.

In parallel, the workload of women in agriculture has increased. Whereas men spend a greater proportion of their time in income-generating activities, enabling them to monopolize the community's access to the monetary economy, women are left relatively powerless. A study in Nepal examined the workload of rural women in the context of availability of environmental goods collection over the past two decades. It found that although all household members spent less time collecting various local resources, such as water and wood, the amount of time women spent on collection fell by the largest proportion and the female share of the total collection time also decreased. Given the large amount of time women in the region spend on collection and the burden it entails, this finding suggests a positive trend, which may be a result of the increased availability of local environmental resources.

For instance, each of the sites studied had installed at least one water tap, and some also had noted an improvement in their community forest during the 14-year period in question. A study on women and food production in the Pacific Islands of Samoa, Fiji, the Solomon Islands and the Marshall Islands found that the quality of home gardens depended on land availability, amount of land, soils, women's access to planting materials, training, labour availability and knowledge about pests and diseases. On some atolls, problems of poor soils and garden washout from rain and sea spray also presented difficulties. In each of the countries studied, the women with the most successful gardens belonged to dual income or high status families. This suggests that training alone might be insufficient to achieve family food security.

LOCAL GROUPS AND SOCIAL CAPITAL

The development of women's groups is a strategy to expand women's access to information, increase their comparative bargaining power and create opportunities for collective action to access economic inputs. In reality, however, persisting gender biases, deep-seated community dynamics and women's time constraints prevent women from actively participating in these organizations which were intended to bring about social capital benefits and female empowerment. The widespread trend to transfer responsibility for irrigation management from the state to communities or local user groups has by and large ignored the implications of intra community power differences on the effectiveness and equity of water management. Gender is a recurrent source of such differences.

Despite the rhetoric on women's participation, a review of evidence from South Asia shows that female participation is minimal in water users' organizations, in part because the formal and informal membership criteria exclude women. Factors that constrain women's participation in formal institutions for environmental management include rules, norms, perceptions, entrenched territorial claims, the household's economic and social endowments and women's individual economic endowments and personal attributes. For example, women who have primary responsibility for both domestic and farm work have extremely full days and are unlikely to have the time to attend meetings.

Some women in rural areas may also lack links to male-dominated and government hierarchies. A Food for Work Programme in Cambodia found that women without husbands and those who were poor tended to be isolated from other villagers because of the amount of time they must spend working alone, foraging for food, hauling water and caring for the home. In Thailand, a study found gender differences in participation in local organizations. Women tend to belong to local organizations that are focused on home economics and household tasks. Men are more likely to join local organizations that seek to improve agriculture productivity and generate income. A minimum level of assets - in the form of land, livestock or human capital - is normally required as a precondition for participation in local organizations.

Often poorer households and women lack sufficient assets to be eligible for membership. Additionally, women have less access than men to decision-making processes in local organizations. An excessive workload that involves managing multiple tasks as unpaid workers in farm and rural production, domestic work and care giving responsibilities leaves little time for women to be active and effective participants in local organizations. Yet another facet of participation is that although women are visible numerically in the local organizations, they have limited opportunities to articulate their needs and concerns by themselves during the planning process which is dominated by men.

EDUCATION: FORMAL AND INFORMAL

Gender difference in access to education is a key contributor to inequality in rural women's access to other resources. Many studies carried out in different parts of the world have documented the importance of women's education for positive outcomes in child schooling and nutrition. Yet education also is critical for female empowerment. Women must have at least basic education if they are to develop the skills needed to participate in knowledge-intensive agriculture and economic activities. Women who lack access to basic education are likely to be excluded from new opportunities and, where longstanding gender gaps in education persist, they will be at increased risk of falling behind men in their ability to participate in development.

Across Asia, studies have documented women's unequal participation in education and training. One such study carried out in 25 villages in Pakistan found that a number of serious supply-side constraints (inadequate primary schools for girls close to villages, lack of female teachers) deny girls access to primary education. Similarly in South India, research has identified factors that keep poor boys and girls out of the classroom. These include poverty, the opportunity cost of children's labour and entrenched social and cultural norms that give rise to inequality of caste, class and gender.

A survey undertaken by the Asia-Pacific Economic Cooperation found that the time allocated for unpaid work was the major barrier preventing women from improving their skills and training. Existing rural disparity in educational infrastructure, combined with inadequate quality control, partially explains lack of access to good learning as well as social perceptions that undervalue the importance of education for girls among the current generation of rural girls. For adult women farmers and producers, literacy deficiency is a legacy in rural areas for cultural and economic reasons held by their families. In the present generation of adults, rural women's illiteracy is the major barrier to their social and economic advancement; for the future generation of rural women the major barrier is rural girls' lack of access to formal education.

TECHNOLOGY

Rural women in their dual roles as producers in farm and home production and as caregivers need technologies to ease their work stress and improve productivity and family welfare. According to one renowned Indian scientist, "If women are empowered with technological information and skills, all the members of the family will benefit". However, traditional biases, which are internalized by scientists, technocrats and technology disseminators, contribute to the gap between gender differentiated technology needs and actions for gender responsive technology development and technology transfer. Access to technology is not neutral, and is particularly not gender neutral.

> *"Access to technology is not neutral, and is particularly not gender-neutral. Internalized traditional biases contribute to the gap between gender differentiated technology needs and actions for gender responsive technology development and technology transfer."*

In developing countries, technology development and dissemination programmes have not been responsive to household drudgery associated with different production activities routinely undertaken by women. In particular, these programmes have failed to recognize rural women's demand for technology that improves their productivity. For instance, in Nepal, little effort has been made to develop and diffuse new and improved agricultural tools tailored to women farmers even though national policies and programmes have sought to promote women's empowerment. A participatory assessment of the intrahousehold effects of modern agriculture technologies in Bangladesh identified reasons why poor women fail to utilize knowledge of new technologies; those reasons included unfavourable land tenure, gender division of workspace that is validated by purdah and limited size of homestead plots.

Most technical solutions in the livestock sector, even those directed specifically at women, have ignored women's actual needs. Imprbvements designed to intensify the production system generally have increased women's workloads. Appropriate technologies should be designed to consider not only women's workload, but also the potential effect of the technology on their status and the economic control over resources and property. Although some efforts have promoted participatory technology development, the participants most often were defined to be male farmers, an error perpetuated by traditional perceptions held by extension service and agricultural education providers. Such a limited understanding by the agents of technology transfer placed a low value on women's ability to learn and to use technologies, thus making women farmers invisible.

A major finding of the recently completed Asia-Pacific Gender Science and Technology Project in Kiribati, Fiji and Samoa that focused on biotechnology, green health, water, energy and information technology, was that women's main access to technology is through women's NGOs such as Ecowomen Fiji, Wainimate and research institutes affiliated to the University of the South Pacific that tend to rely on donor funding. Agricultural research and extension services still tend to direct their attention to men and export crops. Rural infrastructure in Asia and the Pacific region must be improved to increase access to off-farm employment opportunities and to facilitate the adoption of new technologies and information and support services by women farmers.

Credit

The provision of microcredit - usually collateral-free and group-guaranteed - has provided an important source of capital for rural men and women in Asia and the Pacific region. High economic rates of return have been attributed to the excellent repayment performance of rural women. The group-based microcredit and microfinance approaches have served the short term credit needs of rural households well, improving cash flows where petty trade opportunities have been available. In the Asian region, the mixed effects of microcredit have been documented. These include the incremental benefits of microcredit on women's livelihood and social solidarity as well as the potential for changing social relations. On the other hand, negative effects are increased social conflict in the community, the tendency of men to control women's access to economic assets and women being used as the front person for control over the loans or financial decisions.

Most often the microenterprises are based on the existing domestic production skills. Expansion of the microenterprises is limited by the loan sizes and by the poor access to opportunities to improve skills or to cost effective technology and knowledge of market complexity. Microfinance programmes exhibit clear differences in terms of their approach - particularly the commitment to build rural women's capacity to become self-reliant producers and confident credit holders in their individual right - and the results they achieve. The collective effect of rural women's small savings on the national economy is not categorically established. The critical relevance of women's efforts is inadequately acknowledged and women's due status as partners contributing to local economic vitality and national capital is denied.

Women not only contribute to national production as unpaid workers, but they also increasingly are the key economic actors who contribute to the financial flow of the national economy through their participation in microcredit and microfinance programmes. The illustration below conceptualizes microcredit and women's economic contribution. Women's small enterprises collectively result in the cash flow within the local economy, and their savings deposited in national banks result in capital formation for commercial investments and middle class loans to support consumption of life style consumer durables. The current rationale of microcredit as an instrument of mobilising women or as an investment in social capital should be re-examined in the light of the economic reality that these women contribute to the national economy by creating capital for other investments including bank loans to urban middle class to support their consumption.

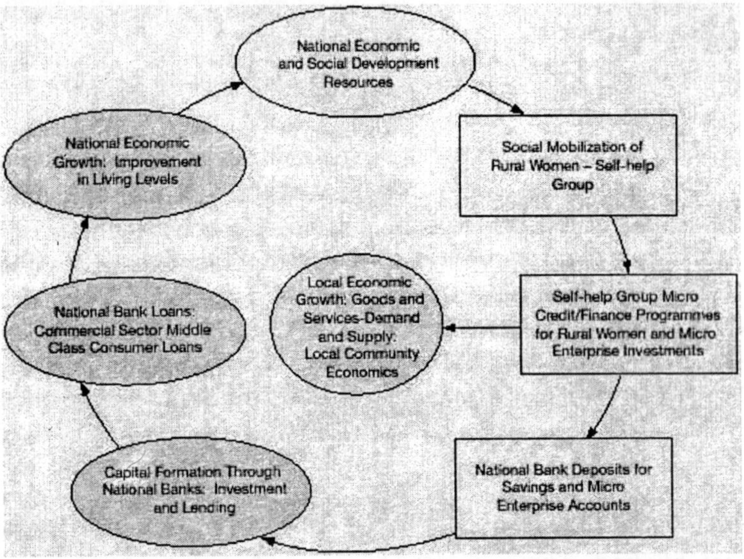

Fig: *Microcredit and Rural Women's Economic Contribution*

The repayment terms dictated by microcredit tenets (compulsory weekly repayments plus a contribution to savings) and interest rates have not been appropriate to meet the fund needs of agriculture households, which do not normally have a weekly cash flow given their reliance on longer term agriculture production and livestock rearing cycles. Consequently, the women-centred credit model has pressed rural women to pursue additional, alternative income-generating strategies to keep up with repayment schedules, thereby causing an increase in their workload.

Recent studies questioned the assumption that microcredit is an effective instrument for women's empowerment by indicating that, in some cases, women serve as a front to access credit for men in the household, thus lacking direct control over the credit obtained in their name. In short, a preoccupation with performance - measured primarily in terms of high repayment rates - has affected the incentives of those who grant and recover credit, resulting in less attention being paid to whether and how women can have meaningful control over their own investment activities.

In the Pacific Islands, women tend to experience difficulties obtaining credit through commercial banks given their lack of collateral and the small size of the loans requested. The fact that banks are normally located in urban areas, coupled with women's lack of knowledge about banking procedures, further impedes female access to capital. In this context, many women's groups have developed savings and loans schemes where members make regular deposits and have the option to borrow at reasonable interest rates. However, major constraints associated with these schemes have included management weaknesses as well as the high costs of running small schemes and making them available in rural areas.

FEMALE-HEADED HOUSEHOLDS

Female-headed households in rural areas demonstrate specific vulnerability in terms of access to resources, access to social networks to improve their access to development resources and at times the labour requirement to undertake agriculture practices to improve productivity. An assessment by IFAD recognized the feminization of rural poverty in Asia and noted two key dimensions of this trend. Notably, female-headed households in the region usually are poorer than male-headed households, and poverty is more severe and binding for women in that it is more difficult for women and their children to escape it.

According to this study, female-headed households represent a significant proportion of households in Cambodia, Nepal and Bangladesh. In Cambodia, 35 per cent of household are female-headed; in Nepal and Bangladesh female-headed households are 16 per cent of landless and marginal households. The migration of men and grown children in Cambodia has had both positive and negative consequences. Some men and children who work away from the village may send money home, significantly improving the standard of living for the family there. On the other hand, wives whose husbands leave for long periods may suffer some of the same deprivations as poor women without husbands. For instance, a study by the World Food Programme has shown that women in households with no men have inadequate access to decision-making networks, legitimate knowledge and assets like rice and labour.

Similarly, the Vietnam Living Standard Survey identified labour shortage in female-headed households as an important resource constraint in expanding economic assets and agriculture productivity. For instance, in rural parts of Vietnam median profits of female-operated enterprises are 84 per cent of those of men. Specific hardships faced by women in the Pacific Islands include a shortage of family labour as a result of migration and children at school, a reluctance of youth to perform agricultural work, as well as seasonal male labour trends. For example in Kiribati and Tuvalu, men are engaged in waged employment on sea vessels for long periods at a time.

At the same time, family support systems that traditionally protected women from negative changes in the economy are being eroded, an increasing number of marriages are breaking up and the number of unmarried pregnancies is increasing, all of which contributes to an increase in the number of female-headed households. In short, such factors substantiate that women are the group most vulnerable to poverty throughout the Pacific Islands today.

RURAL WOMEN'S RESOURCE ACCESS INEQUITY MATRIX

The interlinked, complex relationships among various gender-based inequities vis à vis rural women's access to resources are highly relevant to achieving sustainable food security and rural economic vitality.

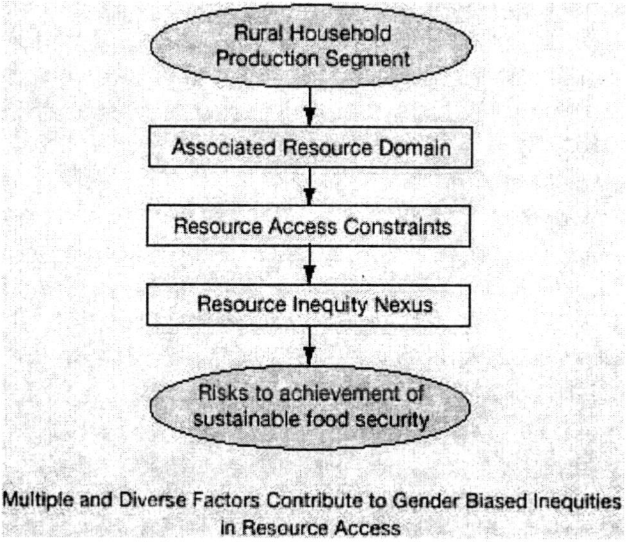

Fig: *Gender Based Access Inequities and Food Security*

This matrix illustrates the nexus of inequity and its relationship to sustainable food security across a range of production segments. Major food security risks include limited incentives to improve land and productivity, inadequate opportunities and restricted capacity to diversify income sources, women's insufficient time to improve agriculture production, poor nutritional gains for rural households, uncertain access to food at times of family crisis, seasonal unavailability and crop loss. These factors have major implications for the availability of sufficient food to ensure national food security.

2

Group Membership, Inheritance, and Resource Distribution

Women have come to be recognized as a proper subject for study 'by social science disciplines in the ASEAN countries only in recent years. They have been referred to in different contexts in many anthropological and related studies of tribal groups, communities, religion, politics, and kinship and family systems conducted during the last few decades by American, Dutch, British, Australian, and indigenous social scientists. In works like Kinship, Status, and Sax in South Celebes, Malay Kinship and Marriage in Singapore, Housekeeping in Malaya, The Javanese Family, The Position of Women in Batak Society, and The Indonesian Women Struggles and Achievements, the focus has been on women.

Anthropologists took a long time to lose their preoccupation with unilineal descent systems and accept the fact that sizeable parts of Asia and Oceania follow the bilateral pattern. Studies of a number of communities in the countries of the ASEAN region provided rich material for generalizations about non-unilineal systems. Most of these studies were not, however, specifically concerned with the position and roles of women in their respective societies. Some collections of essays dealing with the women of countries in particular regions, with roughly the same ecological base, or at similar levels of development, had begun to appear in the fifties. But the publication in 1963 of Women in the New Asia, edited by Barbara Ward, more properly marks the beginning of planned women's studies in Southeast Asia.

This book was the outcome of a UNESCO project, and its introductory chapter clearly describes the comparative approach that was envisaged. The contributors came from the various countries that the book covers. Women in the New Asia remained, for quite some time, the principal publication about the women of the ASEAN countries. It would be facile to suggest that this reflected the state of the social sciences in these countries. The fact was that many of the issues concerning women that were thought important in the sixties in the West, particularly in North America and in Britain, were of little relevance in the cultures of the ASEAN region.

Nor should it be assumed that there were, in these countries, no efforts to assess and to improve the position of women. A good deal of writing, of semi- popular or technical (pertaining to laws, for instance) nature, had been done on a vast range of themes related to women. In the fifties and the sixties, 'area studies' became popular in many universities in the developed countries; this led to the establishment of several centres for research on, among other regions.

Much of the proliferation and diversification of social science research on Southeast Asia since the sixties has stemmed from this development. Such centres, besides supporting the research of their own scholars, have trained some research students from the regions that they have been concerned with and have assisted and collaborated with indigenous scholars. The contribution of such centres to the knowledge that we have about women in Southeast Asia is evident in the bibliography that follows this report. In Indonesia, recognition of women's achievements and strengths, and concern with the limitations imposed on them, had begun to be articulated in semi-popular literature well before the sixties, when social scientists – many of whom were attracted by the novel kinship pattern and by the role that women played in the family and in the economy – started to produce studies on the country and on its women.

In the Philippines, consciousness of the need to assert women's rights developed in the sixties, while at the same time interest was arising from contact with Western scholars, and a few studies resulted on matters related to women. In Women's Role in Economic Development, Ester Boserup (1970) examined the place of women in the labour force in Africa, Asia, and Latin America. While discussing the importance of women's contributions to productive activity as a determinant of their status in society, Boserup referred to the vital role of women in rice cultivation in some countries of Southeast Asia.

She did not, however, take into account the full social and cultural contexts of women's lives (women's access to strategic resources, the nature of control over land, rights over children, rules of inheritance and the sharing of property, residence patterns, and so on) in these areas while comparing them with other parts of the world where intense wet rice cultivation is practised. Boserup's main hypothesis, that the change from traditional to modern economic systems adversely affects women as part of the labour force, has been tested – in large samples as well as in small-scale studies – by researchers in various developing countries.

Some social scientists working in the ASEAN region have made efforts to understand the socio-economic constraints placed on women and to identify fundamental issues related to their status. Social scientists outside the ASEAN region have found these studies valuable in the creation and the testing of theoretical formulations. Some social scientists indigenous to the countries of the region see them as a first step towards the introduction of reforms. The branch for equality between Women and Men of the UN Centre for Social Development and Humanitarian Affairs encouraged the establishment of commissions and committees on the status of women in various countries.

To help these bodies assess the status of women at different socio- economic levels, in different life contexts, and among diverse ethnic groups, indigenous social scientists undertook a series of studies concerned directly with women.

It may not be an exaggeration to say that in the ASEAN countries, much of the involvement of social scientists in studies of women's problems and of basic issues related to women's status was a consequence of the activities of various agencies of the United Nations System.

Many development assistance agencies based in western countries have also initiated studies on women by social scientists in the ASEAN countries. Some of these studies involve the compilation and collation of data already available; others combine available data with fresh research. Preparatory work for the International Women's Year consisted of seminars, conferences, and workshops. In 1975, there was a profusion of such activities. The World Conference of the International Women's Year focused attention on the integration of women in development.

The ASEAN seminar on "Integration of Women in Development", sponsored jointly by the Indonesian Human Resources Development Foundation, the Indonesian National Secretariat for ASEAN, the Indonesian National Committee for International Women's Year, and the Friedrich-Ebert-Stiftung of the Federal Republic of Germany, was held in Jakarta in December- 1975. Each member nation presented a country report and an expert paper. The country reports attempted to give a comprehensive picture of the status of women in various areas of life, such as law, economy, education, and family. They tried not to ignore the rural component of the population.

Although not many social scientists, strictly defined, participated in the seminar, it generated a good deal of research activity aimed at obtaining a proper understanding of the situation of women in these countries. Since then a number of seminars, conferences, and workshops on the women of the ASEAN countries and of those in Asia and the Pacific have been organized in these regions. More and more social scientists from these countries are participating in such meetings.

United Nations agencies based in these regions, such as the Asian Pacific Development Administration Centre, the

Asian and Pacific Development Institute, the Economic and Social Commission for Asia and the Pacific (ESCAP), and the Social Welfare and Development Centre for Asia and the Pacific (SWDCAP), initiate and support action research as well as other research aimed at development} some of their programmes are concerned directly with women. These agencies also co-operate with the Asian and Pacific Centre for Women and Development, which has been established by the United Nations specifically to promote the welfare and development of women through research and training programmes.

In addition, ILO, UNESCO, UNFPA, UNICEF, and WHO support, directly or indirectly, some research on women in the region. In the ASEAN region, research on women is in the process of being recognized as a major endeavour of the social sciences. It is encouraging that women's studies in these countries are seldom handicapped by antagonisms of the kind that commonly exist among the social sciences in the West. While Thailand, and perhaps Malaysia, may take some time to recognize the importance of research on women and to identify those issues that are most relevant in their socio-cultural contexts, Indonesia and the Philippines seem to have firmly accepted women's studies as-a legitimate and necessary pursuit.

Scholars in Singapore have yet to explore the research potential of their multi-ethnic society. In the following Section, a review of researches done in Indonesia, Malaysia, the Philippines, Singapore, and Thailand – the five countries of the ASEAN region – is attempted. The survey identifies the main trends of research and indicates some of the areas on which research may be carried out. Following the country-based review, the last section of the Report, summarises the findings and offer suggestions for further work.

INDONESIA

The women's movement which was active during Indonesia's freedom struggle lost much of its momentum after the attainment of independence. As articulated by an Indonesian scholar, the women's movement appears to have been "swallowed by the new feudalism". After independence the educated women in the professions, who were trying to establish themselves in their careers and to prove that they were the equals of men, forgot that the opportunities available to them were made possible only because of the nationalist movement.

The feminist movement of the West is not unknown, but Indonesian wife involved in women's movement and concerned with women's problems have not reacted favourably to it. In fact, there has been strong opposition to the essentially culture-bound approach of the American feminists. There is pronounced skepticism among scholars regarding any artificial separation of women's and men s problems. The deliberate emphasis placed by international agencies on women as an independent category for the purpose of research and action programmes has, however, succeeded in attracting some good women scholars.

These women have been able to interest many scholars in the problems of women. The United Nations System's efforts to involve the governments of member states in programmes focused on women have been responsible for the growth of some research and action ventures here. In Indonesia, there is a pattern of close collaboration between the government and social scientists. They are involved in the formulation and implementation of plans, sit on various committees and boards, and hold permanent or periodic positions in institutions for research and planning like BAPPENAS and LIPI.

Literature on the culture and society of various parts of Indonesia dates from the colonial period. For the Dutch, their Southeast Asian colonies provided subjects for anthropological study. University training in ethnology was imparted to civil servants; a thorough understanding of the customs, beliefs, and socio-economic systems of the subject populations was considered desirable for maintaining efficient rule. Besides the primitive tribes of the region, the mainstream of the population also interested Dutch scholars and administrators. The Royal Dutch Institute of Linguistics and Anthropology has been publishing a series of English translations of major Dutch works in the two fields.

These indicate the range of the material on Indonesia that was prepared during the Dutch regime. During the sixties and the seventies, considerable social science research has been done in Indonesia by scholars from the U.S.A., Europe, and Australia. The number of scholars and the volume of work have steadily increased. Much of this work has been in the disciplines of anthropology, demography, economics, and social history. Kinship, economy, and religion have been the themes of many studies. While some of these have dealt directly with the life and problems of women, others provide very good source material for understanding the status of women in Indonesian society.

In recent years, Indonesian scholars have been contributing to research in fair measure. Koentjaraningrat, who is known for his study of the people of south central Java (1960) and for his description of Gotonq Royonq practices in two villages of central Java (1961) based on work diaries of village women and men, deserves credit also for bringing together the work of a number of Indonesian anthropologists and for compiling material from different culture areas of the country. His Villages in Indonesia (1967) is particularly notable. Women in Indonesia have formed the subject matter of many articles and books, some of them of a semi-popular nature.

A few works that were published before 1963 have already been mentioned. Hurustiati Subandrio (1952, 1953) was one of the first Indonesian women to write about her countrywomen for the outside world. Masdani (1969) wrote about the psychological conflicts of educated and so-called emancipated women. Nani Soewondo has been active in fighting for women's legal rights; besides writing on law, she has considered the status of women in its various aspects. Hanna Papanek (1975) has made use of her Indonesian experience in surveying the source material on women in South and Southeast Asia and in suggesting relevant research concerns.

There is a considerable literature on women's movements and women's organizations in Indonesia. Suryochandro's doctoral dissertation (1976), written in Bahasa Indonesia (the

Indonesian language), is a study of women's organizations. Purawidjaja's (1972) is a bibliography concerning the Indonesian women's movement since 1945. The journals Archipel (1977) and Prisma (1975) have each devoted an issue to the problems of women in Indonesia. Indonesian Women; Some Past and Current Perspectives, edited by B.B. Hering (1976), is a collection of papers prepared during the International Women's Year. Women in Indonesia (1975), brought out by the Overseas Educational Fund of the League of Women Voters, is a useful compilation of material.

We may now turn our attention to research on the women of particular geographical areas and ethnic groups and to that on specific aspects of women's lives and problems. A fairly clear understanding of the position of women among the Minangkabau in the traditional as well as the changing settings is available. The role of Batak women in the household and in agriculture, handicrafts, and trade was competently described by Nasution (1943). Singarimbun has made a study (1975) of kinship, descent, and alliance among the Karo Batak.

In a short paper, "The Status of Buginese and Makassar Women as Seen by Their Own Societies", Mangemba (1975) points out that while they accept temperamental differences between the two sexes as a general proposition, the Buginese recognize the possibility of a person's having the temperament of the opposite sex and also give such a person the right to adopt the role and activities of the opposite sex. Thus, the right to a directive role is determined not by sex but by personal qualities. That is how women in these societies could share with men the highest positions of authority and be rulers and military chiefs.

It would be worthwhile to study, as Mangemba did, cultural notions regarding natural differences and similarities, and the possible overlap of qualities and temperament, between the sexes, as well as allowances that can be made to a person who acquires qualities of the opposite sex, among peoples such as the Javanese and the Balinese. The matrifocal character of the Javanese family was emphasized by Hildred

Geertz (1961). Buddiasantoso (1971) attributes the matrifocal family in a village in West Java to men's inability to fulfill their roles as husbands and fathers. Many students of Javanese culture and society have taken notice of the prominent roles of women in the family and in the economy.

Alice Dewey's description (1962) of women's predominance in small-scale trading in east central Java and Robert Jay's account (1969) of women's pivotal place in child-rearing, decision-making, and small-scale trade are widely known. Clifford Geertz (T9Ç3) also dwells on the role of women in cottage industries and tride. The studies of the seventies, which have been concerned mainly with land distribution, population pressure, exploitation, adverse effects of technological changes, and time allocations have not, however, failed to take note of the prominent place that women have in the family and the economy.

We discuss a few of them here. Edmundson's doctoral thesis (1973) on land, food, and work in chree eastern Javanese Villages also studies time allocation. Gillian Hart (1976b) shows how returns from labour are lower for the landless than they are for the landed, and how the poorest women have to waste their time searching for remunerative opportunities. Displacement of women due to technological innovations has been the concern of many scholars. They have analysed the effects of changes in the method of harvesting, the adoption of hullers in rice-milling, and the gradual disappearance of handicrafts and cottage industries.

During the last few years, demographers have made substantial contributions to the study of women in Indonesia. Demography has developed here through the cooperation between Indonesian scholars and their Australian and Western counterparts. "The Demographic situation in Indonesia" provides information on the growth and distribution of the population and on mortality, fertility, and migration. Dey (1975) presents a demographic analysis of the progress of women in literacy, education, and the labour force during the decade 1961-71.

There has been other important work on fertility, mortality, and family planning; on labour absorption; on underutilization of labour; and on marriage and divorce. Mely Tan's reports on surveys of nutrition in rural areas reveal some interesting facts about the socially and culturally determined nutritional problems of women. For instance young girls, pregnant women, and nursing mothers are denied even easily available nutrients because of beliefs about what they should and should not eat. Women also tend to sell a large part of the vegetables they grow. Vulnerable sections of society, such as pregnant women, nursing mothers, and small children, are the main concern of students of nutrition.

Statistics for small samples, collected through field-work and from available records, have been fruitfully utilized in recent research on rural Indonesia. These studies deal with subjects such as the economics of fertility; fertility, socio-economic class, and the position of women; population pressure and poverty; marriage and divorce; organization of production and utilization of labour; and the measurement of labour inputs. T. Hull and V. Hull (1977) have found a 'positive relation between economic class and fertility. They have shown how, within Javanese society, the fertility of the poor is kept lower than that of the rich by such indirect and involuntary factors as infecundity, divorce, and accidental abortions. In addition the poor breastfeed, and abstain from sex, for longer periods after childbirth, and thus keep the fertility low.

Benjamin White's work on fertility is part of a large project on the value of children which was based on the argument that since the basic unit of demographic and economic behaviour is the family, "if we wish to examine the economic rationality or otherwise of demographic behaviour, we must transfer our attention from large-scale statistics to individual couples in their individual economic environments". Children were seen as possessing two kinds of economic value for their parents: immediate, since they begin to contribute their labour at an early age; and potential, since they are expected to provide support when they grow up.

The study has great relevance for understanding the position of women. For instance, it was found that in almost all age groups, girls devoted more time to work than boys did. In some age groups they made a considerably greater contribution to production. This was ascertained by calculating the average time spent per day by male and female children of different age groups in activities that contributed to their household's economics. Some of the circumstances that can create a close bond between parents and daughters – and at the same time induce parents to value daughters as much as they value sons – are described in the following words: "In the Javanese village, daughters rarely end up far from parental homes after their marriage. They also do substantial work before they leave their parental homes. These two factors are perhaps responsible for the fact that Javanese, unlike parents in many other Asian countries, do not appear to express any significant preference for sons over daughters".

In "Class Structure and Female autonomy in Rural Java" Ann Stoler argues that women in the villages are disadvantaged more by class than by sex. Her paper is based on field data from a Javanese village. Mayra Buvinic (1976) has summarized Stoler's argument thus: "At all socio-economic levels, women have more autonomy than the men of their own level. The major subsistence resource of the village is intensive wet rice cultivation. Women invariably manage the rice-harvesting operations, and harvesting provides the highest returns to labor of all agricultural activities.

The profits from trading are important supplements to the household economy; women constitute the majority of the traders in the village (40% of the adult women, versus 1.2% of their male counterparts, were active traders). Women also have unequivocal authority over the household. However, this independence does not necessarily imply high status. According to the author, the social and economic position of women in society depends on the social relations of production between strata as well as the organization of labor within them." Stoler gives an excellent description of women's role in the ceremonial allocation of food and in decision-making within the household. Her study can form a starting point for a research programme to compare women in rural Java with women in other areas of wet rice cultivation, in India and Bangladesh, for instance.

The legal status of women has been one of the best-studied aspects of Indonesian women's status. Because it is bound with Islamic law for the majority community and is also rooted in Adat (customary) law, it is viewed with the greatest concern. Nani Soewando's work on the legal status of women in Indonesia is widely acknowledged. Reflections on matrimonial legislation during the last forty years or so form an important part of her work. Differences between norms based on Islam and those based on Adat law pose problems in both matrilineal and bilateral kinship systems and have a bearing on the status and role of women.

Harsja Bachtiar (1967) has studied the matrilineal Minangkabau from this angle and Taufik Abdullah has written on modernization among the Minangkabau. Adat Law in Indonesia, by B. Ter Haar (1962), has been read widely, even outside the country. Indonesian women's status under civil law, Islamic law, and Adat law is assessed by Hornick (1973). Aden (1974) discusses the effects of Islamic concepts on the status of women. Koesnoe (1975) discusses the status of women according to Adat in village communities of Madura. Empirical accounts of marriage and divorce (often with quantitative data for small communities) are found in monographs based on field work. Guritno (1964) has studied divorce in a Javanese village in Yogyakarta. Singarimbum and Manning (1974) report the results of a quantitative survey in a village near Yogyakarta.

Some demographers and population experts are interested in studying patterns of fertility in relation to divorce. This concern with the legal status of women is reflected in all statements on the status of Indonesian women in the social science literature of the country. Since action is also associated with it, studies on this theme are encouraged. As Mely Tan

(1973b) says: "In fact, ever since the establishment of the first women's organization (about 1912), regulation of marriage by law has been mentioned as being one of the most important aims. It includes regulations in regard to polygamy, child marriage, grounds of divorce, financial support and alimony in case of divorce, and registration of marriage and divorce".

The new legislation passed in 1974 has brought about quite a few changes. Various aspects of the passing of the National Marriage Law of Indonesia have been studied by Jean Buah Adeh (1974), K. Hadiati (1972), June and Ronald Katz.(1975), and Nani Soewando (1975). Soewando (1977) also looks into the implementation of the marriage law; she is now involved in working towards the passing of a comprehensive inheritance law. There have been no empirical studies to evaluate the implementation and the effects of the new National Marriage Law. It is necessary to assess the functioning of the legal system among different populations of the country.

Well-planned micro—level empirical studies of the actual operation of the laws in various spheres of life are needed. Between the cultural patterns recorded by Dutch scholars and the written law, there is what the people actually do in regard to inheritance, marriage, and divorce. Do urban women, rural women, and poor urban women look at the law in the same way? And how have communities that adhere to Islam but follow different Adat reacted to the changes? There is no doubt that a new type of research is needed in the field of law to understand the legal status of women in Indonesia.

Education is recognized as an important indicator of women's status; its various facets engage the attention of scholars from disciplines like education, statistics, and demography, and to some extent sociology and psychology. It must be mentioned, however, that so far very little serious work on the sociology of education has been done, and still less so on education of women. Some work on this has been initiated both by the National Commission on women, and the international agencies. Participation in economic activity is another important issue on which comparative statistics and analyses are available.

The ILO report of May 1978, titled Women's Participation in the Economic Activity of Asian Countries, is an example of the use of available statistics. Many of the recent and ongoing projects on women have been inter- disciplinary in nature and conducted as collaborative efforts by scholars from disciplines like anthropology/sociology, demography, economics, and law. For instance, The Status of Women and Family Planning in Indonesia (1973) was prepared by six scholars belonging to different disciplines, under the directorship of anthropologist T.O. Ihromi.

This report draws upon a whole array of works by Western as well as Indonesian scholars dealing with social structure, values, religion, the legal system, etc. In her excellent contribution to the study, Mely Tan reviews the social and cultural context of the status of women in Indonesia. The review is based on social science literature in Dutch, English, and Bahasa Indonesia, on the writings of people involved in the women's movement, and on the available demographic data.

For the collaborative work, seven geographical areas were selected on the bases of ethnicity, religion, type of family, and kinship structure. Both rural and urban dimensions were taken note of in each selected area. The areas were: Acehnese, Muslim, parental (bilateral) Batak, Christian, patrilineal Minangkabau, Muslim, matrilineal "Melting pot", the most urbanised area of Indonesia Sundanese, Muslim, parental (bilateral) Madurese, Muslim, parental (bilateral) Balinese, Hindu-Balinese, parental (bilateral). The interview guide used while collecting data emphasized information on the role of women in family and society, and also sought information concerning activities in the family planning field.

The authors themselves acknowledge that "there is very little information on the status of women in Indonesia because the family planning programme has only been implemented on a large scale since 1970-1971". They also mention that the unevenness in the quality and thoroughness of the information obtained through field work was partly a result of the patchy training that some of their research associates had. The interview guide was an adaptation of the guidelines provided by the United Nations Commission on the Status of Women.

Perhaps an assessment of the status of women was to be made on the basis of socio-cultural indicators and this was to be correlated with patterns of family planning. It is not clear whether this could not be done very well because the programme of family planning was relatively new or because the research plan provided by the international agency could not cope with the socio-cultural specificities of different countries. It is, however, a comprehensive work containing a review of the social and cultural settings of women's lives; a history of legal changes; data on education and employment among women; and information obtained, through a survey, on matters like the value placed on children, attitudes towards family planning, changes in women's roles due to modernization, and so on.

It carries on extensive bibliography of relevant works in Bahasa Indonesia, Dutch, and English. One important study which is being finalized seeks to present a profile of Indonesian women. In this study again, social scientists from disciplines like anthropology, sociology, demography, and law are collaborating. Its content includes demographic data and information on the education and employment of women, women's role in various economic activities, health services and family planning, and networks of communication, as well as time budgets for typical rural men and women and a series of chapters on various aspects of legal rights relating to marriage, custody of children, property, and so on.

There is also to be a discussion of the effects of customary law and tradition on the ability of women to exercise legal rights. This study will be comprehensive and, hopefully, will be able to point to the shortcomings of demographic and other kinds of data. In each of these collaborative studies, the Indonesian scholars have faced immense difficulties in taking account of the diversity of cultures in the country. Studies on nutrition, health, and family planning are being undertaken in various parts of Indonesia. A new action project, "Statistical Profiles of

Children and Mothers", which has been prepared by UNICEF for Indonesia, is part of a larger project which will also cover Bangladesh, India, and Pakistan.

One significant project being carried out by the Agro Economic Survey in cooperation with the Centre for Rural Sociological Research, Bogor Agricultural University, is a "Study of Rural Households and the Role of Women in Two Villages of West Java". The schedule being used is extensive. It is aimed at obtaining data on labour inputs, produce obtained, income generated, and patterns of consumption. An enormous and really imaginative effort will be needed if a worthwhile understanding of the role of women in rural Java is to emerge from the materials gathered for this study.

Women's studies started relatively early in Indonesia because they received social acceptance easily, and partly because they happened to interest some Western scholars. Recent years have been marked by the development of new lines of research in studies of rural Indonesia. Indonesian social scientists now have before them the difficult task of critically evaluating and carefully assembling the available material on women. They cannot afford to ignore either the diversities in their country or the various processes of change if they are to consolidate their position and to plan appropriately for the future.

Malaysia

It is well known that in Malaysia, all the major social sciences with the exception of economics have received recognition only in the last decade. However, the areas that form today's Malaysia have attracted a series of western scholars since the thirties. There is, for example, the excellent research of Raymond and Rosemary Firth on Malay fishermen and peasants (1946, 1943); Derek Freeman's work on the Iban (1955); and William Geddes's book about the Dayak (1954). Accounts by ethnographers-cum-administrators, like H.D. Noone who worked in the thirties, and Dick Noone who worked in the fifties, also need to be mentioned.

Also available are descriptions of aborigines who had different degrees of contact with the mainstream of the population. Studies with a specific focus on women have slowly emerged in the seventies. A number of regional seminars on various themes concerning women, mainly supported by United Nations agencies, were held during the last few years. They have given much impetus to the study of women by creating a concerned interest in the problems of women and by identifying new talent among researchers. Academics in the universities are being drawn more and more into this field of research.

Some action programmes of the Government of Malaysia relate to women as a category, or to households, and deal with problems like family planning, nutrition, employment, and education. The collection and collation of data on women is an integral part of these programmes. Economists and demographers are engaged in research on population, using sex as a basic variable and thus providing valuable statistics about women. A Bibliography of Demography in Malaysia, by Ng (1977), gives some idea of what is available. James Palmore has written, in collaboration with others, about marriage patterns and cumulative fertility in West Malaysia and about the demographic situation in Malaysia.

The Department of Population Studies of the University of Malaysia is undertaking a new programme of research with the help of the United Nations Fund for Population Activities. The vital statistics of the population of West Malaysia have been published by the Department of Statistics of the Government (1976), and help in understanding the condition of the country's women. It must be stressed, however, that the value of collecting information sex-wise (in regard to health and education, for example) is not fully recognized. Such information would make possible proper comparison of the relative positions of males and females in the country; it would also help in understanding how Malaysia compares with other countries.

Because money is available for them, many studies on family planning are being taken up. Family planning, however, is a matter that anyone in Malaysia, particularly social scientists, would find very difficult to deal with. The ethnic divisions in the population can strongly influence the selection of target groups for action. The issue of numbers is a sensitive one, for there is full adult franchise and each group wants effective political participation. The Malay, who come from varied backgrounds and include the indigenous tribes, are represented in both rural and urban areas. They constitute 52.7 per cent of the population of Malaysia.

The Chinese, who are principally urban dwellers engaged in trade, business, and finance, form 35.7 per cent; and the Indians make up another 10.7 per cent of the population. The economic and political interests of the three communities clash; differences in religion, language, dress, and food habits are obvious even to a casual observer. Research on family planning has, however, made available some worthwhile material on women in Malaysia. For example, the Federation of Family Planning Associations of Malaysia has produced a report, Women Today in Peninsular Malaysia (1975).

The position of women in the labour force and the special problems of young village women who migrate to urban areas to enter factories or to join the labour force in the unorganized sector are being taken up as subjects for investigation. Plantation labour is also being studied. While the lead has come from foreign social scientists, Malaysian scholars have recognized the importance of such research; and a few research scholars and young teachers are already working in these areas. Studies on rural labour throw light on labour by women and on their conditions of work. Jamilah Ariffin, a Malaysian scholar trained in Australia, has written on rural-urban migration and the status of women factory workers in Malaysia (1975).

Her paper, "Industrial Development in Peninsular Malaysia and Rural-Urban Migration of Women Workers: Impact and Implications", prepared for the Tenth International Congress of Anthropological and Ethnological Sciences held in December 1978, shows how the interplay between the pattern of industrialization and the New Economic Policy of the Government has been crucial in attracting migrants from rural areas. Ariffin gives a candid account of the situation in which the immigrant girls find themselves and describes the reaction of urban society to this relatively recent phenomenon: it is called a 'social problem.

Studies of plantation labour have not so far been focused specifically on women. It appears to be a field with particular potential for studies on exploitation and discrimination, division of labour, time allocation, and authority patterns within the household. We may mention here M.I. Komanyi's doctoral work, The Real and Ideal Participation in Decision-Making of Iban Women: A study of a long house community in Sarawak, East Malaysia (1973). If tribal and rural ethnography now directs its attention towards such problems, our knowledge of the position of women in Southeast Asia is likely to be placed on a sound footing. Research as an intellectual exercise finds a fertile ground in Malaysia, and the country's tradition of collaboration with Western social scientists has brought about some worthwhile results.

One such collaboration, which involves the Australian scholar Gavin Jones, is a very interesting project on marriage and fertility being launched by the University of Malaya. The objectives of the study are:

a. To measure time trends in age at marriage, age difference between spouses, and outcome of marriage among each ethnic group in traditional and "modern" settings;
b. To investigate factors influencing age at marriage and changes in these factors (e.g., education of girls, the switch from parent-arranged to self-arranged marriages) which may make for further changes in age at marriage;
c. To investigate the relationship between age at marriage and patterns of marital dissolution on fertility; and
d. To investigate attitudes to inter-ethnic marriage, together with their correlates.

The study is to be conducted among Tamils on rubber estates, Chinese in new villages, rural Kelentan Malays, and rural Johore or Malacca Malays; the "modern" sample is to be drawn from urban middle-class Indians, Chinese, and Malays.

Anthropology and sociology, which go together in Malaysia, are gradually being drawn into studies of women mainly by some of the younger researchers. A doctoral dissertation on the status of women in Malaysia is being prepared, along with a bibliography, in the Department of Anthropology and Sociology at the University of Malaya. Those who are interested in the study of development are also paying attention to problems created for women by the processes of development.

The measurement of the working hours of women is of interest to anthropology and sociology as well as to economics, psychology, and education. The common theme of role conflict, attitudinal variables involved in the choice of careers and courses, and the notion of femininity, etc., are receiving attention in the Departments of Psychology and Education. The discipline of education appears to have developed a keen interest in the problems of girls and women and in aspects of women's status. Dr Fatima Don, Dean of the Faculty of Education, is on the National Advisory Council for the Integration of Women in Development. This is a coordinating, consulting, and advisory body on women's affairs. The government expects it to look into legislation affecting women and to examine standards and regulations which affect the conditions of working women. Dr Don prepared a comprehensive paper on Malaysian women for the training course in leadership conducted by the Asia Pacific Centre for Women and Development (APCWD) in Bangkok in September-October 1978.

A few research projects are in the per cent. Her colleagues are also involved in research on women's education and in studies of the conditions of women workers in factories, plantations, etc. The Department of Anthropology and Sociology at the National University of Malaysia has organized a seminar on women in Malaysia in which various aspects of the position of women received attention. In the first session, the position of women from the legal point of view was presented by Kin Arifah of the Faculty of Law, University of Malaya.

Women in the labour force were an important subject at the seminar and were discussed by Jamilah Ariffin, Selvaratnam, and others. The consequences of the exploitation of women on the verge of delivery, rural-urban migration, the socialization of children, and women and nation-building were other topics on which papers were prepared. A significant feature of the seminar was the involvement of a number of scholars from different disciplines like economics, political science, law, psychology, anthropology, and sociology.

Legal aspects of the status of women which have been a major concern of researchers and social workers in Indonesia and the Philippines, have received barely any attention from those who are concerned with the status of Malaysian women. It needs to be ascertained whether the women of the majority community have been able to use Muslim Personal Law mainly to their advantage, with the help of the traditional social organization, and hence have not bothered to raise their voice against whatever constraints are imposed by it. An important fact to bear in mind in this connection is that Malaysia did not have a women's movement comparable to that which existed in Indonesia.

The relatively new social movement demanding a return to Islam which is gaining ground in Malaysia, deserves a mention here. Young women involved in the movement have started wearing a specially-designed shroud in order to cover the hair, neck, arms, and hands, which remain exposed in the accepted attire for women. The shroud also covers the bust with a double thickness of cloth. This is in keeping with instructions in the scriptures. Many of the ideas regarding the roles and the status of women which are being accepted by those young women come in direct conflict with the efforts of other women who are cooperating with international agencies, pursuing academic research, or involving themselves in action programmes aimed at the betterment of women's status.

Modernized women as well as those who follow traditional ways come into conflict with the ideas of these young women. Bitter debates on the status of women in Islam and on the definition of proper behaviour for Malay Muslim women go on. Departments of languages have just begun to realize that studies on women are an essential component of the study of society through language. So far there is no clear understanding of how literature – written as well as folk – as also the structure of a language, can be used for studies on women.

The Department of Tamil has produced Women in Tamil Society: the Classical Period and Women in Modern Tamil Literature. These can only point to the need for well–planned socio- logical studies based on qualitative and quantitative content analysis of literature in order to understand the situation of women in it. The study of oral tradition should also be kept in mind.

A few projects on women being taken up by social scientists at the University of Malaya will give an idea of the academic interests that are developing in this country: "Employment and Career Development of Women: A Study of Their Needs and Aspirations in an Urban Society (Seremban Town)", "A Study of Rural Women in Economic Development", and "A Study of Women's Needs and Aspirations in Society and Their Priorities in Employment and Career Development: An Exploratory Study of the Faculties of Arts and Social Sciences, Science and Economics and Administration Undergraduates, University of Malaya". The last one, which is being conducted by the Faculty of Education, is being supported by the National Council for Integration of Women in Development.

THE PHILIPPINES

There has been a spate of studies on women in recent years in the Philippines, and a considerable volume of research is now available. In terms of the training of its social scientists, subsequent communication through the flow of visiting scholars from and to the Philippines, and easy availability and use of social science literature produced in the West, this country may be considered the most developed in Southeast Asia. Earlier Spanish influence has been overshadowed by American influence in the present century. Facility with the English language is a distinct advantage when compared with the difficulty in communication faced by social scientists in Indonesia, Thailand, and, to some extent, Malaysia.

Several institutions engaged in research and in action programmes, which make use of social science concepts and methodology, are functioning in the Philippines. Concern for the integration of women in development is bringing forth many kinds of studies on various aspects of women's lives. The National Media Production Center, the Bureau of Women and Minors, and the National Commission on the Role of Filipino Women, among others, are also actively involved in promoting studies on women. Alzona's The Filipino Woman, published in 1934, did not represent an established area of academic interest.

By and large, the society and culture of the majority community in the Philippines did not attract social scientists until the fifties; most studies related to the tribal communities and other minority groups. As Zamora (1976) observes, work in urban anthropology and in the anthropology of education, and studies of lowland Christian peasants and of values came to the Philippines in the sixties. By the mid-sixties, women had been recognized as a subject for systematic research; over the years, interest in this area has grown and diversified.

Castillo's paper "Occupational Sex-roles as Perceived by Filipino Adolescents" was published in 1961. Facts on women's participation in the labour force were made available by the Women's Rights Movement in 1963. By this time, the access of women to training and employment had become an important concern of people who were interested in the progress of women. In general terms, the progress of Filipino women and their status and role in society have interested social scientists since the mid-sixties.

The literature includes Castillo's study of the multiple roles of the Filipino woman (1969); her evaluation of the Filipino woman as 'manpower' (1976); The Development and Progress of Filipino Women by Guazon (1968); The Filipino Woman: Her Role and Status in Philippine Society by Montiel and Hollnsteiner (1976); Filipino Women as Partners of Men in Progress and Development by Gonzalez and Hollnsteiner (1976); and the report of a national survey on the status and roles of women in the Philippines by Bulatao (1977).

The cultural minorities, consisting of Muslims and tribal communities generally divided between non-Christian groups and Negrito groups make up 15 per cent of the total population. Filipino anthropologists should have been able to provide necessary information about women's status and roles in these communities; but in the surveys based on available empirical data these communities are either not touched upon at all or, as in A Profile of Filipino Women, only some broad cultural patterns are presented. Very little systematic information is available on Muslim women.

Some anthropologists-both Western and Filipino-have written on tribal women in the Philippines. To be sure, most of the tribal studies did not specifically focus on women. Little effort has been made by the Filipino anthropologists to draw relevant materials relative to. women from existing literature or to plan studies that would help to bring out those essential features of these societies that have a bearing on the position of women. In point of fact, the bilateral principle governing group placement and the right to strategic resources, and a broad non-discrimination between sexes combined with some differentiation of sex roles, provide a rich field for anthropologists.

A few recent anthropological studies of tribal groups have given some attention to the status of women. A notable mention should, however, be made of Jill B.R. Chuneff's research project entitled "Sex Roles, Economics and Power: A Study of Bontoc Village, Philippines". She says that in more traditional, non-industrial societies, the gender dichotomy between the public sphere and the domestic sphere has little or no relevance for understanding the social structure. Her central thesis is that control of the economic resources of the society gives women access to legitimate power, and therefore, to authority, in both domestic and public spheres.

The project is to study the social structural interrelationship between sex roles and economics and its effects on power and influence in decision-making in the village in a situation of neo-colonial encroachment. Political scientists' interest and involvement in women's studies is extremely limited. Sex is used as a variable in studies of political behaviour, like voting, and of political participation and decision-making, and sometimes trends in women's political behaviour are discussed; but that is about all. Studies concerned with law generally reflect a commitment to the introduction of reforms.

While authority and decision-making in the family are egalitarian, legally the husband has the right to decide for the wife in matters of residence, work outside the home, etc. This is probably a result of Catholic and Spanish influence. Some important aspects of law that are being studied are the legal rights of women in the family and in society; laws relating to marriage which impose specific constraints on a woman in relation to her husband; laws pertaining to separation, which tend to be unfavourable to women; the legal implications of abortion; and the status of children born out of wedlock.

The Forum on Women's Rights in the Philippine Law is also engaged in work along these lines. Women lawyers are actively concerned with removing the legal disabilities of women. The National Commission on the Role of Filipino Women also welcomes the co-operation of eminent women from the field of law. Demography and economics, the former more than the latter, are involved in women's studies in a big way. The National Demographic Surveys of 1968 and 1973 and the National Sample Surveys have resulted in a good statistical profile, particularly for the majority community. The survey data have been utilized further in analytical and correlational efforts to understand the situation of women.

The Population Center Foundation is doing extensive work on "Women Power: Development and Utilization" and on "Female Work Experience and Fertility in the Philippines". The Population Institute of the University of the Philippines has done, and is engaged in, work on women, particularly on cross-cultural variations in demographic characteristics. The study of social and economic aspects of fertility provides much information on women's life concerns and roles and on their place in decision-making. Contributions of this kind include the work of Harman (1970) and that of Madigan (1977). Bulatao participated in and wrote on the cross-national study of the value of children.

This effort at understanding the motivations that determine fertility includes a design for studying patterns of the division of labour and the relative values placed on sons and daughters, both in the immediate context and in terms of security for the future. Economists have been cooperating with international organizations to bring out studies on economic participation, particularly labour participation of women; on the role of women in development, including their contribution to the economy; and on nutrition and health programmes. Measurements of work inputs and outputs for women interest economists as much as they interest sociologists.

The study of woman power in the Bicol River Basin by Jeanne Frances Ilio, Involvement by Choice; The Role of Women in Development (1977a), reviews extensive data on income, labour force participation and life concerns gathered from women as well as men in rice-farming, coastal fishing, and urban communities, and comes out with a proposal for involving women in development efforts. The Institute of Economic Development and Research also has an active interest in research on women.

Its publications include Bonlier's work on children and household economic activity in Laguna (1976); Jayme Ho's on time budgets and labour force participation of married women; King's on time-allocation in rural households (1976); and Popkin's on child welfare in rural Philippine households, the role of the rural Filipino mother in child care, and the relation of the earnings and the time-allocation of a working mother with the nurture of her children.

Education is another discipline which has evinced an unequivocal interest in developing an adequate understanding of the status, roles, and opportunities available to Filipino women. Curricula, institutional frameworks, sex-linked variation in enrolment in different courses, and attitudes to and perceptions of the performance of females in various disciplines and professional training courses are some of the themes studied. Both empirical studies and analyses of available data are taken up, often in combination. Sociological, economic, educational, and communicational aspects have been approached in this fashion. Studies conducted during the last four years by the Fund for Assistance to Private Education (FAPE) on manpower resources, sex differences in performance, and educational aspirations may be mentioned.

It will not be an exaggeration to say that the initiative of Filipino scholars has been of great help to their counterparts in other Asian countries in the study of the various facets of education for women in developing countries. In 1970, the very well-attended Conference on the Education of Women in Developing Countries was held in Manila under the auspices of the National Science Development Board. In the same year, the Philippines Women's University published The Educational Dilemma of Women in Asia edited by Alma De-Jesus-Viardo. This university has a special interest in the education of women and in the sociology of educated women. Job-oriented education was the focus of some of the studies made by sociologists.

Filipino Women as Partners of Men in Progress and Development by Anna Miren Gonzalez and Mary Hollnsteiner advocates reform for shared and equal partnership between men and women, and stresses the potential of the educational system for bringing this about. Studies on women have become a special concern of sociology, social work, and social psychology. Any bibliography of publications on women, of which there are now several, shows a preponderance of studies from these disciplines.

The bibliographies given in Filipino Women as Partners of Men in Progress and Development (1976) and A Profile of Filipino Women (1977) may be mentioned in this connection. The status that women have traditionally held in various sections of society, the roles they have played, and basic issues concerning women's status are treated in the studies carried out by scholars in these disciplines. In studies of socialization, attitude formation, role differentiation by sex, and the values nurtured by women, the twin notions of machismo and femialsmo have received attention.

People's perceptions of occupations as sex-linked or sex-neutral, the opportunities open to women in various spheres of activity, the division of labour and the patterns of authority in the family and in society, the implications for women of the role of housewife and mother, and the dilemma of work versus home are some of the other subjects that have been dealt with. Many studies of small samples or those generalizing about Filipino women have, often unconsciously, focused on urban middle and upper-class women.

Gradually, however, research interests appear to be shifting towards the rural sector and poor and lower-middle levels in the country. Whether some sociologists are not carrying their preconceived ideas about the traditional roles of Filipino women into the study of these populations, with whom they are less familiar, is a debatable issue; but the trend towards studies of rural women and those belonging to poorer sections is unmistakable. There is a growing demand for the authentic description of conditions in the rural areas and for programmes of reform to improve the situation of women.

The participation of women in income-generating activities is viewed with enthusiasm. In research programmes, a conscious effort is made to take up projects in rural areas and to cover different geographical areas of the country. The effects of poverty on the role of lower class women in development are being studied. The much-emphasized role of Filipino women as managers of the household and controllers of purse-strings is being reviewed in the light of situations of deprivation in which exigencies decide how the meagre income should be spent. Anna Miren Gonzalez (1977) has successfully shown how poverty limits "the life concerns of the women to eking out existence of the family and getting seemingly endless household and child-rearing tasks done each day".

The new interest in the study of women in the unorganized sector is likely to grow. Some interesting small-scale studies on the issue of professionalization of housekeepers, hostesses, waitresses, and similar callings, and on hospitality girls and massage attendants, "who engage in totally unproductive labour and function as sex symbols and ego-builders for the élite" have been carried out. They demonstrate the need for pursuing sociological analysis in a proper socio-economic perspective. The contribution that the Institute of Philippine Culture of the Ateneo de Manila University has made to the advancement of research on women cannot be overemphasized.

Studies on women thrive in an interdisciplinary environment; rigid disciplinary boundaries are likely to impose severe constraints on them. At the Institute, scholars from the various social sciences, and even some from the humanities, interact and collaborate with one another. The interdisciplinary character of the research conducted under the auspices of the Institute is evident in the work done on values by Frank Lynch and others, which has relevance for understanding the concerns of Filipino women; in a study of women and development; in Gonzalez and Hollnsteiner (1976), which has been mentioned earlier; and in the project to study manpower in the Bicol River Basin, on which Jean Ilio's report (1977) is based.

The Institute's most recent achievement in the field of women's studies is Philippine Women and Development; An Annotated Bibliography by Elizabeth Eviote (1978). In the Philippines, interest in research on women seems likely to grow. There is no dearth of women social scientists in the Philippines. Moreover, many men are also involved, in varying degrees, in programmes to study women. The social sciences in this country have by now accepted that women cannot and should not be viewed in isolation. There is no doubt that the field of women's studies is in competent hands in this country.

The use of new approaches and of hitherto untapped sources of data is likely to carry it forward, as is already happening in the study of various facets of Philippine culture. The study of women will profit, for example, from the growing interest in folklore and ethnoscience.

SINGAPORE

The activities of social scientists in Singapore in the field of women's studies are divided into two parts: work being done specifically on Singapore society, and compilation, documentation and empirical work being done at the Institute of Southeast Asian Studies, As is clearly put forth in the country statement for Singapore in Policy Towards Social Sciences in Asia and Oceania, social sciences are expected to be relevant and useful within the developmental framework of Singapore.

The exigencies of socio-economic development are the fundamental factors in guiding social science activity. There is a tight integration of governmental and semi-governmental units. Family planning and population control have been integral to the programme of development in Singapore, and there are a number of studies on these subjects. Most of these studies take into account the situation and the role of women; a few focus directly on women.

Several works on aspects of fertility, family planning, and population in Singapore, for instance those by Peter S.J. Chen, Chang Chen-Tung, James Fawcett, and Eddie Chen-Yu Kuo, have been published during the last five years or so. Forthcoming publications include Dilemma of Parenthood; A Study of the Value of Children, and The Dynamics of Child Bearing Decisions; The Singapore Experience, both edited by Peter S.J. Chen and others. Aline Wong's extensive writings on women also include some that are concerned with fertility and family planning.

Work on subjects such as the family, abortion, and housing contains some observations on the status of women. That researchers have a keen interest in the study of the female labour force in Singapore is evident. The relation between fertility and the employment of women has also been examined. By and large, we may say that interaction with social scientists in other countries and contacts with international agencies have helped social scientists in Singapore to develop an interest in the study of women.

For example, An Exploratory Study on the Effectiveness of Population Disincentives in Preventing Higher Order Births in Singapore, by Aline Wong (1977) was done for the International Development Research Centre of Canada. Wong wrote "The Persistence of High Fertility: Population Prospects in the Third World" for the Family and Fertility Change series edited by John C. Caldwell of the Australian National University. Her other paper "Chinese Women at Work" forms part of The Fertility of Working Women: A Synthesis of International Research edited by Stanley Kupinsky. Another of her papers on "Women in Singapore" was published in Signs.

The research project on the "Value of Children" is another example of international collaboration between scholars. The research activities of the staff and the academic exercises of the students of the Department of Sociology and Anthropology of the-University of Singapore give evidence of interest in studies of women. The following projects can be mentioned: "The Value of Children", "Comparative Status of Women in Hong Kong and Singapore", and "Culture and Fertility".

Subjects covered in academic exercises by students include the present status of women in Singapore (different aspects); factory girls in Jurong; female delinquency in the light of the quality of the adolescent's home background; female construction workers; university students: their self-images and images of society; unwed mothers in Singapore; the sex of the first child and the family relationship; drug abuse among female addicts; marital conflict and divorce in Singapore; and the social consequences of maternal employment.

The only member of the staff whose major research interest is women are Aline Wong. She has contributed to edited volumes and has presented papers at seminars and conferences. In the Department of Social Work, subjects like adoption, prostitution, and divorce are being studied. Studies of inter-ethnic relations, which both social work and sociology/anthropology departments undertake, also touch upon women. But these studies often lack historical and cultural perspective, and tend to ignore many relevant features of the societies to which immigrants like the Indians, the Chinese, and the Sinhalese originally belonged.

In social science disciplines, sex-wise data are often collected and a good deal of information on women is, thus, available. This information, however, is not always adequately used either in preparing statistical profiles or as a guide for further qualitative research. This is not to say that new lines of research are not emerging: Noeleen Heyzer's work on the "Peripheral Workforce: Young Women and Migrant Workers in Singapore" is evidence that they are. Here the role of the Institute of Southeast Asian Studies is notable. It draws scholars interested in Southeast Asia from various countries and has perhaps the best collection on Southeast Asia.

It provides opportunities for social scientists from Singapore to interact personally, and through their writings, with other scholars. Some of the work on women done at the Institute may be referred to. The Status of Women and Fertility in Southeast and East Asia: A Bibliography with Selected Annotations, by Betty Jamie Chung, was published in 1978. The same author has written, in collaboration with Ng Shui Mug, The Status of Women in Law: A Comparison of Five Asian Countries. Rural Asian Women: Status and Environment, by Robert Orr Whyte and Pauline Whyte (1978), is based on studies conducted by social scientists from various universities, Western as well as Asian and Australian.

This small publication was only a prelude to their voluminous bibliographical work on the status of Asian women which is now nearing completion. Chang Heng Chee's paper on "The Mobilization of Women into the Economics and politics of Singapore" published as an occasional paper by the University of Singapore (1978) was originally published in Southeast Asian Perspectives brought out by the Institute. The Oral History Programme of the Institute is launching a long-term project entitled "An Oral Ethnography of Singapore's

Cultural Communities". Some women are likely to be included in those who are selected for in-depth interviewing in the course of this study. Besides social scientists, many educated women in Singapore are actively involved in promoting the cause of women. They include social workers, doctors, and lawyers. Newspapers frequently carry reports on issues concerning women and serve as a forum for debate on the subject.

THAILAND

Thailand welcomes foreign researchers and gives them facilities for their work. Between sixty and eighty foreign researchers visit Thailand every year, and some of them are social scientists. They generally pursue their preferred interests. Some of them are interested in religion, others in the relationship between religion and the State; some in politics, others in problems oriented to family planning; and so on. It is only in recent years that the country has started making efforts to develop an understanding of the conditions and specific problems of women at different socio-economic levels in rural as well as urban areas.

The issue of the integration of women in the development process has given rise to a strong emphasis on the rural sector. Employment, literacy, and population control are the three principal areas in which the government, philanthropic organizations, and academic institutions are increasingly involved. The role of UN agencies is notable. They collect statistics for making cross-national comparisons and involve social workers, government representatives, and social scientists in conferences, workshops, action research, and so on. They also make available funds for cross-national studies and for research on specific topics.

The Social Research Institute at Chulalongkorn University (CUSRI) has prepared a bibliography of work on social development in Thailand (1975a). A number of studies conducted under its auspices in rural areas deal with matters such as employment (1975d) and manpower (1975e), the non-formal education programme, and socio-economic condition:

in selected villages. Some of these are written in Thai. Population in Thailand and Demographic Situation in Thailand provide basic data about the population of the country.

Fertility has been studied in relation to labour force participation, education, urbanization, migration, acceptance of contraception, marriage and employment, cultural attitudes, cost and value of children, and religion. Many anthropological studies of the peasantry and of various tribal groups in Thailand indicate a tendency towards equality between the sexes in the kinship system and a relatively flexible pattern of residence. Substantial economic contributions to their households are made by women and they wield considerable power in the family.

These are, however, only isolated descriptions of observed facts; there is a need to systematise these and other related patterns of family behaviour to better understand the status of women in these communities. Robert Cooper's article on sexual inequality among the Hmong perhaps marks the beginning of a new trend. It should be added that social science research with a specific focus on women is still uncommon in Thailand. Only a few projects have been completed, or are still in hand. The National Research Council has the following research projects concerning women on its list:

1. The Comparative Study of Thai Women's Occupations in Urban and Rural Areas, a doctoral thesis prepared for Chulalongkorn University, 1976;
2. The Role of Southern Thai Women in contributing to Family Income, published by Friedrich-Ebert-Stiftung, Federal Republic of Germany, 1976;
3. Employees' Expectation of Their Supervisor's Role, conducted by the Faculty of Social Sciences, Kasetsart University, 1978; and
4. Labour Force Participation, Village Characteristics and Modernism and their Influence on Fertility among Rural Thai Women, Institute for Population and Social Research, Mahidol University, 1978.

Nibhon Debavalya, Director of the Institute of Population Studies at Chulalongkorn University, has conducted a study on Female Employment and Fertility; Cross-sectional and Longitudinal Relationships from a National Sample of Married Thai Women. It forms part of a series of monographs which presents the results of research by the permanent staff of the Institute as well as by foreign advisers and research workers temporarily attached to the Institute. The report says, "We can summarize by saying that the differential in fertility between women who did not work either before or after marriage and those who did is evident for both urban and rural areas.

The facts indicate that the pattern is considerably more pronounced among urban women than among their rural counterparts. In rural areas, working outside the home is relatively easy since the majority work as farm labourers or related workers in the same community. For both urban and rural areas, it is obvious that work for pay before and after marriage are more critical independent variables influencing fertility than the present work status. The differences in average number of children ever born, standardized for age, between women who worked and those who did not work for pay either before or after marriage seem to be greater, on the whole, than the differences in relation to current employment status.

In addition, within each current work status, those who worked for pay all the time after marriage seem to have a stronger negative association with fertility (as measured by the difference in the standardized fertility levels) than the same group of women who worked for pay before marriage and their present work statuses. For instance, among total working women in Bangkok, those who worked all the time after marriage have an average of 2,385 children ever born per 1,000 married women, as compared to 3,199 children when they worked before marriage and 3,798 per 1,000 for those in the work force at present.

"Among rural women, having worked for pay before marriage seems to have a stronger negative relation with fertility than having worked for pay after marriage or the present work status. Since family planning methods are being practiced by only a very small minority of rural wives, the evidence suggests that there may be an association between female work for pay before marriage and a later age at marriage, thus, in turn, making a fertility differential between women who did work and those who did not work at all".

From the above quotation it will be seen that even with sophisticated methods of analysis, really significant results regarding the status of women are not forthcoming. During a meeting which I had at the Population Centre with him and a few other social scientists, Dr Debavalya began with the remark that the status of women in Thailand was already high. The statement is not wrong; but some relevant indicators of women's status are not given sufficient consideration in research that is undertaken. It seems that some of the assumptions on which studies on fertility are based do not apply to Thailand in the same way as they do elsewhere, particularly to South Asian countries.

It is also open to doubt whether they apply to the majority of the populations of other Asian countries. Recent findings of studies on population control and family planning support this doubt. Small research studies undertaken by students of the social sciences in Thailand also indicate that role conflict is mainly a problem of women white-collar workers who have to come away from home leaving their children behind. Even here the role of the extended family is not unimportant. The two roles, of homemaker and of worker, appear to be compatible for workers in hotels and restaurants; employers provide facilities for the care óf young children, as this is considered essentially women's work.

In her or her family's own business also, a woman can manage to make the two roles compatible. Among industrial employers, however, there is a distinct preference for unmarried girls. A disturbing consequence of this is that when they get married, girls try to keep this information back from their employers; if they happen to become pregnant, they resort to abortions. Thus, because of indirect pressures, their right to become mothers is taken away from them. In many cases, when such girls become mothers they leave their babies with their own mothers or with other relatives and continue to withhold the facts from their employers.

This situation needs careful study so that it can be remedied. The woman's role as homemaker is clearly recognized in Thailand, but questions that can elicit valuable information from rural women about the overlapping of sex roles, authority patterns, and about the traditional situations, followed by effects of changes, are often not asked. A study of the roles of women in three villages, undertaken by a doctoral candidate, also illustrates the need for asking incisive questions based on the situation in Thailand and not mechanically drawn from research done in other countries. Another area of research interest is literacy and education.

According to general findings the per cent age of drop-outs is higher among girls, who are needed at home to help their mothers; in out-of-school programmes, moreover, men can continue to practise reading and writing but women cannot, for they have too much to do and are too tired to attend these classes at the end of the day. One of the major problems mentioned in Thailand was the "lack of responsibility on the part of men and over-work on the part of women". Whether women are treated on par with men by promoters of such educational programmes also needs to be investigated. In analysing data on drop-outs, it is perhaps necessary to weigh the significance of sex-linked activities in childhood and the family's and society's expectations of future roles by the two sexes.

The distinction between literacy and illiteracy made in the census needs to be reconsidered. Thailand has had compulsory primary education since 1921. Boys and girls thus study for a few years and achieve some literacy; but when they take up adult roles and become preoccupied with household work and agriculture, they tend to forget much of what they had learned at school. Should these people be called illiterate in the same sense as those who have never been to school? In the Thai census, these people (understandably, women predominate in this category) were asked if they could read and write and were also asked to demonstrate the claim.

Out of shyness, women often adopted the safe course of denying any knowledge of reading and writing. Some women officers interested in women's development are of the view that if they are properly approached, such women can demonstrate that they are not totally illiterate. To consider how plans could give enough attention to women and children, a governmental sub-committee was appointed in January 1978. One working group was set up to advise on data collection, and another looked at the possibility of establishing a permanent office. A survey on the status of working women was planned, which would also examine the working conditions of women in industry in the provinces. The results are yet to be analysed.

According to the Chairman of the Task Force for the Planning of Women's Development, who was also the organizer of the 1975 Women's Year Programme, funds from the Voluntary Fund are still available for supporting research. Two themes which are engaging the attention of the National Economics Social Development Board (NESDB), and in which social scientists will be involved, are:

i. How working women in the agricultural sector apportion their time, and
ii. The attitudes of women towards their roles in the family and in the community.

The attitudes of men towards women and towards women's roles are also sought to be studied. An exciting experiment currently being carried out in Thailand has great potential for social science research. This is the work of Community-based Family Planning Services (CBFPS), a non-profit private organization which specializes in the training of voluntary family planning motivators, contraceptive distributors, and agents of change at the community or village level. CBFPS has a Research and Evaluation Division which analyses the information gathered in the course of the institution's activities, which also include helping women with abortions, or with childbirth if abortion is not possible, and the promotion of family planning?

Only 20 per cent, of the clients of CBFPS come for contraceptives alone; the others come initially to get rid of unwanted pregnancies. It may be mentioned that abortions, except under certain conditions like rape, or when the woman's social and economic situation makes her unfit to bear a child, are still illegal in Thailand. Women lawyers, however, are trying to get it legalized. The Thai government is also aware of the considerable propaganda work for population control that is being done by this institution. A careful analysis of the material which is collected at this institution from its clients can provide a useful insight into the place of women in Thai culture and society. It was for instance said that the fact that prostitution is found on a rather large scale, cannot be attributed mainly to the coming of foreigner.

In Thai culture it is not disvalued that men have mistresses and minor wives or visit prostitutes. The work of prostitutes or massage girls is considered a profession, though not a very valued one. Systematic study on these issues will certainly be useful in under- standing the position of these women in society.

Observations And Suggestions

It is not an overstatement to say that studies of women and of action programmes aimed at elevating their status have been handicapped by a general lack of understanding of cross-cultural and intra-cultural variations in the organizational principles of societies and in the life contexts of women. Organizational principles shape basic notions regarding male-female relationships and determine spheres of activity of the two sexes as well as their rights and responsibilities. In different life contexts, the various components of women's roles are accorded different relative values and collectively tend to form varied configurations.

The frequent over-generalizing, even universalizing, of issues concerning women has encouraged the view that women's problems are rooted in the fact of human existence. With sound cross-cultural evidence, including in-depth studies in societies that have not so far received scientific attention, the validity of many of these generalizations can be disproved. Anthropologists have amassed considerable data on this subject from many parts of the world. Undoubtedly, further careful research on the Southeast Asian situation will provide useful evidence.

There are studies of.various aspects of social structure and culture which illuminate the conditions of women in these countries. In one of the recent publications of the Institute of Southeast Asian studies, Singapore, Rural Asian Women; Status and Environment (1978), Robert Orr Whyte and Pauline Whyte refer to many studies conducted by scholars from Australian, American, and other Western universities and also by indigenous scholars. They also bring out the differences between Asian and East Asian women, on the one hand, and Southeast Asian women, on the other, on the basis of social science work done so far. However, it remains a fact that studies on women are generally not informed systematically by such baseline data.

Problem-solving and action-oriented research has tended to look at women in a developmental perspective. Urbanization, education, employment, mobility, and changes in family organization and values — in fact, social and cultural change generally — are now sought to be studied specifically in relation to women. Factors like exposure to mass media and education, independent earning, and the breakdown of the extended family are regarded as basic criteria for evaluating the emancipation of women, and they are, therefore, used in studies of the status of women. The relevance of these criteria needs to be examined carefully.

One of the important concerns of women's studies is the adverse effects of development on women. It is essential to study the particular economic and political conditions of every country. Those who use demographic data in assessing the situation of women, and those who pursue action research on employment, literacy, nutrition, health, and so forth, attempt cross-national comparisons. Such comparisons often use predetermined and inaccurate categories of analysis and classification. It is now accepted that the interests, objectives, and problems of women are not similar all over the world.

The differences between North America, Europe, and Australia, taken as a group, and the rest of the world are widely recognized. There is also awareness that Africa, South America, and Asia should be considered independently. In many recent research and survey endeavours, Asia has been treated as one unit. For certain operational purposes this will have to remain so, but it is time for us to recognize the dangers inherent in the use of a single Asian model. Research on women is an area in which the use of, or even the search for, such a model must be cautioned against.

Even where the activities of women at particular socio-economic levels are similar in different societies, the structure of rights in respect of these activities and the quality of man-woman relations can differ widely. Superficially, similar situations may have radically different explanations and cannot be treated as identical. For example, the low levels of literacy and education among females, the acceptance of lower wages by women and the consequent preference of employers for female labour, and the overburdening with work of many women appear to be common features of the condition of women in many Asian countries. But the forces that bring these features into being are not the same in each country.

It follows that any remedial measures that are planned would have to take note of these differences. One tends to agree with Whyte and Whyte (1978) when they say that with regard to the quality of relations between men and women, Asia can be divided into three regions: South Asia, East Asia, and Southeast Asia. In Southeast Asia, while familial control over unmarried daughters may be fairly strict in Islamic countries, women generally have a freedom of action and decision-making not found in South and East Asia, While there are some patrilineal groups and also a few matrilineal groups, the predominant pattern of kinship in Southeast Asia is bilateral, with rights of inheritance for women, relative flexibility of marital residence, and considerable interdependence between mothers and daughters.

There is a distinct tendency towards sex equality in formal kinship. Another notable feature of the societies in Southeast Asia is that their women do not practise seclusion (Purdah) and, by and large, are not constrained by a rigid segregation of the sexes. In making cross-national comparisons, these differences need to be kept in mind. Studies of population control are being confronted with their own findings like the one regarding absence of preference for a son in most of the populations in these countries. Understanding of motivation is necessary before undertaking steps to remedy the situation.

In the Philippines, in the programme of promotion of contraceptive measures in the Catholic population the main focus will have to be on women. Family planning research in the Philippines needs some qualitative studies so that a sound basis can be provided for action research. Quantitative techniques alone will not be sufficient. The questions to be asked must partake of the culture of the people. Recent research on women in the ASEAN countries has indicated two dangers. First, the use of Western notions and methodology sometimes leads to irrelevant and superficial findings; this is because the categories used in data collection and analysis may not be related to the cultural realities of the region. Second, use is made of the nonexistent 'Asian' model discussed above.

The use of Western (specifically, American) concepts and methodology is most pronounced in the Philippines. The emphasis that some research gives to sex-role differentiation and inequality of status did not represent real conditions. In many situations, class and economic differences are more significant than sex-based ones. Women may have an egalitarian relationship with menfolk within the family and in kinship networks and close social circles, and yet may be objects of exploitation in the outside world. The forms that this exploitation takes need to be properly identified and studied.

The attention that is being given to kinship systems must not be misunderstood.

The kinship system need not be regarded as a set of moral principles alone but as something that is rooted in material conditions. It should be viewed as a set of principles pertaining to the distribution and control of resources within and between socio-economic classes. Within a kinship unit, regardless of class, women and men may or may not have equal access to resources; and this difference is usually consonant with the kinship rules that apply to the unit. In recent years, many studies have been undertaken – some dealing with individual nations, others cross-national – on various aspects of women's lives: participation in labour, economic and social development, acceptance of family planning, literacy and education, mortality and morbidity rates, and so on.

There is a trend towards the use of available macro-level data, often supplemented with other information specially gathered. Impressive as some of these studies are, meaningful results often cannot be obtained from them. Besides the limitations of available data and of procedures adopted for collecting fresh data, there is the problem that the definitions of terms and categories that are implicit in macro-level data drawn from various countries are not always comparable. The interpretation and explanation of numbers may also follow different methods. Predetermined categories and equations, as well as the use of hastily-adopted common denominators, often distort the data and detach analysis from the living contexts.

An apparent comparability of numbers does not necessarily indicate the existence of similar social patterns or conditions. For instance, the drop-out rate of schoolgirls in Thailand does not have the same explanation as drop-out rates for them in India or Afghanistan. The segregation and vigilance imposed on girls in India and Afghanistan which are responsible for sexual disparities in enrolment and for dropping-out among girls, are not features of Thai society. Nor does the unequal allocation of scarce resources have the samo import for Thai girls. Instead, the pattern of life, in which women have considerable rights but need to shoulder far greater responsibility than men, has more relevance.

In Thailand, while the division of labour is not inflexible, role expectations and motivations differ. This situation can be more easily remedied than that in South Asian and West Asian countries. Of course, intra-country variations are quite considerable in some countries and they must not be ignored. In demographic comparisons of female infant mortality, Indonesia gives a worse account than India; but in Indonesia infant mortality is higher among males than among females. It would therefore be misleading to compare female infant mortality in India with that in Indonesia without reference to male infant mortality in these two countries.

The same is true of average life expectancy. Differences in nutrition and in health care among the various socio-economic levels are important; within particular strata or classes, females may not be discriminated against. Nutrition may be tied up with many subtle factors: the state of knowledge regarding nutrition, the supposedly different nutritional requirements of male and female children, the content of the mother's role, how much time a mother can devote to her children, and so forth. It is reported that in Thailand and in the Philippines, mothers tend to pamper sons, who therefore become irresponsible about contributing to the income and participating in the activities of the family, and even about sharing the available food.

There is, however, no conscious discrimination between male and female children in regard to the food they are given. It is noteworthy that in a sociological research project on nutrition in a rural community in Indonesia, the interview schedule did not ask for sex-wise information on the intake of food among children.

Objective Search for the Roots of Filipino Culture and the Position of Women

In the Philippines, it appears necessary for social scientists, particularly historians and anthropologists/sociologists, to attempt in-depth-analyses of the ancient heritage, traditions, value systems, and socio-economic structures in order to identify the roots of the existing social system. Old Malay traditions still persist at the inner level, often in an unobtrusive way. It became clear in discussions with some perceptive social scientists that the egalitarian authority pattern in the Filipino family, the custom of spouses holding common property, and the dependence of parents on daughters in old age, all have their roots in the Malay tradition.

About four centuries ago, the male dominated Spanish culture, combined with patriarchal, Catholic ethics, was superimposed on the older cultures. The ideal behaviour for women, according to Spanish Christian norms, was to stay at home and take care of children. In the Philippines, this ideal is repeatedly described as the traditional ideal and there is no doubt that it may have influenced the well-to-do to some extent. But one can safely assert that it did not constrain the majority of women in the Philippines. There is very little evidence that it has been internalized, and women can change easily when circumstances demand or when the emerging contexts are conducive to change.

Today, Filipino women can be found in all walks of life. Many are being trained in agricultural colleges, belying the assumption that women have only a supportive role in agriculture. Several researchers regret that some of the present programmes for women in the Philippines overemphasize the role of women as home-makers and seek to train them in the domestic skills and in handicrafts. They feel that something extraneous to the culture is being brought in through such programmes. Programmes related to nutrition and to the augmentation of home Income need a careful look -from this angle.

An objective search for the roots of Philippine culture so as to identify the position and fields of operation of women is urgently indicated. Perhaps in this interdisciplinary endeavour, some collaboration of scholars from other ASEAN countries, and contact with the Institute of Southeast Asian Studies, Singapore, will prove useful. What is being suggested is not a book of history that would stand by itself, but a study that can explain, by examining specific cities, the situation of women today. In Islamic countries of the ASEAN region also, indigenous social scientists can fruitfully undertake such studies.

Evaluation of Existing Baseline Data and Collection of New Data

Much baseline socio-cultural and historical data on these countries have been provided by foreign scholars. Neither are the data sufficient, nor have they been properly used in studies on women. It should be worthwhile to subject these data to careful evaluation and systematization; after filling various gaps, better baseline data can be built up for these countries. Collecting new data on the status of women, planning comparative studies within individual countries as well as cross-nationally, and correctly interpreting and explaining data, all demand that social scientists make efforts to extend the coverage of such baseline data. It is also necessary to avoid the adoption of prevailing stereotypes without assessing their applicability in various situations.

Content Analysis of Folk Literature and Oral Traditions

Folklore and written literature, old as well as modern, are among the richest sources of data, but they remain largely untapped. Content analysis of these sources, perhaps in combination with field-work, will be most fruitful. The subtleties of the relationship between man and woman can be understood through this approach. A despairing statement often made by women in Thailand, the Philippines, and Indonesia is that men need to be taught to be responsible.

A woman has rights in the familial context, but she often has to bear the entire burden of running the household and caring for children. If divorce or separation does not alienate her children from a woman, it leaves the man free to follow his inclinations with almost no responsibilities. Women work very hard, while men take life easy. Literature can throw much light on these matters and on people's attitudes towards them.

Language and the Position of Women

Unbiased studies of the use of language may be helpful in knowing the quality of relations between the sexes in the communities of the ASEAN region. The grammar, speech forms, and intonation in a language can point towards the differentiation in sex roles. Language is one of the most potent instruments for creating and maintaining sex typing; its study, therefore, can help us know the relative place of sex as a principle of organization.

A reference may be made to what has been mentioned in connection with the study of Indonesian population: It would be worthwhile to study cultural notions regarding natural differences and similarities and the possible overlap of qualities and temperament between the sexes, as well as allowances that can be made to a person who acquires qualities of the opposite sex. Comparative studies of language in different communities may be very helpful in this connection.

Beliefs Regarding Reproduction

Ethno-reproductive beliefs appear to be a promising area of inquiry for this region. Notions about the nature of male and female sexuality, and about the role of the two sexes in procreation, provide insights into some fundamental aspects of man-woman relations. Rights (or lack of them) over children, which are a crucial aspect of the position of women in a society, are often tied up with ethno-reproductive beliefs. Not only rights over children but rights of inheritance and succession may also be shown to derive their justification from these beliefs. Their study in some Southeast Asian communities may partially explain why the problem of women has to be viewed in a different perspective in this region.

Legitimacy of Children

In Southeast Asia, the meaning of legitimacy/illegitimacy in relation to children needs careful examination. For this, it would be necessary to study the legal point of view, the cultural understandings, and outlook of the society towards children born out of wedlock. The circumvention practised by the people of the inegalitarian laws imposed by the legal codes of the great religions will have something to tell about the position of women in these societies. Do any orphanages, meant primarily for children born out of wedlock, and hence clearly indicative of social non-acceptability of such children, exist in these societies? Comparative studies of such institutions, along with those of unwed mothers and of children born out of wedlock, may be undertaken with profit.

Law and Women

The legal status of women could be better understood by examining the actual working of law through empirical studies and through the analysis of recorded cases. The differences between the written law, the people's view of it, and hew it really functions, need to be examined. An understanding of these would indicate the kind of work that is needed to bring about an improvement in the conditions of women. A similar understanding of laws relating to abortion, prostitution, massage parlours, and so forth, is called for, together with an understanding of the social origins and consequences of these phenomena.

Here again, each country must be treated as a specific case: there are too many differences between the various ASEAN countries to permit an identical approach to all. In Thailand, for instance, girls can enter and leave prostitution with comparative ease. This is probably because of the relatively few constraints placed on women and the absence of rigid ideas regarding the legitimacy of children.

Women in 'Sex'-related Professions

In all these countries prostitutes, call-girls, massage girls, and hospitality girls need to be studied with cultural specificities in mind. The contribution of feudalism and neo-colonialism to these practices has to be clearly understood, and mechanical explanations derived from other cultures should be avoided. The study of the people's perceptions of these practices is also essential if their cultural place is to be understood. Perhaps the absence of a clear demarcation between prostitutes and non-prostitutes indicates greater freedom for women; but it has implications for health and, moreover, it encourages a form of exploitation.

Division of Labour between Sexes

A relatively flexible division of labour often leads to women being overworked, but it can also form the basis for change. There is a need for more research on the division of labour, and for accurate measurement of the labour put in by each sex, at various socio-economic levels. If the sexual division of labour is more a matter of convenience than a result of rigid rules about male and female behaviour, and if there is much overlapping of work between the two sexes, this has to be made explicit; it should be taken into consideration while designing welfare programmes for women. In such programmes, treating the family or the household as the receiving unit of welfare may be better than concentrating on the female sex. The adverse effects of development on women can also be avoided if a better understanding of the role of women in the economy is acquired.

Social Hierarchy among Women

Not only relations between the sexes but relations within a sex have to be studied in order to analyze the sources of women's oppression. For instance, oppression of women by women is in a way characteristic of the patrilineal extended family system. In the bilateral or matrilineal setting, on the other hand, the female kin of a woman play a supportive role. They enable the woman to hold her own in situations of conflict, and to work out smooth arrangements for sharing the work of child-rearing and running the household. It needs to be examined whether socialization and experiences acquired within the familial and kinship groupings tend to develop in women a more co-operative attitude towards members of their own sex.

Women in Extended and in Nuclear Families

Examined in the light of the above statements the blanket assumption that disintegration of extended family system is invariably indicative of a rise in women's status does not seem tenable; it needs further examination, particularly in the Southeast Asian countries. Indeed, the point needs to be made that among the social scientists, and among those who are interested in the problems of women, there is not enough awareness of the compulsions and constraints that are a part of the nuclear family pattern. In a nuclear family of the Western variety a woman is much more inescapably bound to her wifely and motherly duties than in a family unit in Southeast Asia which may either be embedded in larger kinship or be composed of extended kin.

Studies of Adoption

Adoption which is a common feature of these societies will be a fruitful theme for comparative research. Adoption may not always be viewed as only a mechanism for rearrangement of property; it should be examined as a mechanism to provide flexibility of arrangements for child care and socialization in societies where marriage is unstable, women are engaged in activities of production, and residence pattern has an element of option. Case studies of adoption may also be helpful in understanding the relative value of male and female children in these societies.

Studies on Patterns of Socialization

Well planned research on socialization should include the area of perception of both adults and children in regard to sex-linked attributes and behaviour in the first few years of life. It is useful to obtain guidelines on what to look for in this research area from the studies done elsewhere, but ASEAN social scientists should be cautious not to rely on structured tools with borrowed categories lest the subleties and actualities of the situations and processes being studied are lost.

The same care needs to be taken in obtaining sex-wise information on nutrition, health care, child labour, access to education, and so on. As part of the study of socialization, analysis of the content of textbooks for possible sex discrimination should be undertaken. Besides using the method of content analysis for such a study, it may also be worthwhile to find out how the school children who are exposed to these textbooks themselves perceive their contents.

Role of Women in Decision-Making

There is a great need for some well-planned studies, at different socio-economic levels, of the role of women in decision- making in the household and the kin group, as well as in the wider society. Malaysia and Thailand, in particular, have to fill big gaps in their data base relative to women. The role of women in development can no longer be illuminated by country papers, or more papers produced officially and based on impressions, macro data, and examining a few populations from various countries for the applicability of census categories will be very useful.

A consideration of the practical problems of language and utilization of talent in these countries will not be out of place here. There are scholars who can do excellent work in regional languages but are hamstrung by the necessity of having to use a foreign language. The difficulty is very real in Indonesia, Malaysia, and Thailand. UNESCO should try for greater involvement of talented and knowledgeable people from these countries in the work on women. Translations of works from the native languages into English should form one important scheme for expanding the base of UNESCO activities. The need for culture-specific data on women cannot be over- emphasized.

In order to plan cross-cultural studies and thrash out categories for obtaining comparable data for various countries in Asia, some assessment of available data needs to be done. UNESCO may develop a plan for understanding women's problems, in the wider socio-cultural context. For this, it would be necessary to plan delineation of the sources of data and their evaluation, to identify talent, and to make plans for sharpening the research capabilities of researchers. A collaborative effort on the part of social scientists for assessing the research needs in the area of women's studies in these countries is urgently indicated.

3

The Management of Female Sexuality

The sex industry in Asia is changing rapidly. It is becoming increasingly complicated, with highly differentiated sub sectors. The majority of studies, together with anecdotal evidence, suggest that commercial sex is becoming more common and that it is involving a greater number of people in a greater variety of sites. Assessing the size of the market is difficult because the trade is largely illegal and often underground. The most authoritative studies available suggest that the market is vast.

The industry in four Southeast Asian countries has been estimated to account for between 2% -14% of Gross Domestic Product. Estimates of the Japanese sex sector's annual earnings suggest figures of between 4-10 trillion yen and that the industry accounts for approximately 1% - 3% of Gross National Product. Between 1993 and 1995 profits from the Thai sex industry were thought to be three times higher than profits from the drugs trade.

We have limited knowledge of commercial sex in the region. There is an acute lack of accurate statistics on sex work and although the numbers that are commonly cited have little basis in reality they have been repeated so often that they have become accepted as fact. All statistics on sex work need to be treated with caution.

Research and publications on sex work within the region fall into five main categories:

- Reports, polemical works and newsletters produced principally by NGOs that?often either seek to promote prostitution as work or to portray all sex work as exploitation.
- Reports, particularly by international agencies, focussing on the issue of?trafficking for prostitution and children in prostitution.
- Academic books and articles that concentrate?especially on Thailand.
- Surveys and reports written with reference to?HIV/AIDS.
- Sex guides aimed primarily at visiting?foreigners.

These sources give us a partial view of commercial sex within the region - and there are major gaps. This applies to whole sub sectors of the industry - particularly the activities of indirect and part time sex workers, MSW and also to the sex industry as a whole in certain countries (e.g. Pakistan and Burma). Even the best works are sometimes one-dimensional: the most authoritative and widely quoted survey of sex work in Asia, for example, approaches the industry as if it can be explained primarily in terms of economics. There is a notable absence of detailed work on clients.

And research related to HIV/AIDS, which generally provides the most sophisticated available analysis of commercial sex, is limited in large measure because it concentrates on behaviours at sex work sites rather than on the broader socio-cultural context in which the sex acts take place. This report has been compiled from an examination of these sources coupled with extensive fieldwork in sex work sites throughout Asia between 1997-2001.

THE STRUCTURE OF THE MARKET

The Asian sex market is highly segmented. There is an international market catering to foreigners. This market is relatively small in terms of the number of sex acts performed but it is comparatively lucrative for workers because of the ability and willingness of relatively affluent foreigners in less developed Asian countries to pay higher prices per act than most domestic sex consumers. The domestic market catering to local men is much larger but far less visible.

Neither of these markets is sealed - local men may patronise sex workers who entertain tourists, and tourists may visit sex work sites that are patronised by local men but, in general, there is a division based not only on price but also on the preferred form of sexual advertisement. The sophistication and level of differentiation between sub-sectors of the industry varies according to a country's level of economic development. As economies develop, more men have greater spending power. They can spend this on commercial sexual encounters and upon doing so in increasingly luxurious sites.

Less developed economies have a large mass market for sex work, a far smaller middle-income sector and a tiny group of elite sex workers. Highly developed economies have a far greater number of sex workers operating in the middle-income range and in a variety of sites, often catering to niche markets. This breakdown of sex work into sub sectors defined by income-levels mirrors class and income distribution within society as a whole.

THE CLIENTS AND THE DEMAND FOR COMMERCIAL SEX

The bulk of research and literature on sex work in Asia focuses on the supply side of the trade: on the women who provide sexual services as opposed to the men who buy them. The nature of client demand and its cultural foundations are rarely analysed. This is a major failing because the success of the sex industry is dependent not only on there being a supply of women to the trade but, perhaps more importantly, on there being consumer demand.

A strict sexual double standard operates throughout the region. Sex outside the confines of marriage is not considered acceptable in the official codes of most Asian societies - at least for women. In practice, men's purchase of commercial sex is tolerated and, in some instances, may be actively encouraged by local definitions of masculinity. Cultural models in the region foster the sex industry by dividing women into two principal categories: good women who are wives and who are not suppose to enjoy sex very much; and bad women -the prostitutes - who do like sex (or who have no choice in the matter).

It is a common expectation that men will turn to sex workers when they do not find sexual satisfaction in marriage or when single men do not have sexual access to women because of strict norms prescribing virginity and chastity as essential characteristics of respectable unmarried women. A flourishing sex industry and a supply of prostituted women therefore contribute to the construction of sexuality and the maintenance of gender roles in some Asian societies.

It has been argued that they are the logical outcomes of sexually repressive cultures and highly unequal gender relations. There is a reluctance to acknowledge the size of the sex industry within the region. In some countries, most men will pay for sex at some point in their lives and many will do so on a regular basis. In South Asia the practice of commercial sex appears to be less prevalent but it is still grossly underestimated by governments, health departments and by public opinion. This unwillingness to confront uncomfortable issues extends to all aspects of sexuality including basic sex education, the prevention and treatment of STDs.

Throughout the region mobile populations of men form a large proportion of sex consumers. Transport workers, seafarers, businessmen and men who are separated from their families and communities either by migration or by joining the armed forces are regular clients. Urbanisation, the associated loosening of traditional social controls and the emergence of new avenues for sexual expression are encouraging the growth of a market for commercial sex. The spread of consumer cultures has also had a dramatic impact on the Asian sex industry.

It has created a growth market by commercialising sex acts. Sex can be seen as a product through which men define themselves. Men wish to buy the commodities they associate with an exciting, modern, urban lifestyle: women are one of these commodities. Materialism has also created a supply of women for the trade. It encourages women's involvement in sex work by offering them the opportunity to buy coveted symbols of modern consumer culture and it has simultaneously turned women into a tradable commodity.

In this context, materialism and the financial benefits to be gained from selling sex outweigh customary social disapproval. This process is occurring at different speeds throughout both developed and less developed parts of the region and is encouraged by the fact that women's traditionally low social status in Asian societies, and their unequal access to economic resources, permits their easy exploitation within the sex industry. In some areas of Thailand, Nepal, India and China prostitution is socially accepted.

THE LIMITATIONS OF STATISTICAL ANALYSIS

A narrow definition of prostitution limits our understanding of commercial sex. If we assume that prostitution is the exchange of sex for some form of material reward then sex work involves a substantial proportion of the general population. Sexual intimacy may be exchanged for a variety of resources - food, shelter, clothing, transport and social capital. Some people do this on a regular basis. Others do so occasionally - sometimes for fun and sometimes because of need.

Many of these individuals would never perceive themselves to be sex workers and sex work is not their primary occupation (even if it is their primary source of income). The sex industry in Asia is moving out of traditional sites and concentrations in red light areas and becoming dispersed throughout cities, in suburbs and along highways. It is straddling international borders and growing wherever there is a high density and movement of people. There is a clear move away from direct sex work and towards indirect prostitution in all Asian countries.

Bars, clubs, massage parlours, karaoke bars, restaurants and hotels are typical venues. Sex workers increasingly operate in private houses in suburbs and they may use mobile phones or the internet to contact and negotiate with clients. This makes mapping of sex work sites, the control of exploitation within the industry and dissemination of advice on sexual health extremely problematic because the industry has no geographically defined borders and only a minority of sex workers can be labelled as having a sex worker identity.

Customers may believe that there is more to their relationship with an indirect sex worker than an exchange of sex and money and, indeed, this may be true. The worker maintains the fiction that they are not selling sex and the client is not alarmed that he is courting health risks by having sex with a prostitute. The perceived nature of a commercial sexual encounter may be changing and this has implications for the mapping of sex work sites, gauging the numbers of sex workers, and in particular, the promotion of condom uses in high risk situations.

Amongst many sex workers and their clients there may no longer be a perception of high risk precisely because they are not self-identified as 'workers' and 'clients'. A false sense of security is gained in mapping and analysing known sex work sites. NGOs and health departments concentrate their activity in these areas while the industry is changing around them. Statistics can mislead because they appear to impose order on an infinitely complex industry.

Figures produced by anti-prostitution NGOs are inaccurate in that they probably overestimate the number of trafficking victims. Statistics produced by governments, by contrast, probably underestimate the number of sex workers because they are based on a very restricted view of sex work and fail to adequately enumerate indirect and part time sex workers.

Quantitative medical epidemiological analysis of sex work is troubled by the fact that surveys and questionnaires rarely establish 'truth'. Both clients and sex workers may not wish to give interviewers accurate descriptions of their lives, work and sexual behaviours for complex reasons of pride, status, shame and fear. Long-term, qualitative ethnographic research coupled with quantitative studies will produce more reliable results but, to date, this kind of work is almost totally absent.

Most of the people who sell sex in Asia do so because they are compelled by economic and social inequality and by terribly restricted life chances. Especially in the poorer countries of the region, they have no other realistic option. Some moreover are physically coerced and a large proportion of women staffing the brothel sector have been trafficked into the business. Those women who are held in debt bondage may receive only a fraction of the money paid by clients.

On the other hand, in patriarchal societies in which women have inferior access to economic resources, sex work gives many uneducated and unskilled women an income that far exceeds that which they can obtain in any other occupation. The same is true for MSW. Elite sex workers in both developed and less developed countries can earn substantial sums in a very short time. Many people are selling sex because of relative deprivation rather than absolute poverty. An undocumented number of young women from Asia's middle classes are now selling sex – often on a part time basis - to supplement salaries or to provide extra money while they are in education. Anecdotal evidence suggests that these part time sex workers are attracting business away from traditional sex work venues and full time workers.

Contentious debates over sex work in the region have done a great injustice to many sex workers and those who are held in sexual slavery because it creates an artificial dualism of passive victim versus the sex worker who exercises agency. Most sex workers in the lower ranks of the industry are victims of many kinds of social and economic injustice and it is inaccurate and patronising to exaggerate their degree of agency and their power to negotiate with clients and the management of the industry. Some sex workers profit well from their work but the sex trade, as a whole is exploitative of the women and men who work within it.

TRAFFICKING, MIGRATION AND THE LINKS WITH CRIME

The conflation of trafficking and migration and the muddling of definitions have obscured the fact that many sex workers are increasingly mobile and will migrate in search of work. There are increasingly complex regional linkages throughout Asia that are expressed in terms of economics, trade, population movements and sexual networks. This phenomenon is apparent, for example, in the Mekong Delta, the 'Golden Triangle' island, Southeast Asia, and the Indo-Nepal border. The financial rewards of elite and middle-income prostitution have also encouraged sex works from outside the region to migrate to Asia.

It is possible, for example to find highly visible sex workers from the former Soviet Union and Eastern Europe working in clubs, bars and hotels throughout both poor and affluent Asia. In most Asian countries prostitution is illegal. The sex industry is regulated by legal codes, social custom and organized crime. These factors determine the type and form of sex work. They also penalize the sex worker in different forms: either by punishing workers with imprisonment or fines, stigmatizing and shaming them, or economically exploiting them.

Organized crime reaps enormous profits from the sex industry. In more developed Asia the forces of poverty bring many girls and young women into trafficking networks and agents. Within cities, organized crime is heavily involved in the sex trade. And throughout Asia police forces are often involved in the sex market. In areas where efforts have been made to tackle abuses the result has been to clean up recognized sex work sites but also to push the most exploitative aspects of the industry further underground. In particular, young, vulnerable, trafficked women and girls find themselves locked into socially invisible systems of sexual exploitation.

THE DEMAND FOR YOUTH

Youth is an essential prerequisite of sex workers throughout the world but in Asia there appears to be an even greater client demand for the very young. The premium age for sex workers in many Asian societies is between the ages of 12 and 16. A complicating factor is that the transition from childhood to adulthood, commonly defined in the West as occurring at eighteen years of age, does not have cultural resonance in many Asian countries – especially less developed South Asian countries. Here the acknowledgement of a female's adult status may occur at puberty or marriage - whichever is the sooner.

Definitions of child prostitution as the prostitution of those under eighteen years of age may seem meaningless in a context in which cultural norms encourage females to marry when they are fourteen, fifteen or sixteen-years-old. Like females in their early teens, adult women may also be vulnerable to economic, social and psychological pressures. There is nothing magical about a girl's eighteenth birthday that guarantees that she can make free and unpressured choices. What is important in the context of prostitution and the controversy over 'choice' is an individual's ability to manage power hierarchies and to retain an element of control within them.

For the youngest women and for those from ethnic minorities, fragile communities despised social groups and castes (in other words, those who commonly fill the lowest rungs of the sex work ladder) this power and ability to control their lives is negligible. The youngest girls are too young to make an informed choice to join the sex industry. They are extremely vulnerable. Their youth contributes to their powerlessness and makes them less able to negotiate with clients on anything approaching an equal basis.

The understandable preoccupation with HIV/AIDS has sidelined many other problems relating to sex work. HIV/AIDS intervention programmes correctly identify workers' powerlessness as an important factor in transmission of the disease because it makes them less able to negotiate the terms of the sex act and client condom usage. Reports throughout the region consistently state that sex workers' ability to negotiate condom usage is limited. Many programmes seek to empower women and hence, by extension, to tackle a whole range of problems.

Yet for many women involved in the trade, avoiding the threat of AIDS does not appear high on their list of priorities when they are faced with more immediate concerns such as debt, violence, ill-health and social exclusion for themselves and their children. It appears that condom usage has been increasing in key sex work sites but that safe sex practices are not necessarily followed by those who are most vulnerable: particularly by young women.

Nor is condom use thought to be high or consistent amongst indirect sex workers. Condom promotion programmes have been extremely successful amongst direct sex workers in countries like Thailand and in select sex work sites in other countries. The link between the condom and commercial sex is reflected in consistent reports throughout the region that indicate that although many sex workers use condoms with their clients they do not do so with their regular partners or lovers. This behaviour expresses the non-commercial nature of their relationship.

MALE SEX WORKERS

Analysis of sex work in Asia concentrates on FSW and child prostitution. Female sex workers outnumber MSW in most Asian societies. The failure to address the incidence of men who sell sex and therefore the failure to meet their health needs derives from cultural patterns that do not allow the social expression of male-male desire. Homosexual behaviours are commonplace. Frequently these behaviours are non-commercial but they also take the form of commercial encounters that fulfil sexual desires whilst at the same time posing no challenge to heterosexual norms and family structures because of their fleeting and anonymous nature.

Many men who sell sex will have a variety of partners - some commercial, some non- commercial, some male and some female. They may not identify themselves as homosexual. Crucially, just as with indirect FSW they will not necessarily see themselves as sex workers. Neither will anyone else. Many will be married and will have non-sex work occupations. In terms of analysing sex work it is important not to apply western categories defining sexual identity to people in non-western cultures and to recognise the fact that many of those involved in sex work have overlapping identities. This applies to both workers and clients.

JAPAN

Japan has a big and lucrative sex industry. Prostitution is illegal but the country's long tradition of prostitution and the highly advanced stage of its economy have given rise to a proliferation of sex work sites often catering to much specialised niche markets. Low-income prostitution consists of brothels, clubs and bars where men can purchase sex acts. Higher in the market hierarchy are health and fitness clubs, *onsen* (hot spring resorts), saunas, 'soap lands', massage parlours, and theme clubs. Bars and clubs cater to clientele from widely different socio-economic backgrounds.

Many of these employ workers that have originated from a specific foreign country. At the top end of the market are call girl services, private clubs and hostess bars. The primary function of these bars is to provide sophisticated entertainment in the form of conversation and a highly stylized serving of drinks and lighting of cigarettes. Hostesses may not necessarily provide sexual services and those that do so will negotiate with clients to perform sex acts in other sites.

Many of these workers will not identify as prostitutes: they may have very few clients and may view these as generous boyfriends. High school and college girls also offer sexual services to middle-aged businessmen in return for gifts and extra pocket money. This system of 'compensation dating' is increasingly popular. The lower sub-sectors of the industry tend to be dominated by trafficked women and those who have migrated from developing countries to work as prostitutes because of the high profits to be made from selling sex in Japan.

Women come principally from the Philippines and Thailand but also from other countries such as Columbia. Other groups of migrants come from the former Soviet Union and Eastern Europe. They generally enjoy better conditions than women from Asian countries. Japanese women tend to dominate in the higher sub-sectors and there is a close relationship between skin colour and place within the sex market hierarchy. Elite sex workers tend to be white-skinned, educated Japanese women and blonde, blue-eyed Europeans and Americans. Many Japanese men will buy sex at some point in their lives. Today, men go in small informal groups on sex vacations to a variety of sites throughout Asia where they can purchase sex.

CHINA

The Chinese government's crackdown on 'social evils' led to a dramatic decline in the sex trade after 1949 – although this was never as thorough as the party claimed. Since the late 1970's, and the advent of economic liberalisation policies, the numbers involved in prostitution have 'increased rapidly'. The resurgence of prostitution was intimately associated with market oriented economic policies which made it acceptable to be wealthy and opened up new economic opportunities. It was associated with greater mobility: the estimated 120 million migrant labourers in China today are mostly sexually active young men who can be assumed to be potential or actual clients of sex workers.

There has also been a tendency towards sexual liberalisation that has affected non-commercial sexual relationships as well as commercial ones. In some instances greater materialism has diminished the social stigma against prostitution. Sex workers today may be poor, ill-educated women in difficult financial circumstances but they may also be well-educated women who choose to sell sex because of the high monetary rewards.

The expansion of the sex industry began in the special economic zones -particularly areas in the south and south east where a rapidly developing economy linked to Hong Kong and Macau led to the creation of entrepreneurial classes eager to buy sexual services. Today there are extensive sexual networks linking the fast developing parts of China with Hong Kong and the men who pass back and forth are frequent clients of sex workers in the mainland. In Hong Kong in 1993 an estimated 20,000 sex workers serviced a predominantly local market.

There is a high turnover of women in the industry and many of these are trafficked or migrate to Hong Kong. Demand for sex workers is increasing and appears to be common in both urban and rural settings and amongst both local men and visitors. China's unbalanced sex ratio may also be contributing to the demand for sex workers because men cannot find women with whom to have more formal sexual relationships.

The shortage of women is increasing demand for trafficked brides in rural areas and, in the coastal provinces; it is leading to the trafficking of women for prostitution. The conditions under which these women and girls work are not well understood and there is no real idea of their number. Prostitution is a criminal offence and sex sites tend to be indirect: clubs, bars, teashops, dance halls and hairdressers. The authorities organise periodic clampdowns on the industry and a small per cent age of the women are re-educated and rehabilitated.

SOUTH KOREA

Most analysis of sex work in Korea is concentrated upon military prostitution: in the form of sex work around US military camps and Japan's record of forced military prostitution during the Great East Asian War. Sex work in Korea is divided into two categories - those catering to the foreigners and a local market. There is a large demand for commercial sex in Korea. Prostitution has long historical roots and, despite the illegality of sex work, sexual services can be bought in a multitude of sites: in brothels, tea-houses, saunas, Turkish baths, karaoke bars, hotels and barbershops.

These venues vary from the most basic to extremely luxurious and their diversity reflects the rapid development of the Korean economy and rising standards of living in the post-Korean War years. Sex workers increasingly come from all socio-economic classes. Poorer women work in the lower sub-sectors of the market and service American military forces, but there is also anecdotal evidence that educated middle class Korean women turn to sex. This was thought to become a marked trend during the economic crisis of 1997-98. These women will not be perceived as sex workers and will not identify themselves as prostitutes.

THAILAND

The best research and analysis of sex work in Asia has been focused on Thailand – much of this associated either with sex tourism, gender and identity, trafficking and migration for prostitution and HIV/AIDS related issues. Thailand provides a good example of the way in which the sex industry has become institutionalised, more sophisticated, diversified and how, in recent years it has altered under the impact of new legislation and changing social patterns. Sex work is intrinsic to the fabric of gender relations and socio-economic hierarchies.

Sex workers are frequently rural-urban migrants – particularly from north and northeastern Thailand, and the money they earn brings buying power to families in poor villages. Many of these women migrate to find lucrative sex work and many others are trafficked in the sense that they leave their homes for sex work in the city when they are still children. In parts of northern Thailand, in particular, sex work is socially accepted. In addition to these rural-urban migrants are tribal girls from the north and women from Burma and the southern Chinese province of Yunan. Since 1990, around 80,000 women have moved to Thailand for prostitution.

The majority of these women are from Burma. Many of them have not been 'trafficked' but have migrated - yet their status as illegal migrants in Thailand makes them vulnerable to abuse. Most of these women work in shadowy brothels and venues at the very cheapest end of the sex market. They have little negotiating power and very little awareness of health issues. There are an estimated 16,423 foreign prostitutes in Thailand – 30% of whom are younger than 18. This may well be an underestimation given the clandestine nature of their work. The sex tourist industry in Thailand is well documented by the international media.

It is staffed, in general, by women who are ethnic Thai. Despite its high profile this sub sector of the industry is comparatively small. It appears to be of greater significance than it really is because it is visible and highly concentrated in a few tourist destinations. The domestic market is far more important both in terms of its economic turnover and the numbers of workers and clients. Low priced services are provided by Burmese women. Their clients may be both low-income Thai men and male Burmese migrants.

Often they work in a brothel-like setting: many of these establishments are underground and many of the women are held in debt bondage. The middle income market has diversified greatly over the past ten years. The government has clamped down on child prostitution and in 1996 the Prostitution Prevention and Suppression Act whilst still retaining the illegality of prostitution concentrated its force against activities associated with prostitution.

A result of this has been for the sex industry to reorient itself away from direct prostitution and turn towards indirect prostitution. Brothels disappeared and then reappeared as karaoke bars, massage parlours and restaurants. During the mid-1990s commercial sex was thought to have declined in Thailand, even though the level was higher at the end of the decade than at the beginning. This decline was thought to be a result of demographic and economic factors but was interpreted principally as an outcome of the AIDS epidemic, which reduced the supply of Thai women willing to work in the industry.

Men were also supposed to have decreased their use of sex workers and compensated for this by increasing their number of casual female partners and girlfriends. However, it is possible that the changing structure and visibility of prostitution masked similar levels of commercial sexual activity. Estimates of the number of sex workers in Thailand are subject to wide variation. The most reliable suggestion is that there are between 150,000 and 200,000 sex workers. Certainly a large proportion of sex workers enter the trade before they are eighteen.

A third of women working in massage parlours and brothels started sex work before they were eighteen and a fifth of brothel based women were between thirteen and fifteen. The problem of child prostitution is particularly acute in border provinces and to a lesser extent, in Bangkok and tourist centres. Many of these youngest and most vulnerable children and women will work in the cheapest establishments and service large numbers of clients. There has been a proliferation of sex work sites. Fitness clubs, massage services and beer halls are increasingly popular.

Sites may not necessarily be in the entertainment sector but can include shopping malls and department stores. Indirect sex workers generally have fewer customers who pay higher fees. Frequently they may work in the sex industry on a part time basis and may not classify themselves as prostitutes. Similar trends mark the market for MSW. The most authoritative estimates on the numbers of MSW suggest that there are around 5,600 workers in Thailand – but this figure is likely to be an underestimation.

Like FSW sites venues have been diversifying away from bars and a-go-go bars and towards saunas, fitness clubs, massage services and beer halls. Sex workers work in department stores, can be contacted through callboy services and through internet-based services. A number of excellent NGOs and sex worker organisations operate in Thailand. Significantly however they do not work extensively in the south of the country. Little is known about sex work venues in the area bordering Malaysia.

CAMBODIA

Prostitution in Cambodia has expanded greatly in the past few years. There is a large market for commercial sex. Visits to brothels are a routine activity for young men in urban areas. Prostitution outlets have been opening in boomtowns such as Siem Reap to cater to both the tourist market and the male migrant labour force involved in construction work. Following the pattern throughout the region, there are sex work sites along highways and in border towns. Most of the client groups are local men. The tourist market is far smaller.

Sex work sites have been diversifying rapidly. These now include indirect sites and the sex workers may be 'beer promotion' girls, waitresses, guest relations' officers or be employed in entertainment/service sector occupations without identifying as sex workers. Although prostitution is illegal the government has taken a pragmatic line, and is in the process of implementing a 100% condom use programme nation-wide. Estimates of the number of sex workers are unreliable and the high turnover of FSW makes the task of enumeration difficult.

Workers tend to stay in the trade for a short period and not to stay in any specific location for any length of time. Very young females are found in the brothel sector. Lower ages are associated with increased numbers of customers and brothel-based women as a whole report a higher number of customers than indirect workers. There is anecdotal evidence, however, that this commonly reported link between indirect workers and lower numbers of customers may be changing in Cambodia.

A significant proportion (perhaps as high as 30%) of sex workers are migrants or trafficked women from Vietnam. Some of these women are culturally and socially isolated and have communication problems. Cambodian FSW suffers problems of disempowerment particularly within a brothel setting. The youngest debt bonded girls have very little control over their lives. On the other hand, in a society in which there are few avenues for female employment that will provide a basic standard of living, women who are successful in negotiating their way through the exploitation of the commercial sex market can make a relatively good living selling sex.

VIETNAM

Client groups include those that are usually cited in the region as important consumers: mobile men; workers in the transportation sector; construction workers; traders; seafarers and businessmen. Widespread rural unemployment has led to the migration of young, unaccompanied men to the cities thus increasing consumer demand for commercial sex. Prostitution is illegal and the government periodically organises heavily purges of the industry.

This encourages the camouflaging of sites so that around 70% of the market comprises indirect sex workers. Sex sites are increasingly indirect and sex work is largely non-brothel based. Low income FSW work from the streets or in brothels near transportation hubs and important routes like the north-south Highway One. Other low and middle-income workers are based in 'hugging bars', hairdressing salons, restaurants and karaoke bars.

High income prostitutes work out of dancing clubs and through call-girl networks. Significantly middle-income workers will not necessarily see themselves in the mould of the average sex worker. They are less likely to use condoms in commercial sexual transactions because their perception of risk is reduced by their 'non-sex worker' identity and because they believe that wealthy clients will not be infected with HIV. This phenomenon is repeated throughout the region.

In addition to local client groups there is also an expanding sex tourist sector. Many of the sex workers are very mobile, moving from one area of Vietnam to another and sometimes to Cambodia. This puts them beyond the control of the police and the health sector. It is thought that there are approximately 300,000 sex workers and that the commercial sex market is most vigorous in southern Vietnam.

LAOS

There is little research on prostitution in Laos and it is generally believed that Laos does not have a very large commercial sex market. This however is likely to change as the commodification of sex spreads from neighbouring countries. There is evidence of child and adult female trafficking from Laos to Thailand for the purpose of prostitution.

BURMA

We know little about commercial sex in Burma. What information we have has been based on anecdotal evidence, work by journalists and travel writers, short-term assessments of a few sex work sites by NGOs and testimonies of Burmese FSW in Thailand. There is an increasing commercial sex market in Burmese cities and there is widespread rural prostitution especially around border areas (e.g. on the Burmese- Chinese border and in areas on the northern Thai - Burmese border). As well as cross- border trade in women there is also internal movement as women migrate to serve male migrant workers in mining areas, construction sites and logging camps.

Anecdotal reports indicate that the average age of sex workers is declining. The sex trade is closely linked with the trade in drugs that runs between Burma, Yunan and Thailand. These trades are often run by the same people and making young women dependent upon locally manufactured amphetamines is an increasingly common way of securing malleable sex workers from southern China and Burma. UNICEF estimates that there are between 30,000 and 50,000 sex workers.

MALAYSIA

Comparatively little research has been done on the Malaysian sex industry. The size of the sector is hard to gauge because much of it exists underground. Although prostitution is not illegal, brothel keeping, trafficking, pimping and soliciting are offences. It is illegal to run 'places of assignation', that is establishments which can link clients with sex workers. The result is an underground sex trade that is hard to monitor and control.

The most authoritative source suggests that there are between 43,000 and 142,000 sex workers. They work in highly differentiated sub sectors. At the lower end of the market are workers servicing poorer local men and a large number of low skilled international migrant workers. The sex workers may be brothel based, may work in another form of direct sex work establishment or they may be streetwalkers. Many venues provide access to sexual services: fitness clubs, hairdressing salons, karaoke bars, coffee shops, nightclubs and hotels.

These do not operate openly and the women working in them may not admit to being sex workers. Many will not perceive themselves to be prostitutes because they service a small number of clients or do so for payment in the form of gifts. Many will have daytime jobs as clerks or in factories and will only sell sex on a part-time basis. Because many workers do not wish to be identified as sex workers, and because of the legal restraints upon the industry, the sex market has become very mobile and innovative. Venues move frequently.

In the upper end of the sector clients belong to discreet networks and mobile phones are used to negotiate business. Sex acts take place in hotels or apartments and the existence of the trade is hidden from public view. Relative, as opposed to absolute, poverty pushes many women into prostitution. Sex workers are commonly from large families and they are poorly educated relative to average women. Average earnings in the sex industry are high and have increased over the past few decades. As there is an assumption that the numbers of women in prostitution are increasing – and that there is a regular supply of women to the trade, it is logical to assume that income levels are increasing as a result of growing client demand.

Although there is a market servicing sex tourists in Malaysia it is small compared to that in neighbouring Thailand. There are also other significant international linkages. Malaysian prostitutes migrate to work in Singapore. Indonesian women work in the Malaysian industry, as do small numbers of Filipinos and Thais. Some Malaysian men visit southern Thai brothels for short sex holidays. Sometimes it is simply for a day trip. There are therefore extensive sexual networks linking island and peninsular Southeast Asia. The number of MSW in Malaysia is unknown. Sodomy is prohibited by law.

SINGAPORE

There are a variety of sites where sex work is occurring in Singapore although only some of these are officially recognised. Prostitution is legal (providing a woman is over 21 year of age). Operating a brothel and soliciting in public are technically illegal but in practice they are tolerated in designated red light areas (DRAs). There is a very high degree of control over this sector of the industry. Workers must be registered, have medical checks and carry cards verifying this. Sex work outside the DRAs is extensive and growing.

There is street prostitution, a call-girl system and a network of mobile semi-permanent brothels. Sex workers in this sub-sector are more expensive and the trade is very hard to monitor and control because it is invisible. All classes of people are found amongst sex workers and their clients. There is large local demand and a highly developed market catering to tourists and foreign businessmen and also a low-income market servicing principally male guest workers in the construction industry.

The majority of registered prostitutes are Malaysian and there is a constant flow of FSW to Singapore from neighbouring countries. Workers come from Thailand, the Philippines, Indonesia, Hong Kong and Taiwan, in the process strengthening informal regional linkages in the sex industry - both of sexual networks and of brothel owners who operate exchange programmes. Most of these sex workers are thought to enter Singapore legally but there is also significant illegal trafficking of women and sexual abuse of migrant women domestic workers.

INDONESIA

The scale of the sex industry in Indonesia is perhaps smaller than that of other South East Asian countries. Even so it is still estimated to account for somewhere in the region of 0.8% - 2.4% of Gross Domestic Product. As elsewhere, estimates of the number of women in prostitution vary greatly but the most authoritative study claims that a figure between 140,000 and 230,000 is credible. As a per cent age of the population this is a lower figure than that found in neighbouring countries of the region. Commercial sex is expanding in Indonesia.

Changes in employment patterns, increased geographic and social mobility and a growing tourist industry have created increased consumer demand both amongst local men and visitors to the country. There are also increasing links between the Indonesian sex industry and those in Malaysia, and Singapore with the creation of sexual networks of both clients and migrating sex workers. The best example of this is the Indonesian island of Batam, which caters to a significant number of clients from Singapore, and Malaysia who avail themselves of cheaper prices than in their home sex market.

The increased linkages associated with the sex industry parallel patterns of economic development in the East ASEAN growth area. The women who enter the trade are usually compelled by economic circumstances. They may be divorced and have families to support. There are no available figures suggesting how common this practise is. Certain parts of Java are well-known prostitute recruiting grounds that have traditionally specialised in providing women for sexual services. In areas such as West and Central Java sex work is an acceptable occupation for girls. Selling sex is not technically a criminal act, although aspects of the industry such as soliciting, pimping and procuring are illegal.

Direct prostitution in brothel complexes is regulated by government legislation and regional authorities on the grounds that this concentrates the problem of vice. The brothels, and the women within them, have to follow strict regulations regarding health, length of service in the complex, age of entry into the trade and willingness of the women to undertake 'rehabilitation' courses. In practice, concentrating prostitution in these brothel complexes has not been successful because prostitution has flourished outside the designated zones.

Massage parlours and unofficial brothels provide direct services and there are many other venues offering indirect sex workers. As the economy has grown and men have gained more purchasing power the industry has diversified and there has been a proliferation of sex work sites. These include nightclubs, discos, hotels and bars. They facilitate indirect sex work as the sex acts take place away from the venue. There is also street prostitution catering to less affluent consumers and a sophisticated system of high-class call girls catering to the rich.

Many of these women work independently. There is a very wide variation in income levels amongst sex workers. To date programmes targeting sex workers have failed to appreciate the massive differences between categories of workers. Mass-market prostitution (principally street prostitution, and official and unofficial brothels) is poorly paid but for women with minimal education and skills the earnings are still far higher than in any other occupation open to them.

Amongst elite sex workers earnings are extremely high and are comparable to those of senior professionals. Many women will exchange sexual acts for a variety of rewards, principally gifts, but will not think of themselves as sex workers. This blurring of the division between commercial and emotional relationships can also be seen in the relationships, which sex workers develop with their regular clients. These tend to be more emotional and more in harmony with traditional Indonesian gender roles. Within this context women have reduced negotiating power. This pattern is repeated throughout Asia.

THE PHILIPPINES

The market for military prostitution dried up to a large extent with the closure of US bases in the early 1990s. Today sex tourism has replaced military prostitution. Poorly educated women within it can earn substantially more selling sex to foreigners than in any other occupation open to them. Official surveys indicate that men do not buy sex on a large scale and that sexual networks cannot be extensive because HIV/AIDS prevalence rates are low.

The most reliable study quotes figures of 400,000-500,000 sex workers. The division of the sex industry into sub-sectors parallels that in other fast developing countries: there is a mass market, mainly involving brothel and street based prostitution and indirect forms of prostitution based in cheaper bars and cabarets. And there is an increasingly differentiated market catering to the middle classes, which operates out of a variety of venues (karaoke bars, saunas, massage parlours and more sophisticated brothels).

The top end of the market is dominated by hotel prostitution and call-girl services. Both local men and foreigners patronise the middle and high sub-sectors of the industry. Local men tend to dominate in the cheaper sectors. Most of the women entering prostitution will do so because of difficult economic circumstances. Many will also have come from impoverished and troubled families in urban slums.

Prostitution is illegal in the Philippines but the government requires that women working as entertainers attend social hygiene clinics for regular health examinations. In addition to the registered establishments and official entertainers there is also a large illegal business organised around *casas*, special tourist agencies, escort services and hotel room service. Few of the women in these latter sub-sectors will acknowledge or even recognise themselves as prostitutes. Girls in *casas* will not identify themselves publicly as prostitutes. There are no figures for MSW in the Philippines.

INDIA

Small, geographically concentrated sub sectors of the Indian sex industry are well documented, particularly from a socio-medical perspective. Brothel based prostitution in Calcutta has received especially detailed attention. There are studies on the history of prostitution, sociological studies of temple prostitution, journalistic articles and polemical works on trafficking and low-income sex work, and some important but largely descriptive work on call girls.

This gives us only a partial and inadequate picture and there have been no really reliable regional, let alone national, studies that can suggest the size of the sex industry. Estimates for the numbers in sex work are high - reflecting, in part, the size of the population. The Indian National Commission for Women quotes figures of two million sex workers. The number of child prostitutes as a per cent age of the total is also quoted as being high. It has been suggested that 40% of female prostitutes begin selling sex before they are eighteen.

All figures on sex work in India (with the exception of HIV-related surveys in a minority of sites) must be treated with extreme caution. Very little is known about the demand for sex worker services. Sexuality is not a subject that is much discussed in India. Contrary to cultural ideals that stress chastity before marriage and fidelity within it, men commonly stray from this norm. While this behaviour is generally not as pronounced as in societies in East and Southeast Asia there is consistent, although largely anecdotal evidence to indicate that a large minority of men are clients of sex workers.

Mobile groups of men: male migrants in the cities; truck drivers; those in the armed forces; and travelling businessmen are frequently cited as important client groups. Many young men are initiated into their sexual lives by prostitutes. Rapidly escalating prevalence rates for HIV indicate that monogamy is not necessarily practised. This applies to men from all social classes. There is a large and relatively visible sex industry in Indian town and cities. This is especially true in north Indian cities where there are traditional brothels that constitute entire neighbourhoods.

In the southern cites of Madras and Bangalore there are ill-defined red light areas and a larger population of floating (or in this case 'flying') sex workers who operate on the streets. Agencies and NGOs working on HIV/AIDS, child prostitution and trafficking have focused their energies on brothel-based prostitution in the cities because this is where concentrations of workers and the exploited are most obvious. Yet there are many other sex work sites dispersed along highways, in suburbs and in small towns. The tendency for commercial sex to diversify, expand and to change forms has complicated this further.

In Mumbai, for example, NGO activity is concentrated in Kamatipura yet a recent mapping of sex work in the city revealed that there were at least another thirty-three important sex work sites. These sites did not include those categorised as indirect. Like its counterparts in East and Southeast Asia, the Indian sex industry is diversifying away from traditional sites and dispersing into the anonymity of 'ordinary' society. This process is not as advanced in India as elsewhere partly because of low levels of economic development and partly because traditional cultural norms regarding sexuality are less relaxed and more resistant to the idea (if not the practice) of commercial sex.

Nevertheless there are a growing number of venues for the purchasing of sex and increasingly sophisticated sexual networks involving low, middle and high-income prostitution. The vast majority of women who become sex workers do so because of dire economic circumstances. Those entering the brothel and street prostitution sectors tend to be very young. Many perhaps most will be children. The situation is thought to be especially acute in northern states where a combination of poverty and the low status of females contribute to their exploitation in the sex industry. In many desperately poor regions it is accepted that girls will become prostitutes in order to help their families.

A significant number of new entrants to the cheaper sub-sectors of the trade are trafficked. Despite the high profile given to Nepali and Bangladeshi girls who are trafficked into Indian brothels, the majority of trafficked females in India come from poor Indian states. The situation of the majority of trafficking victims is grim: many are held in systems of sexual slavery with minimal control over their lives. There is large demand for females like these because they are young, cheap and submissive. There is substantial anecdotal evidence indicating that it is not only poor and desperate women but also educated women who are entering the market for commercial sex.

Students, professional women and housewives are also selling sex. Workers in traditional lower class brothels complain of their 'quality' trade being taken by educated women. These women are invisible purposely so within the commercial sex market. They will endeavour to portray behaviours that are not those of stereotypical prostitutes. Research on male sex workers is even more limited. This is to be expected in a context in which male-male sexual desire is a threat to strong, family-oriented social patterns.

However, homosexual behaviours are extremely common. Many of these are non-commercial exchanges but many involve material transactions. There are no clear dividing lines separating the male sex worker from the man who has sex with men. In the same way there is no absolute dividing line between the MSM and the person who is a 'regular' family man with wife and children. In many instances all these behaviours and roles are found in the same individual.

BANGLADESH

The Bangladeshi sex industry has been subject to the same kind of changes apparent in other parts of the region. The trade is dispersing. It is moving out from traditional red light areas which are ghettos in the cities and dispersing through the suburbs. There is increasing 'hotel prostitution': with networks of mobile workers, pimps and clients operating in hotels, hostels, and guesthouses. There may be up to 10,000 women working under these kinds of arrangements in Dhaka and a symbiotic relationship is developing between hotels and the sex trade. Freelance sex workers also operate out of hotels and private apartments.

There is a significant street prostitution scene with workers providing sex services in parks and side streets. Brothel complexes exist in town and cities: over a dozen of these are 'official'. In the past three years, however, there has been a clampdown on a number of high profile brothels in which thousands of women were based. Kandupatti, Tanbazar and Nimtoli brothels were both closed amidst great controversy and the women made homeless.

Although prostitution was not technically illegal (providing the woman was eighteen and of sound mind and had made the decision to sell sex) deep legal, academic and public confusion over the status of prostitution existed up until March 2000 when the High Court ruled the profession to be legal. Estimated numbers of workers vary significantly. A total of 36,000 workers in the entire country are suggested by one study. Another study quotes police figures of 25,000-30,000 sex workers in Dhaka alone. Whichever estimate is used there is general consensus that the commercial sex trade is expanding, with some sources claiming that there is a 'phenomenal growth' in the number of sex workers.

Most sex workers in low-income brothels are the children of workers have been forced into the trade by desperate economic circumstances. Many are children and a majority are debt-bonded. There is significant client demand for young girls, with a positive correlation between the youth of the worker, the number of clients she services and her level of income.

There are an estimated 700,000 clients of sex workers (although this figure is based on the assumption that there are 36,000 sex workers). Principal client groups include rickshaw pullers, transport sector workers, students, police, sailors and dockworkers. There is a significant population of MSW and transgender workers. Homosexual behaviours are common in Bangladesh and many of these will be mediated through some form of commercial exchange. The men involved in these exchanges may not see themselves as possessing a 'homosexual' or sex worker identity.

SRI LANKA

Anecdotal evidence suggests that the size of the commercial sex market has increased in recent years. There is a market catering to local men and a sex tourist market. Contrary to popular perceptions this tourist market does not dominate the local one. Prostitution thrives around the conflict zones: poor widowed women make likely candidates for the industry and there is a large demand for sexual services from men in the armed forces.

Sex work sites include beaches, street prostitution, massage clinics (mainly in Colombo) different classes of brothels and 'satellite' brothels around guesthouses. The growth of free trade zones and the low wages paid to the women who work there propels some into sex work – often on a part time basis. There appears to have been a growth in this type of part time sex work. These FSW will have other regular occupations and not necessarily see themselves as prostitutes. Trafficking of women does occur in Sri Lanka and over one third of sex workers who took part in a pilot study revealed that they had been trafficked into the trade.

Estimating the number of sex workers is difficult and there are some very wide variations. The most authoritative study suggests that there are around 4,200 street sex workers (the majority in Colombo), around 1,700 based in massage parlours and another 4,800 in the brothel sector. This is probably a very conservative estimate. Although there have been a number of unsubstantiated reports of enormous numbers of children in prostitution, it is likely that they do not exceed 2,500.

These children include both girls and boys although client preference appears to be for boys between the ages of twelve and fourteen. Sexual behaviours amongst MSM appear to be altering with growing contact with other cultures. Anal sex, which was not traditionally practised on a large scale, is now becoming far more common.

NEPAL

Debates on prostitution in Nepal have been dominated by the issues of trafficking and the migration of females from Nepal's middle hills to north Indian brothels but comparatively little research has been done on prostitution in Nepal itself. The subsistence nature of large parts of the rural economy meant that there was no mass market for commercial sex until comparatively recently.

Economic development and urbanisation and the increasing integration of Nepal within global consumer cultures has altered this so that there is now an expanding domestic sex market in all parts of the country. There is also a small but expanding trade catering to sex tourists and expatriates. Sex work sites tend to concentrate in urban areas of the Kathmandu Valley, Pokhara and in the cities and towns of the Terai where there are dense sexual networks linking the Indo-Nepal border areas.

There are many sex work sites along the main north-south transport routes and along porterage routes. Sex work sites can also be found in the bazaars of the hills. Usual sex work sites include 'drinking pubs', hotels, restaurants and lodges, the worker's own home, roads, bus parks and jungle areas. Much of the trade is underground and FSW tend to be extremely mobile. Women of all castes and classes become sex workers, although those who are trafficked or migrate to India come primarily from ethnic minority groups in the hills.

Contrary to popular belief not all females working in the Indian or Nepali sex industries have been trafficked as a result of abduction, drugging or deception. Many young women and girls are sent into sex work because they can earn relatively high wages that can be remitted back home to support families in impoverished villages. Confusingly prostitution is neither legal nor illegal in Nepal although sex workers are subject to police harassment and arrest.

The estimated number of sex workers is over 25,000 with about 5,000 based in the Kathmandu Valley. Around 5,000 children are thought to be exploited in prostitution 88 and around 35% enter sex work by the time they are fifteen. Around 100,000 Nepali women and girls are believed to work in the Indian sex industry although this figure is open to question with some estimates being significantly higher.

PAKISTAN

Pakistan's sex industry is very poorly documented and analysed. It operates largely underground because prostitution is illegal (as is all sex outside the confines of marriage). Despite this, the sex market in Pakistan is increasing. There are only a handful of identifiable traditional red light areas remaining in Pakistani cities: most prostitution began a process of moving out from traditional sites in the 1960s.

Today prostitution is dispersed throughout urban areas in residential suburbs; it operates in guesthouses and hotels and it is very hard to identify either workers or sex work sites. Anecdotal evidence suggests that buying sex is common. It is more usual in the urban areas but rural men also buy sex at travelling fairs and when they visit the cities during holidays. More affluent men may have a series of 'second' or 'third' wives: these may be sex workers with whom they will have a semi-permanent sexual relationship in return for financial support.

These men and women do not perceive their relationship in terms of client and sex worker. The vast majority of FSW are socially isolated. Even when they are based in large red light areas, *purdah* practises mean that they have restricted social networks. Typically females will enter sex work at fourteen or fifteen years of age. Most are trafficked from rural areas in Pakistan, are the children of sex workers or have been abandoned by their husbands and families.

Many will be married and pimped out by their husbands (who are often drug addicts) and, in much of Pakistan; the management structure of the trade has a 'family' basis. These women have little control over their lives. In contrast, there are also groups of women who approximate a sex worker 'caste'. Their families have been in the profession for generations and women within these families do exercise a significant degree of independence because they earn and control economic resources.

These women, however, are in a minority. In the north of Pakistan, both female and male refugees from Afghanistan are selling sex in order to survive and in parts of Pakistan the sex trade is closely associated with the trade in drugs. Women working in the higher levels of the industry have more control over their work and some young women operating in affluent suburbs can command high fees.

Many of these young women are educated and middle class. Workers in brothels complain that this new breed of worker is depriving them of business. Homosexual behaviours are common in Pakistan and many sex acts will be non-commercial. HIV/AIDS awareness is minimal or non-existent in traditional red light areas.

4

The Seclusion of Women

Fertility in the Asian and Pacific region has been falling with notable uneveness over the past one and half decades and there has been considerable variability in the decline among the subregions. Fertility in the region declined 36.8 per cent from 1960-1965 to 1980-1985 and most of the decline (30.8 per cent) occurred during the period 1970-1975 to 1980-1985. East Asia experienced the steepest decline (53.1 per cent), almost all of which occurred since 1970-1975. The remarkable transformation in East Asia was greatly influenced by the decline in China where fertility dropped by 54.9 per cent during the more recent period.

The decline in South Asia (28.1 per cent) closely followed that of the Pacific (30.8 per cent), where a significant decline started in the earlier decade. East Asia is close to reaching replacement level fertility. In contrast, the total fertility rate (TFR) is close to 5 in South Asia and 4 in South-east Asia. The future rate of decline for the Asian and Pacific region as a whole depends primarily on these two subregions. Large countries in the region such as Bangladesh, India, Pakistan, the Philippines and Vietnam have fertility rates that are still very high, i.e. TFRs are in the range of 4 or more. Out of 14 large high-fertility countries, six have Governments that are pronatalist or have no major family planning programmed.

Of the remaining eight, four are from the Indian subcontinent, namely Bangladesh, India, Nepal and Pakistan.

Two other countries, Afghanistan and the Islamic Republic of Iran, border the subcontinent; however, not much is known about their current fertility situation. Three countries in the subcontinent, Bangladesh, India and Pakistan, constitute about 35 per cent of the population in the region. They are characterized by high fertility in the range of TFR = 4.5+ to 7+. It is evident that the fertility transition has yet to begin in full force in the countries of the subcontinent. By contrast, the South-east Asian countries, Indonesia, Malaysia, Singapore and Thailand, have made remarkable progress with regard to socio-economic development and fertility reduction.

However, slower progress in economic advancement alone cannot explain the lag observed in the three countries of the subcontinent. For example, Pakistan has continued to enjoy appreciable economic development without any corresponding success in family planning, while certain States in India have made remarkable progress in family planning despite only moderate improvements in economic conditions. Bangladesh also has made some progress in family planning in the absence of any significant improvement in economic conditions. The persistence of moderate to high fertility in the subcontinent appears to be deep-rooted in the structure of society and its culture.

When resistance to change lies at the structural and cultural level, policy intervention, the emphasis of which is on service delivery only, is not likely to bring any appreciable shift in the behaviour of the population. This chapter explores several important dimensions of the socio-cultural milieu in the subcontinent that seem relevant to answering the question: "Why do a large majority of women in the subcontiment still not practise family planning?" Most demographic surveys of the subcontinent consistently report that large majorities of women of reproductive age do not want any more children after the initial few births. Survey results also show that these women do not practise family planning.

SOCIO-CULTURAL FACTORS

These findings are often dismissed on the ground that they are not capturing the realities of the situation. However, not only are they valid, but those findings are also inadequate. The results truly reflect the individual desires of women, but they are inadequate in that they fail to identify the social and cultural constraints which prevent women from translating their desires into practice. All too often, explanations of fertility change concentrate primarily on the dynamic influences of social and economic change or organized interventions to spread fertility control.

Very little attention has been paid to the particular mixture of cultural features that may facilitate or inhibit fertility behaviour. Such an approach has proved useful in comprehending the recent fertility decline in Thailand. A clear understanding of the social position of women in the subcontinent appears to be the best possible approach to comprehending the discrepancy between reported desires and behaviour.

The concept of female autonomy is more amenable to empirical measurement than the concept of status and is therefore adopted for this chapter. Autonomy indicates the ability (technical, social and psychological) to obtain information and to use it as the basis for making decisions about one's private concerns and those of one's intimates. In the agrarian societies of Bangladesh, India and Pakistan, female autonomy is strongly influenced by kinship, family and marriage relationships. It is also greatly influenced by age, religion, the political system and cultural norms and practices, including the division of labour between the sexes.

KINSHIP, FAMILY AND MARRIAGE RELATIONSHIPS

The kinship structure of the subcontinent is characterized by the principles of village and kin exogamy, relatively close ties among patrilineally related males and control of property by males. Of course, there are minor variations in the three countries. For example, although a Muslim woman in Bangladesh has the legal right to inherit property from her parents, in actual practice it is more likely that her brothers will seize control of her share of inherited immovable property (land) regardless of her wishes. (She normally would not be entitled to moveable property.)

According to the custom of patrilocal marriage, a newly married woman is brought from her family of birth and placed in her husband's house which is usually distant from her parents' house. The preference for lineage and village exogamy attenuates a woman's ties with her family of birth and reduces the possibility that her family will intervene on her behalf after marriage. In the Indian subcontinent, as in most other agrarian societies, kin relationships still constitute the prime avenue of access to such scarce social resources as information, economic assistance and political support for the great majority of people.

An individual's power, influence and social ranking are closely related to his or her ability to exploit kin linkages. Thus cultural practices, such as patrilocal marriage, that tend to constrain or erode personal links between a married women and her natal kin directly diminish a woman's autonomy. At the same time, norms of avoidance (a married woman is regarded as an outsider in her family of marriage) make it difficult for a woman to establish effective links within the household into which she marries; she is, therefore, left almost powerless socially. Arranged marriage and differences of almost 10 years in age at marriage between bride and bridegroom place a woman in a subordinate position relative to her husband at the outset of marriage. Dowry is an essential part of Hindu marriage in India as well as in Bangladesh.

Although dowry is not an Islamic tradition, it is gradually becoming the fashion in Muslim marriage in Bangladesh. The size of dowry demanded usually far exceeds the amount of dowry given (either in cash or kind or both), which again puts women at a disadvantage from the outset of the marriage. When a woman from a poor family cannot bring any dowry with her or has nothing to inherit, she is endowed with neither money nor property that is her's alone. This situation further reduces her influence among the members of the husband's family. Beneath the larger social organization, there exists in each village an organizational subsystem (termed bari in

Bangladesh and caste in India) that regulates the life of groups in the village.

It acts as a source of collective security for its members and as a guardian of their mores. Membership in a *bari* or caste is crucial when individuals are faced with a choice, as in the case of accepting an innovative idea or adopting it in practice. Moreover, it puts a great restraint on female autonomy, particularly the movement of women outside the home and the seclusion of women. Deference for age is strictly adhered to in the subcontinent, regardless of class and creed. As mentioned previously, women are in a disadvantageous position because on average they are almost 10 years younger than their husbands.

Among women, solidarity and potential resistance are undermined by an age hierarchy that allies older women with men in dominant positions. The young bride enters her husband's household to find herself under the control and supervision of her mother-in-law. In general, older women dominate younger women: mothers-in-law dominate daughters-in-law and elder brothers' wives dominate younger brothers' wives, and so on.

RELIGION

Both as an ideology and as a normative force that governs behaviour and expectations, Islam sanctifies male dominance. It is also explicit about the sexual division of labour and responsibility, with men being the providers and protectors of women and women the servers of men. Such beliefs and practices make women subservient to their husbands. Submission to the husband by the wife is also abundantly glorified by the Hindu religion. A Hindu woman regards her husband as her god regard- less of his character.

A married woman's prime task is to produce a male heir so that a son can perform the last religious rites at the death of the husband. A woman's standing among her husband's kin is greatly undermined when she does not produce a son. Whereas Muslim inheritance law allows a daughter to receive one-half of the share received by a son, Hindu inheritance law does not allow even the one-half share to be given to the daughter. Both religions therefore reinforce inequality among men and women and allow female subjugation to be perpetuated.

Another important aspect of Islam, as practised in Bangladesh and Pakistan, which has direct effects on female autonomy is purdah, the seclusion of women. Purdah is a system of secluding women and enforcing high standards of female modesty. Its manifestations in Bangladesh and Pakistan include severe restrictions on a woman's movements outside her immediate homestead and standards of dress that hide face and form. Women who move out of the homestead into the public domain are considered both provocative and offensive.

In India, groups of patrilineally related males would have their honour, reputation and consequently their power undermined should the chastity of their females be subverted. As a consequence, free movement of females is very rigidly controlled. Restrictions on female personal movement and "protection" from other males take the form of seclusion in India too.

DIVISION OF LABOUR

The predicament of dependent women that forces them into relative seclusion within their own household compound also denies them access to economic opportunities outside the homestead. In these countries, a division of labour among household members has evolved whereby women specialize in work inside or near the homestead and men specialize in work outside the home.

This division of labour itself engenders a powerful element of men's control over women, enforcing women's dependence, on men by denying them direct access to income-earning opportunities. The sexual division of labour applies to all women in the rural areas and the costs, in terms of abuse and loss of status, of engaging in types of work that require movement outside the homestead are indeed very high.

SON PREFERENCE

In societies in which women are dependent on men, where they are excluded from inheritance and mainstream economic activities, parents place a great premium on sons. This preferential treatment of the male child severely retards the personal development of girls and hence affects their autonomy in later life.

POLITICAL SYSTEM

Political power in the subcontinent, as in other developing areas, is monopolized by men. Until relatively recently, elected and appointed government officials were almost always male. Village councils, which adjudicate most local disputes, are exclusively composed of men. In part because of male domination of political institutions and in part because formal judicial institutions and administrations are weak, particularly in the rural areas, legal protection of women is nominal. If a female litigant is not closely related to and supported by a man, she is likely to lose a case regardless of its merits. Under the influence of *purdah,* women are discouraged from going to court to establish legitimate claims.

THEORETICAL LINKAGES

The direct relationships linking social structure, female autonomy and family planning acceptance are summarized in the accompanying figure. The complete dependence of younger women on men and older women, deference for age and lack of access to the outside world make it difficult for them to resist pronatalist pressures. Moreover, early marriage increases their period of exposure to the risk of pregnancy in the absence of opportunity to regulate their fertility. Females are brought up to believe that their own wishes and interests are subordinate to those of the family group.

They are, therefore, likely to sacrifice their own wishes to regulate fertility, even at the cost of risking their health from repeated pregnancies. Given the situation of relative social isolation faced by newlywed women, there are clear advantages to high fertility. A wife is encouraged to create her own social group by producing children. Confronted with an insecure future that will probably become more unstable when her husband dies, a woman undoubtedly sees children, especially sons, as a potential source of security, both economically and socially. This lack of female autonomy contributes to high fertility.

The Asian and Pacific region has experienced a remarkable decrease in the fertility level over the last decade, with notable variations in magnitude among the subregions. East Asia, particularly China, contributed much to this decline in fertility but there are still large areas with high fertility (TFRs in the range of 5 to 7) particularly in the subcontinent and its neighbouring countries.

There has not been any major decline in fertility in the subcontinent in the last decade or in the previous one. The reason appears to be deep-rooted in the structure of these societies and associated cultural practices. The forces of modernization, which are gradually gaining momentum, will perhaps help women to gain the necessary autonomy to resist pronatalist pressures. Until such time, fertility will tend to decline at a very slow pace.

5

Bodily Processes and Limitations on Women

One of the crucial issues affecting women in South Asia today has been the growth of state sponsored religious fundamentalism. This is occurring in the context of increasing evidence of violence against women dowry murders, sexual harassment, rape often by the police and army, and the throwing of acid on women in the streets. As a result of campaigns and agitations by women's movements, these incidents have been highlighted and the governments have passed some preventive laws, albeit with many loopholes and limitations. However what is significant is that in recent years there has been a shift away from even the liberal rhetoric of equal rights for women and laws have been passed to withdraw the legal and political rights which women already had won.

These developments are linked with the broader process of economic and political changes which have laid the basis for religious fundamentalist groups to grow, as well as for the support to these tendencies by the governments in these countries. The emergence of fundamentalist groups is not specific to South Asia alone. Fundamentalist forces, often with state support have emerged in Sudan, Nigeria, Egypt, and Malaysia, with Iran offering the best example of what implications this phenomenon has for women. Iranian women took an active part in the anti- imperialist struggle against the Shah, making the veil into a symbol of resistance only to find them pushed afterwards into the restricted roles of mothers and wives. The "chador" became a legally binding requirement, the age of marriage was reduced to 13 years and divorce became nearly impossible.

These trends with very specific injunctions for women can be seen also in developed capitalist countries, thus belying any link of this phenomenon with backwardness and underdevelopment. In fact many of these movements use the latest and most sophisticated technology in modern communications. In the United States, the Moral Majority, with close links with the extreme right, have initiated a reign of "holy terror" with senators opposing the Equal Rights Amendment on the grounds that it undermines the family and "deprives men of their right to come home from work to a fresh martini, cooked dinner and a cheerful and compliant wife".

Electronic evangelists fill the air waves with relentless exhortations attributing all of America's problems to the communist menace and the recent movements for racial, sexual and social emancipation. In South Asia in recent years a number of developments show the increasing hold of religious fundamentalist forces in the region. In 1986 the Indian Parliament passed a bill called the Muslim Women's Protection of the right of Divorce Bill, which withdrew a right from Muslim women to appeal for maintenance under a special provision in the Criminal Procedure Code. This bill was passed after a period of mass demonstrations, strikes and petitions presented by Muslims and Hindus all over the country, as a reaction to a Supreme Court judgement to grant a 73 year old woman, Shad Bano, the paltry sum of Rs. 179 per month as maintenance from her husband.

A simple issue of women's rights turned into an issue of minority vs. majority community interests and led to a withdrawal of legal rights for Muslim women. In Pakistan, the Hadood Ordinance of 1979 sanctioned flogging for adultery and rape, with little to distinguish the two, a Law of Evidence reduced a woman's evidence to half that of a man, and a proposed Shariat Bill, now seeks to deprive women of even more political and social rights, including their participation in politics. In Bangladesh, while there have not been specific changes in the law as yet, attempts are being made to assert "Islamic" codes of dress and conduct for women. Women announcers on television were told not to cover their heads and not to wear "bindis" on their foreheads.

At the moment there is a bill being debated on making Islam the state religion. These attempts to reverse the status of women and withdraw the rights which earlier generations of women had won, all in the name of preserving traditions and the fundamental tenets of a religion needs to be understood in relation to the role of the state. While this is clear in countries where a religion is the state religion, even in countries which purport to be secular, there seems to be support if not outright sponsorship of fundamentalism. Interestingly these trends go alongside government policies and programme to integrate women into development.

These are not just part of the rhetoric of the International Women's Decade which most governments have to project as part of their "modern and progressive image". The apparent contradiction between special programmes for women's employment and skill training and the passing of restrictive laws which raise images of medievalism in the 20th Century can be seen as two sides of the same imperative to control and direct women's labour, fertility and sexualitiy to suit both capitalist and patriarchal interests. Although significant work has been done on the implications of capitalist development on women's work and the fact that the needs of capital and the needs of patriarchy can either coincide or conflict with each other, more work need to be done at a theoretical and empirical level on the relation between the state and women's subordination.

This chapter will look at one phenomenon -religious fundamentalism in the South Asian context. (i.e. Pakistan, India and Bangladesh) with a special focus on India, and its relation to state ideology and the women's subordination. The basis for the emergence of fundamentalism, the connection of this with the increasing attempts to reassert control over women, and the implications of such a state ideology for the women's movements in the region are discussed. It is argued that religious fundamentalism as a state ideology could provide a coincidence of patriarchal and capitalist interests in the present context in South Asia.

THE STATE AND RELIGIOUS FUNDAMENTALISM IN SOUTH ASIA

Post colonial states in South Asia have followed a capitalist path of development, notwithstanding the rhetoric of socialism, whether of the Indian or Islamic variety. There exist differences in the nature of the state, for instance, the specific constellation of class forces, the degree of dependence or independence from foreign capital, or the degree of repression and the right to assert democratic rights. However, development programmes in all these countries for agricultural and industrial growth, have resulted in structural changes in the ownership and control over productive assets, especially land which have furthered the process of class and sexual differentiation.

One contribution the decade has made is the challenging of the notion that development policies are sex- neutral; today there is a wealth of empirical material which documents the differential effect of development policies on women and men. Technological changes, legislation, etc, interact with a pre-existing class and sexual division of labour, both within the community and within the household. This has resulted in a deepening of inequalities between women and men, in terms of their access and control over food, education, health care and productive resources.

State intervention is today, explicitly restructuring not just the arena of the economic but also other arenas of civil society, those which concern the most "private" areas of religious beliefs, reproductive choices and man-woman relationships. Given this pattern of development, the continuous aggravation of inequalities of wealth, income distribution and uneven regional growth, have resulted in various forms of oppositional movements for land-rights, higher wages, regional autonomy and implementation of legal rights.

These movements have usually been repressed by governments and power wielding groups, resulting in a tremendous increase in class, caste, communal and sexual violence since the mid-sixties. The inability of the governments to tackle the roots of these problems has resulted in a crippling crisis of legitimacy. It is in this context that the ruling parties in all these countries are seeking to create an ideological unity through the sponsoring of religious fundamentalism. This is expressed openly in General Zia's Islamisation drives and in a more covert form in India and Bangladesh.

In 1977, the secular principles of the Bangladesh constitution were reversed and since then, the government has been supporting the growth of Islamic institutions and linking up with Islamic state. At the moment there is a bill introduced in parliament to make Islam into a state religion. In India, the complicity of the ruling party in the attacks on Sikh families in Delhi in November 1984, the succumbing to Muslim and Hindu fundamentalist pressures and the total lack of political will to solve the increasing communal tension in the country, have shattered the illusions of the secular ideology of the Indian state. The trend is towards a communal state ideology with majority Hindu fundamentalism as a dominant component.

There are differences in the specific factors necessitating the use of religious fundamentalism to create an ideology unity. In Pakistan, the nationality question is the most important. The only way by which Punjabi domination in the economy, bureaucracy and military could be preserved by the ruling party was by stressing that there were Muslims. A homogenous "Muslim" identity had to be stressed to avoid confrontation with the very real structural inequalities between the provinces, each with their own distinctive culture and language. General Zia himself is said to have stated that without Islam, Pakistan, would disintegrate overnight.

In Bangladesh whose creation, in fact, is the best expression of the fragility of religion as the basis of national identity, the upsurge in Islamic activities is linked to other factors. The dependence for foreign aid on the oil-rich-Middle East, and the cooption of right wing fundamentalist forces in the ruling party, are some of the factors pushing towards the Islaminsation of Bangladesh. In India, the situation is more complex since it continues theoretically at least, to be a secular state. Rather than a direct projection of religious fundamentalism as a state ideology, there is a more indirect sponsorship of fundamentalist forces.

The emergence of state sponsored religious fundamentalism has to be seen in the broader context of the communalization of Indian Society "Communalism" as an ideology projects the "belief that because a group of people follow a particular religion, they have as a result, common social, political and economic interests." Analysis has shown that this assumption of a homogenous identity ignores the real divisiions of caste and class and that in fact, a "communal identity" has no natural basis but has to be created.

In spite of the production of historical and contemporary studies which provide evidence of the above mentioned processes, many commentators continue to see the South Asian region as one torn by inherently antagonistic religious communities, with the roots of this antagonism traced to the medieval past. Recent attempts to analyse the Punjab situation, see the conflicts as the outcome of a "Sikh" history and tradition. Such analysis not only ignores the very significant caste and class divisions amongst Sikhs, but also ignores the role of the ruling party in creating the present communal situation in that region.

The demands put forward by the regional opposition party in Punjab i.e. for water, territorial re-division with neighbouring states and Chandigarh as the state capital for Punjab, which were secular demands, were continuously ignored by the ruling party till they became linked with the communal demand for a separate nation i.e. Khalistan. The emergence of communalism as an ideology which leads to violence between groups who co-existed peacefully before has to be situated historically and in relation to the specific socio-economic and political factors leading to such developments.

COMMUNALISM IN THE COLONIAL PERIOD

Historians have established that communalism in the Indian subcontinent, was a product of colonial underdevelopment, located most specifically amongst the middle classes. The breakdown of existing class identities and status systems, along with economic stagnation forced middle class Indians to compete with each other for the scarce resources. The ensuing frustration, combined with a sense of deprivation and fears of the loss of identity, created a volatile situation in which a religious issue could trigger off immediate violence and extreme brutality.

Given a crisis of identity, the protection of cows, or music before a mosque became crucial issues, issues of life and death, because these religious symbols came to represent symbolically, the preservation or destruction of these middle classes themselves. It is therefore, not accidental that communal struggles during the colonial period occurred mostly over government jobs, educational concessions and the political positions in the legislative councils and municipal bodies which enabled control over them.

Communal struggles were therefore over secular issues. In fact, the "purely religious or theological content of communalism has tended to be meager". In addition, from the end of the 19th Century, communalism became an important instrument of colonial policy in the effort to thwart the rising national movement. Communalists, especially the Muslim League were encouraged through the ready acceptance of their demands, official patronage etc. The Indian national movement itself, though secular in its objectives, also used communal consciousness.

There was a distinct Hindu tinge in the leadership's work and thought. Many nationalist identified nationalism with the revival of Hinduism. Modern literature in Bengali, Hindi and Urdu was partly communal in tone, portraying Muslims as foreigners and oppressive lecherous tyrants, while Hindus were portrayed as heroes struggling for positive values. Many leaders used Hindu symbols, idioms and myths in their political speeches and writings. India was often referred to as the Mother Goddess or compared to Durga, Kali, and other Hindu goddesses. Gandhi too, appealed to people in the language of religiosity, for e.g. his interpretation of independence as Ram Rajya. The same divisions affected women in the early women's movement and national movements.

In their struggle for suffrage, education and legal rights, both Hindu and Muslim women attacked the system of seclusion. However, as communal divisions intensified, Hindu feminists began to see purdah (seclusion) as a custom bought to India by Muslim invaders and a cause for the fall in women's high status in the Golden Age, and Muslim women, fearing that they would be swamped as a minority in a India ruled by a Hindu majority, began to defend passages in the Quran about female modesty. This Hindu tinge in the national movement and the subsequent failure in fostering the development of a national consciousness in the post independence period, left the space for communalism and casteism to grow in spite of a secular Constitution. While communalism in the present period does not have the same causes as under colonialism, at level of ideology, it does find an echo in past memories of communal violence.

CONTEMPORARY COMMUNALISM AND THE INDIAN STATE

In the decade between 1950-1960 communal incidents were few but since the 1960's there has been a tremendous increase in communal violence involving many more communities and creation new divisions as for instance, between Hindus and Sikhs. These incidents occurred mainly in urban areas, though recently, communal violence has spread to rural hinterlands as well. Analysis of these incidents have shown that they were systematically planned with selective targets and were a disguised from of economic competition between the two communities. In many cases, the targets were Muslim artisans and small entrepreneurs who had achieved a degree of relative prosperity and were cutting out the traders who happened, to be Hindus. This competition for scarce resources -markets or jobs has even led to the old caste conflicts being converted into communal struggles today.

Another significant factor behind these incidents of violence was the evidence of the complicity of the ruling party in either engineering these riots or not acting swiftly to prevent their occurrence. Fact after fact in Punjab, Delhi, Meerut, Bhiwandi, all point out the complicity of the ruling party and the state apparatus. Behind the specific "riot" however, is the much more disturbing growth of communal ideology amongst large sections of people. Over the years there has occurred a consolidation of Hindu sentiments, a process which escalated when some dalits converted to Islam in South India. Hindu organisations held conferences, and went on all India pilgrimages carrying holy water from the Ganges. Organisations like the Hindu Manch, Vishwa Hindu Parishad, Hindu Ekta Manch, along the older Rashtriya Swayemsewak Sangh, have initiated militant programmes to counter what they perceive as a threat to Hinduism.

These organisations are highly authoritarian in structure, have para- military wings and an ideology of Hindu expansionism. For instance, the Vishwa Hindu Parishad has openly declared that Hindus are the only people who accept India as their motherland and that national integration is synonymous with Hindu consolidation. This includes the recovery of Pakistan, Bangladesh and Afghanistan as part of Greater India. Like fascist organisations elsewhere, these are all male dominated, if not exclusively male organisations. These organistations have been given state patronage, are allowed to function freely with members of the ruling party publicly supporting and attending their conferences and meetings.

This phase of communalism in India is significant in that it emerges in a context of rising religious fundamentalism. Communal tensions in earlier periods have not necessarily been accompanied by fundamentalist movements. The other significant factor is the role of the ruling party in supporting these religious fundamentalist forces, especially Hindu fundamentalists. In sharp contrast to its positions in the late 1960's and 70's, the ruling Congress Party has now shifted from its earlier public condemnation of communalism and of Hindu organisations and support to the victims of minority communities (in particular the Muslims) to a more generalised condemnation of communalism and the foreign hand in public pronouncements along with a series of concessions to communal demands, a refusal to indict individuals identified as being responsible for the violence, and a stifling of secular opinion, both, within, and outside the ruling party.

This shift in the stand of the ruling party on communalism was partly due to an electoral strategy to cash in on the "Hindu vote", especially in North India. When this strategy did not result in large scale support in the 1986 by elections, there was a shift back to and a succumbing to Muslim fundamentalist demands by pushing through the Muslim Womens Bill. The ruling party played one communalism off another in the electoral numbers game. However, it would be a mistake to see the consolidation of communalism today only as the backlash of a short sighted electoral strategy. There are far deeper factors at work which need further research and exploitation, to enable us to understand the reasons for people's responses to communal propaganda and the increasing crisis of the ideological legitimacy of the Indian State and its need for a new hegemonizing ideology.

An area for further exploration would be to see how far the attempt to forge a national identity after the collapse of anti- colonial nationalism would take the form of a projection of a Hindu nationalism. Such an ideology has today ready recipients in the products of the peculiarly Indian pattern of industrialization i.e. the sections of the population who live of frontier and trading profits, the bulk of whom come from the "intermediate" or backward castes which form the Hindu majority. It is these sections, along with the newly emerging rural kulaks, who today seem to be supporting the fundamentalist movements. Whether India becomes a Hindu fundamentalist state or not is an open question but the fact is that it is today a communal state with government support and even sponsoring of religious fundamentalism.

These developments are occurring in the context of a growing authoritarian state structure. Over the years there has been increased investment in the police, para-military forces and the army, along with the passing of laws like the National Security Ordinance, Terrorist Affected Areas etc. which give wide powers to the police and the state apparatus over the lives of citizens. State sponsorship and the emergence of fundamentalist organisations among Hindus, Sikhs, Muslims, and Christians along with an increasingly authoritarian state structure, has serious implications for the future of democracy in India. These trends in the South Asian region have also very specific and disturbing implications for women. Processes of class formation and the construction of nationhood are not separate from the particular forms of women's subjugation in these countries. In the present context, religious fundamentalism as a crucial component of communalism provides a lethal combination to prop up or resurrect patriarchal controls over women.

RELIGIOUS FUNDAMENTALISM AND WOMEN

The terms fundamentalism, revivalism, obscurantism, are often used interchangeably and loosely. There is considerable controversy over the use of these terms. In this chapter, religious fundamentalism is used rather than revivalism. Revivalism implies a "renewed attention to" or "interest in" while fundamentalism implies an adherence often a strict and literal adherence to a set of basic principles. Thus there could be movements of religious revivalism which could over time become fundamentalist i.e. focusing on only one set of principles can vary, as studies on Islamic Fundamentalism have pointed out.

Commenting on the tendency to club together heterogeneous phenomena under the rubric of "fundamentalism", O. Roy makes distinctions between fundamentalisms in Islam which could be "a return to strict religious practice, as we observe in many émigré milieus; return to the observance of the text (study of the Koran and the hadiths), which is the fundamentalism of the madrasa; and return to the religious law, to the practice of the Shariat, which is the fundamentalism of the "ulama"...

Fundamentalism is the "return to..., the re-reading, the quest for origins". This rereading, return to the origins can take many different forms and therefore is not in itself a political position. A purely textual definition would equate the proponents of liberation theology in Latin America, who base their work on the original Christian communities of Christ, with the ravings of right wing tele-evangelists like Jerry Falwell and Oral Roberts in the United States.

Movements inspired by religion revivalist or fundamentalist have played a revolutionary anti-imperialist role in the national movements of the 19th and 20th centuries, and have also expressed the needs and aspirations of working people. Religious movements therefore are not necessarily conservative. Similarly, religious fundamentalism does not always refer to the past in fact what is being asserted as a basic tenet is often a totally modern practise. This is why it is problematic to call the recent occurrence of sati as a revival. In addition, the meanings that people give to these principles can also vary.

For example, Iranian women who supported Khomeini, and marched in thousands, as organised militant contingents turning the veil into a symbol of solidarity and struggle, were not simply retreating to the past, but were asserting a certain positive conception of the future. Islam offered an alternative to the "consumerism and the modern consumer woman" projected by the Shah's economic and social policies. Similarly, attempts by disadvantaged groups to rise in ritual status by strict adherence to "tradition" or the Shariat are not seen by them as a return to medievalism but in fact as symbols of achievement.

Fundamentalism then, can only be understood in relation to a specific historical context. It is crucial to identify when it emerges, which are the social groups initiating as well as constituting the support base of this phenomenon and what exactly is being projected as the basic principles of adherence. One feature of fundamentalism is its *selectivity* in choosing what the true and original teaching is.

In the sense fundamentalism constructs a *particular* version of Islam/Hinduism/Sikhism/ Chritianity as the only valid representation of that religion. This construction makes little distinction between what is textual and what may be local specific cultural practices. Most significantly it abstracts from history and projects that particular amalgam of belief, ritual and practice with a transcedental validity. In Pakistan for instance, the islamisation process selects elements from 19 schools of jurisprudence as well as customs and practises which existed in the 8th and 9th centuries in what is Saudi Arabia, Iran and Syria of today.

Similarly, the "Hinduism" being projected by various Hindu organisations as the only true Hinduism denies the historical existence of two separate and anatgonistic religious traditions amongst people designated as Hindus. One tradition was Brahmanism which was based on Vedic texts and the Dharmashastras, restricted to the upper castes, buttressed by royal patronage and the creation of a priestly caste. The Shramanic tradition (the Bakthi movements were seen as inheritors of this tradition) was popular amongst lower castes, had a universalistic ethic and exhibited a wide diversity in ritual and belief.

Historically one cannot speak of Hinduism as such but a variety of 'Hindu' religions. The Hinduism being claimed by fundamentalist organisations draws on the first tradition but here too it incorporates elements from caste customs, particularly Kshatriya notions of honour, as well. Social scientists have labelled this very modern Hinduism - "syndicated Hinduism". That this contemporary construction of Hinduism (the same process could be seen in other religions) has no need of either textual or historical verification was brought out very clearly in an interview with Ramanand Sagar, the producer of a television serial on the Ramayan recently.

When asked about the historical sources for the film, he mentioned how during that period women did not cover their torsos but it was impossible for him to allow that on the screen since the image of Sita as a pure, chaste and ideal wife was so strong and important that showing her without a blouse would violate the moral message of the serial! Similarly when the Council of Islamic Ideology in Pakistan was discussing whether women should have the right to vote, whether blood money or compensation paid to a female victim should be half that of a male and whether women's evidence should be half that of a man's evidence in court, there was no discussion of "khula" which is the Qur'anic equivalent available to women, of men's right to the "talaq" form of divorce.

Since then the Hadood Ordinance and the Law of Evidence have been passed and there is now the proposal for a Shariat Bill which will extend the jurisdiction of the Shariat Court to all areas of life. However, even here there is the process of selectivity - while the Federal Shariat Court is seen as having only an advisory role regarding fiscal matters, in matters, of Muslim personal law, and judgement passed by the court will be binding. Almost all the issues concerning women's rights fall under personal law. It seems that the criteriea for selection and implementation of true Islam is the crucial area of man-woman relations rather than more general theological issues. A similar process of selectivity can be seen in the codification and implementation of personal laws in India.

While a common criminal code exists for every Indian citizen, areas of marriage, inheritance, divorce etc. are governed by separate personal laws for Muslims, Christians, and Hindus. More studies need to be done one on the process by which these personal laws were codified involving not only a specific interpretation of each religion but also the incorporation of the assumptions of colonial administrators and native representatives.

Hindu personal law for instance, was interpreted initially in 1772 when Warren Hastings appointed ten Brahmin pandits from Bengal to compile a digest of Hindu scriptural law in civil matters - marriage, divorce, inheritance, succession. These interpretations however were only codified into one uniform law in 1941. Prior to this, there had been separate laws for different castes and communities i.e. separate customary laws existed for Nairs, Nambudris, Kulins, Jats etc. The Draft Hindu Code was thus based on specifically Brahmanical interpretations of Hinduism. Changes were introduced into this as a result of the struggles of women and men in the early women's movement and hence contained some rights for Hindu women.

It is significant, however, that the Hindu Code Bill was only passed after Independence after a great deal of opposition. A process of secular reform to abolish all personal laws for a uniform civil code prior to independence was scuttled on the grounds of political expediency and although the ideal of a uniform civil code is enshrined in the Directive Principles of the Constitution, till today, separate personal laws continue to operate. It is not accidental that issues of religious identity are tied so closely with the regulation of relations between men and women. All personnel laws, including the reformed Hindu law have certain common features which reinforce the patriarchal, patrilineal and patrilocal family.

This is the main family form in India, especially in the north, central and eastern parts of the country. Even where matrilineal forms have existed, as in the taravad of Kerala, economic changes and colonial policy have invested defacto rights over property in the hands of men. Government intervention through changes for example, in laws on inheritance has tended to maintain this patriarchal authority. In situations of the breakdown and emergence of new class / caste / communal identities it is these elements of man - woman relations which become crucial markers of identity.

It is significant that during the agitation in Punjab, a demand was put forward for a separate personal law for Sikhs as well. This customary law deprives women of the right to property, and to divorce and contains the provision for a widow to marry her husband's brother. All these features link patriarchal control to newly emerging class interests particularly the need to maintain and keep control over landed property by sections of the Punjab peasantry.

It is also not accidental that that while the ruling party ignored the other secular demands for water, territory and Chandigarh as the capital city, this communal demand was being considered. It is this linkage which needs to be explored to understand why religious fundamentalism has very specific implications for women. In this section we will look at two areas which illustrate this linkage - the emergence of fundamentalism as the result of a challenge to and breakdown of traditional patriarchal structures and the process of identity creation in situations of social and economic crisis.

CHALLENGES TO AND BREAKDOWN OF TRADITIONAL PATRIARCHAL STRUCTURES

"If fundamentalists are calling for the return to the veil, it must be because women have been taking off the veil." There are two processes occurring within the South Asian context which are leading women to "take off the veil "- the changing demand for women's labour as a result of capitalist developments in agriculture and industry and the challenge of a newly developed consciousness about the rights of women. In India, since the 1960's agricultural development has been based on a technological package to increase agricultural productivity, marking a shift away from the earlier focus on land reforms.

The effects of the Green Revolution have been extensively documented. Although there are regional differences, depending on prior patterns of landholding and landlessness, as well as technological constraints imposed by the kind of crop, there have been considerable changes in women's participation in wage labour and their position relative to men in the rural areas. Capitalist development has resulted in many peasants and marginal farmers losing their landholdings at the same time as there has been the crystalisation of a new layer of rural kulaks (rich farmers). There has been a dramatic increase in the number of agricultural workers, within which section the number of women is higher and increasing faster than the number of men.

The 1981 Census showed that half of all rural female workers (as against a quarter of all women is more seasonal and as a result, most women are casual workers. The numbers of female cultivators has declined relative to men, highlighting women's lack of independent access to land. In addition, in 15 states, surveys reveal an increase in the differential between male and female wages, with women's earnings being close to half or less than half of men's earnings. On other hand, the emergence of a rich peasant class had led to the withdrawal of women of this section from work in the fields. However, this has not meant an improvement in the status of these women. Seclusion only serves to hide the labour women perform within the household, which sometimes increases as a result of hiring in wage labour. In any case, this process does not result in any increase in women's economic control over resources and property or decision making.

In Bangladesh, there has been an increasing trend of landlessness documented along with an increase in the number of poor female headed households. Female headed households are estimated to range from 6.4% to 16% of all rural households. Around 40% of all rural women are today seeking wage employment. Studies done on rural areas in Pakistan especially in the Punjab point out the high degree of male out-migration and the importance of foreign remittances in changing the rural setting. Although men do return home for crucial production periods, women have begun to enter areas of work and take over decision making in spheres previously the prerogative of men. One study notes the contradictory implications of these changes.

While some women are wearing modern clothes and cosmetics, for many others there is now the introduction of seclusion as women are withdrawn from work in the fields.

The same study also points out to the increase in social networking between women in different households and the issues which are discussed together range from marriage alliances, problems with family members to monetary matters. There are also variations in the effects of industrialisation strategies, but certain broad trends can be identified. In India, women were mainly employed in textiles, mines and plantations.

In all these sectors there has been a decline in women's employment, especially in textiles and coal mines. Of all non-agricultural jobs that women lost during the period of 1911 and 1961, only 8% were due to these jobs becoming obsolete and in the remaining cases (92%) women were simply replaced in their past occupations by men. However it is important to note that women are still employed by these industries either as contract labour or through the decentralisation of production to all sweatshops or home based units, especially in the textile industry.

The decline in the relative and absolute employment of women in the traditional sectors is also a part of the general crisis of these sectors of the economy. in modern sub-sectors like pharmaceuticals, electrical appliances, motor vehicles, machine production, heavy chemicals, which anyway have a low labour absorption, women are concentrated in certain industries like garments, food processing, electronics i.e. the new export oriented factories, many of which fragment production to household units, as well as in the unorganised sector.

A study on the unorganised sector in Calcutta points out that not only is women's employment in this sector increasing faster than men's employment but those men and women are now, competing for these scarce jobs. Census figures with all their limitations, have also registered an increase in the work force participation rate of urban women i.e. from 11% en 1961 to 14% in 1971. Since women's employment in the organised sector is less than 33% of the urban female employment, this increase of registered employment seems to be in the unorganised hence low waged sector.

In Bangladesh, given the low level of industrial development, women are only recently being employed in the new export industries set up in and around Dhaka. 80 to 90% of the garment workers are young, unmarried women, mainly from the urban areas. In Pakistan, data based on the 1975/76 CMIU shows that the total non-farm employment for women was less than 3% of the total. In the manufacturing sector women again are concentrated in the food processing, textiles, cotton ginning, pharmaceuticals, garments and electronics factories. The CMI date clearly does not reflect the level of women's employment since it does not include the category of casual contract labour or subcontracted home based production. Various case studies have revealed high rates of female employment in the unorganised sector.

Contrary to the general impression, there are quite a few single women working in urban based industries, i.e. not necessarily only widowed or divorced women. Broadly then one can see that capitalist development, in agriculture and industry, has resulted in an increase in landlessness, increased dependence of women on wage work which is seasonal, low earnings and the increase as well as invisibilisation of their work in the unorganised sector. In broad terms then more women are being forced into looking for work and the work that is available is in the unorganised sector, with a large section engaged in subcontracted home based production. The new export oriented industries are drawing in a new layer of younger women.

Although studies of these industries show variations of age and marital status thus showing a deviation from the South East Asian model, many of these young girls are having to take over the traditional obligations of fathers and brothers for instance, to provide a dowry for their marriage and are now earning their own dowries. Studies of young women workers in the garment and electronic factories show a sizeable number who come, from disintegrating middle class to lower middle class families, who hope to earn enough to have a large dowry which is seen as the passport to marriage and an escape from factory work.

However the bulk of their earnings were in fact going towards household expenses, as the families struggled to maintain a increasingly threatened middle class status. In these families, the traditional structure of male provisioning could be maintained in practice. The pressures of increasing poverty in the countryside as well are forcing a renegotiation of structures of authority. As women are moving out of the homestead in search of work and therefore away from the direct control of family patriarchs, they are entering "male space" in search of wage labour in addition there is the attempt to reassert control by regulating women's mobility and access to wage labour and product markets.

Marty Chen describes such a process in rural Bangladesh: "... Patriarchal control over poor women's labour is operated not by the family patriarchs but by the village patriarchs The Village patriarchs, men from rich households, control the paid labour opportunities within the village and dictate the norms of purdah and status that discourage women from seeking wage employment or engaging in trade outside the village. Indeed to show their disapproval of women who break these norms, village patriarchs have been known to stop hiring those women to work in their households and to stop extending them credit or other forms of patron-client service."

These material processes which are threatening traditional patriarchal structures, can create conditions for the emergence and support for ideologies that stress women's traditional roles. In Iran, this took the form of a move to drive women out of office jobs, the closure of workplace nurseries, and the restoration of the husband's right to bar wives from paid employment. There has been extensive documentation of the link between the demands of the capitalist economy and the emergence of ideologies which justify the exclusion or incorporation of women into the labour force.

The best example, is of course pro-natalism in Nazi Germany in the early thirties and its reversal in 1937 when women were exhorted to contribute to the war industry. These ideologies do not always functionally respond to the needs of capital in a purely economic sense. Ideologies of domesticity for women are being forced to seek work. Religious fundamentalism as a state supported ideology in the given economic and cultural context of South Asia could provide a similar justification for controlling the mobility, fertility and sexuality of women. Already communal organisations have started issuing aggressive statements about the right place of women.

In the communal violence recently in Ahmedabad, Hindu fundamentalists put forward what they called a "theory of truth" (satyawad), in which they condemned abortion as murder and advocated that women return to the home and give up their jobs in favour of unemployed men. "These communalists prescription for us is that we stay at home and lose ourselves in our husbands, children and religious texts. To do otherwise is to be a witch, a fallen woman and an insult to manhood". Apart from the changing structures of women's work, the other factor which could lay the basis for support to fundamentalist ideas is the growing strength of the women's movement and a generalised awareness about women's rights in the region.

There has been a rich tradition of women's struggle against patriarchal structures in the history of South Asia. The nature of these struggles has depended on the specific historical circumstances and options available for women during these periods. The early 20th century women's movement for example, did not question the sexual division of labour within the family, but did build independent organisations and fought militantly for equal rights, whether for the right to property which benefited few women, or for the vote, which (at least potentially) benefited all women, as well as for higher wages, food and the right to organize which benefited working class and peasant women.

After independence there was a lull but in the late 1960's and early 1970's in India a new women's movement emerged. The economic crisis of the sixties led to numerous working class and peasant movements all over the country, and in the early seventies, women's issue began to be taken up in the context of these general struggles. In urban areas, small women's groups emerged, constituted by women who were or had been linked with radical left groups as well as activists involved in development work. After the lifting of the Emergency in 1977, women's groups mushroomed in the larger cities of Bombay, Delhi, Hyderabad, Bangalore.

What was new about these groups was the fact that they autonomous organizations (i.e. not linked to political parties), used different forms of organising based more on the consciousness raising model rather than the mass recruitment strategy followed by the party linked women's organisations, with a stress on non-hierarchical internal organization structures. Since the seventies, the new women's movement has grown tremendously and has taken up the issues of dowry murders, police rape, domestic violence, reproductive rights and recently the issues of rights for Muslim women and sati. There are two levels at which the issues of patriarchal control are being challenged.

The first, and the dominant trend is to expose and agiate around the most extreme manifestations of women's subordination in India - dowry murders, police rape, abortion of female foetuses after amniocentesis, sati etc. This is done often within the terms of the argument of the early social reform and 20th century movements of condemning these as social evils and therefore mobilizing a much wider layer of public support. The second level is the less publicized work that women's groups particularly the women's centres in Bombay, Delhi and Bangalore are doing in connecting these extreme forms to the structural violence against women within the existing patriarchal family system.

The issue of dowry murders is linked to the much more hidden and more widespread issue of violence within the family and the fact that women do not assert their right to property. Such issues provide a far greater challenge to patriarchal authority and as a result provoke a more violent reaction from conservative sections of society. A case which has not received that much publicity but which I feel is significant in illustrating this second level of the women's movement's struggles is that of a 21 year old girl Asha who wanted to study and work rather than get married. A women's center took up her case, found her a room in the hostel and informed her family of her decision to study and live in a women's hostel.

The men of her family arrived at the centre; manhandled the volunteers and then filed a case of Habeus Corpus in the Supreme Court accusing the centre of kidnapping and running a prostitution racket! After many dramatic incidents, the Supreme Court finally passed a judgement stating that a 21 year old was mature enough to make up her own mind and decide what to do with her life. Such a simple judgement yet it was the first issues where centre volunteers were attacked physically as well as slandered in the press.

This violent reaction which agitations against dowry murders have rarely provoked was due to the recognition that this simple judgement was in fact eroding one of the pillars of patriarchal authority within the family and therefore had radical long term consequences. In fact, after judgement the centre recieved numerous letters from young girls requesting support to leave their families and work, requests which the centre with its limited resources could in no way handle!

Athough many of these struggles are occuring in big cities and movement has yet to extend to the larger number of women in rural India, there has been the emergence of a generalised awareness of women's rights and women are becoming aware of options that are available to them. This implies that they are no longer willing to submissively accept traditional patriarchal controls. Even if they may not directly challenge men's authority, in every family which has access to the radio, T.V. and newspaper (and that includes a large section of rural and urban people) there is a process of questioning, a shaking of the grounds of legitimacy. Such a process is extremely threatening and it is natural that attempts will be made to reassert traditional controls.

In this context religious fundamentalism could provide a ready ideology specially since the pre-existing structures of the patriarchal household with intra-household discrimination between male and female access to food, health care and other resources has often been justified in the name of religious traditions. The pre-existing culture of son-preference has already made the South Asian region significant in having a declining sex radio i.e. the decline in the number of women relative to men in the population.

While in most countries, developed and developing, women outnumber men, the populations of India, Bangladesh, Pakistan, and Nepal are exceptional in having an adverse sex ratio. In Bangladesh in 1981, there were 94 females of 100 males, in Pakistan there were 87 females to 100 males and in India there has been a long term decline in the proportion of women to men in the country's population. According to the 1901 census there were 972 females per 1000 males while in 1981 there were 935 females per 1000 males. The recent rise in the latest census is restricted to certain regions and does not seem to project a reversal of the earlier trend.

Although there are regional variations, studies have now established that this unusual sex radio is due to higher female death rates which are a result of unequal access to food and health care within the household. Numerous studies have by now established that son-preference is not linked to religion but has a close correlation with labour force participation of women. The practice of dowry for instance has spread in the last 30 years in India to entire communities and castes who had no tradition of this form of marriage payment. Even in the predominantly Muslim countries of Pakistan and Bangladesh, the practise of dowry has increased and both countries have a Dowry Prohibition Law.

While labour participation is an important variable, the increase in dowry practises do not always relate to the withdrawal of women from work outside the home. 'Cost-benefit ratio' analysis (i.e. dowry as a form of compensation for the addition of a non-productive member and bride price as compensation for the loss of a productive member) is not only narrowly economistic, but cannot account for the fact that large numbers of women have been earning their own dowries and continue to work after their marriage. The increase in dowry has to be seen in the context of rising consumerism (commodities and bank loans openly for dowry), the competition to get men with jobs in the organised sector (a new form of hypergamy), which is also a form by which certain men are accumulating seed capital to set up new businesses or investments.

There have been quite a few cases of men marrying two or three times, each time collecting a dowry and murdering the wife. While further research has to be done in this area, it is also important to look at what kind of ideological belief system legitimises these practices and its violent effects in dowry murders. If we are not to fall into the biological trap of seeing inherent evil in these acts of violence, then it is necessary to look not only at the material basis but also the legitimising belief systems which sanction such practices.

The recent incidents of sati, where large crowds gathered to watch a woman being burned and the subsequent defence of this in the vernacular press and by sections of the intelligentsia can only be understood by examining the ideological systems which legitimise this. Specific cultural practices can acquire a more widely embracing religious sanction and in a context of pre-existing son preference, religious fundamentalists could find support for asserting 'traditional' roles for women.

It is significant that Hindu fundamentalists have not condemned the burning of Hindu brides though they have been vociferous over the issues of Muslim women's rights! The challenges to patriarchal structures of authority, arising from the demands of the capitalist labour market and as a result of the confrontations by the women's movement, leads to attempts to reassert control and reimpose systems of domination. It is in this context that religious fundamentalism with its emphasis on circumscribed roles for women can find ready support. However, the significance of man-woman relations in understanding the emergence of fundamentalism also lie in the broader process of identity formation in the context of socio-economic changes.

Communal identity and Control Over Women

In this section, some tentative links between notions of masculinity/feminity and the construction of communal identities are explored. This is an area which needs a lot of research as well as conceptual reflection since there is always the danger of a crude psychological reductionism. In this chapter it is only possible to make some connections which would have to be developed much further. Communal identities do not exist as fixed primordial essences but as we have seen emerge in particular socio-economic contexts and are created identities, which attempts to homogenise other differences within the community.

In this process of identity creation women figure in crucial ways at a symbolic level they become symbols of culture and tradition, i.e. identity markers while at the material level their particularised feminine identity forms the complementary role to enhancing a particularised masculine identity. The crux of the fundamentalist rhetoric - a call for a return to culture and tradition, is almost always a call first addressed to women.

When western dress is rejected, no one demands that men stop wearing suits and ties. Once again the sex-selectivity of fundamentalism becomes obvious as women who "cut their hair, speak English, and wear national dress without the chador..." are attacked for being western while "men do all these without their national or Muslim identity being challenged." Women are neither acknowledged nor allowed to be producers of theology, although they are the main practitioners of religion and hence the reproducers of culture and tradition. `The culture and tradition that is resurrected is, of course, a particular one. Along with the myth of a "Golden Age" another common feature of fundamentalism seems to be the stress on a martial tradition.

The Rashtriya Swayam Sewak Sangh from its inception built its ideological and organisation structure around the "akhara" (traditional gymnasium) with "lathi" (a five foot stick used as a weapon) training by former army officers, uniforms and strict military discipline. This "kshatriya (warrior) model which combined elements of militancy, vigour, and domination, was called upon to overcome the perceived cowardice of Hindus."

In May 1922, the Dehra Dun branch of the Hindu Mahasabha made a statement of warning: "The Hindu race once so great and glorious is truly speaking nobody's child now. The result is that it is usually the Hindus who fall an easy prey to the aggression of those more unitided and virile". This emphasis on virility occurs as a constant theme for instance in the reminiscences of older RSS members who attributed the popularity of the paramilitary training among young middle class Hindu men in Nagpur to the fact that it proved that these young men were equal in manliness to the British soldier.

Its ultimate expression is conveyed by the statement made by Gopal Godse, the brother of Nathuram Godse, an ex-RSS member who assassinated Gandhi: "Our motive was not to achieve control of the government ;... we were simply trying to rid the nation of someone who had done and was doing great harm to it. He had consistently insulted the Hindu nation and had weakedened it by his doctrine of ahimsa. On his many fasts, he always attached all sorts of pro-Muslim conditions... He never did anything about the Muslim fanatics.

We wanted to show the Indians that there were Indians who would not suffer humiliation-that there were still men left among the Hindus." (Emphasis mine) An area that needs further investigation is how the "traditions" that were resurrected by different groups -social reformers, cultural critics and fundamentalists -during the anti colonial struggle in India, were in many ways based on core values of colonial ideology.

Colonial ideology itself was based on changes in man-woman relations and cultural models in Britain an its incorporation into oppositional nationalist ideology in India, simultaneously created a model of "hyper masculinity" for men. In the present period one can see a similar emphasis on the military model amongst fundamentalist groups. In Punjab, for instance the Sikh fundamentalists have drawn on the Jat culture and the warrior legacy of the tenth Guru Gobind Singh rather than the tradition of the first and earlier Gurus who emphasised peace and reflection.

The same process of selectivity occurs in the choice of the female symbol. The ideal of "Indian womanhood" -Sita- as the passive, chaste, faithful wife who worships her husband, is based not only on a choice between other known female figures like Draupadi or Radha, but is also a choice of a popular version of the epic Ramayana written by Valmiki and Tulsidas as against other versions which show Sita as a more assertive person.

The reiteration of the "pati-parameshwar" (husband as god) model through the yearly performances of the Ramayana, in films and television has a clear function in ensuring that women had to be confined within the household and that "tradition "sanctioned violence to ensure that women remained within these boundaries. It is this alternative tradition, especially amongst the adivasis (tribals) where women were independant and sexually uninhibited. These symbolic representations of masulinity and feminity are crucial to the process of identity creation.

Communal consciousness arises as we have seen in situations of insecurity and fear of the loss of social or economic status. Notions of "izzat" (honour) and "biradari" (brotherhood) are the main elements which link a family's honour with the conduct of women. A family's public position is lost if the honour of a family's woman is lost. These notions get generalised to the community having total control over their "own women". Communal propaganda is full of the fall from greatness in the past, challenge of foreign domination today, the need to prove strength, courage and manliness.

What better way to prove manliness than by showing that your women are under your control. If the community is losing its economic status, its social status, at least it still has one form of property within its reach. The fact that women are raped during communal riots is an expression of the same principle. Rape of the other man's woman is a way to humiliate him and show access to his property. Many riots are sparked off by alleged acts of harassment of women of one community by men of the other community. Threats to or the loss of their women, in a situation of economic competitiveness, is seen as a direct threat to manhood. In the Jabalpur riots of 1961 for instance, the cause of the riot was the economic competition between a local Muslim bidi (cigarette) magnate and his Hindu competitors, but what sparked off the riot was the fact that the son of the Muslim owner had eloped with a Hindu girl.

COMMUNAL IDENTITY AND CONTROL OVER WOMEN

The imagery of communal riots is full of sexual stereotypes. "They captured beautiful Hindu women, forcibly converted them and used them as temporary partners of life. Hindu women were threatened, molested and compelled to run half naked for shelter to forests... ". In the communal image, a Muslim was/is a man of low morals and uncontrolled lust, who was/is never ready to seduce, abduct, and assault Hindu women. The Hindus were seen as mild, docile and emasculated. These stereotypes have often been transferred to other communities without much change.

The same stereotype as the Muslim now exists for the Sikh, or the adivasi or the dalits. During the caste riots in Ahmedabad in 1981, it was said - "... the harijans do not really want reservations, they want our women. Once they could only come as far as our toilets. Then we felt sorry for them and let them come into our homes. But now they want our women. We must beat them and teach them a lesson."

The speeches of communalists are similar peppered with references to the "violation of our sisters and mothers" and exhortations to take revenge and prove that the men of that particular community are still men. Whether it is an attempt to reassert traditional authority, or to create a certain identity in the context of economic dislocation, the symbolism of the community gets tied closely with a particular meaning of femininity and masculinity. This process of identity construction results in a series of measures which leads to increasing patriarchal control over women. We have already discussed the trends towards controlling women's labour.

This process can also have implications for women's right to birth control. The rhetoric of communalism is full of the increase in numbers of the other community, the excessive breeding of the Muslims, etc. For instance, the Vishwa Hindu Parishad has published a pamphlet which argues that due to polygamy, by the year 2000, Muslims will outnumber Hindus. In fact, studies reveal that the fertility rate of Muslims has been declining and anyway has no relation to polygamy.

It is not too far fetched to imagine that population policy, in a context of state - supported fundamentalism, could be directed not just on a class basis, as it has been so far, but also on a community basis like other countries in South-East Asia. On the other hand, the fears of a minority community can mean additional pressure to produce more and more children. In either case, women increasingly loose control over their own bodies. Control over woman and the exercise of patriarchal authority has to be differentiated across classes as well as decomposed to allow for the variations that emerge if the control is over women's labour, or sexuality or fertility.

Given these differences, however, in South Asia today, this control is exercised by *particular men* (usually on the basis of kinship relations) i.e. it is fathers, brothers, maternal uncle or husbands who have rights over their daughters, sisters, nieces and wives. *What is significant about state sponsored religious fundamentalism is that it not only gives further legitimacy to this control but, more importantly, shifts the right of control to all men.* The legitimacy given by the state to follow and enforce a particular interpretation of a religion means that any man on the street can stop any woman who does not conform to the "traditional" and "proper" role assigned to her. This can be seen clearly in the countries where the State is declared a mono religious state. In Iran, the "Hezbolahis" (members of the party of God) attack women on the streets with guns or knives if they are not wearing the chador.

In a multi-religious context, this right would extend to all men of that community. Recent press reports from Punjab mention that in the campaign by the extremists against liquor, meat and tobacco shops, women who wear saris, pluck their eyebrows and put on lipstick will face dire consequences"! There were reports of such control by Muslim fundamentalists when they shaved the head of Shabana of Perunthura and Zulaikha Bibi from Kerala who was given 101 lashes as punishment for the violation of Muslim personal law. At the moment such incidents are few in South Asia but continued state sponsorship of fundamentalism would intensify and sanction such acts of violence. Given the context and background sketched above, the emergence of state supported religious fundamentalism clearly has very serious implications for women.

The contradictory tendencies at the level of government policies for women and development with the aim of drawing women into the labour market, and the attempts through legislation to restrict women's access to the public world are part of one process by which the interests of patriarchy and capital are ensured. Religious fundamentalism as a state ideology thus provides the possibility of a coincidence of interests between patriarchy and the demands of the capitalist economy. This remains of course an uneasy coincidence but it would be a mistake to continue seeing the logic of the market as necessarily leading to a liberal ideology of women's work. An ideology of restriction even though large numbers of women are being drawn into work outside the home and therefore competing with men, can be a viable ideology of legitimation.

There are however, other countervailing tendencies within South Asia which could reverse these trends. One of these are the growing social movements which are challenging and questioning the overall paths of development as well as specific issues of patriarchal control. In India, for instance, feminists from the women's movement and the democratic rights movements have entered the arena of general politics. Women's groups have been one of the first to condemn communalism, have been actively involved in supporting victims of communal violence, and held special investigations into the situation of women during communal clashes. Most significantly, feminists have taken initiatives in supporting proposals for political solutions for instance in Punjab and are engaged in a national discussion on the dangers of rising fundamentalism.

At present, there is a debate on the issues of the demand for a uniform civil code. While all sections of the movement agree in principle to the demand for a uniform civil code, there are differences on strategies and implications, since this demand has also been put forward by Hindu communal groups, and as a result creates fear in the minds of minority groups. Some sections of the movement support a strategy of reform within separate personal laws while others have pushed for a uniform civil code. In Pakistan, women groups have been fighting on the terrain of religion itself and have argued for improving the conditions for women within the Islamic structure.

In Bangladesh, there are strong representations being made by minority groups and women's groups against the proposed bill to make Islam the State religion. These developments have led women's groups to directly confront the ruling parties in their countries. This is a significant development since in spite of militant struggles and anti-government and anti-patriarchal slogans, most of the campaigns were directed towards changes in the laws and often demanded more intervention by state authorities in implementing these laws. In practice, the movement has operated with the assumption of a liberal state. Today, it is clear that even demands for legal changes are not going to be granted easily.

This implies that womens groups will have to develop a fuller understanding of the State and State ideologies and evolve strategies which go beyond reflex actions. It would mean tackling the wider questions, not just of the relationship between patriarchal control and the socio-economic changes in the region, but also the problematic issue of cultural identity creation. Although the present constitution of communal identities is repressive for women, there are positive elements which lie behind the need for cultural identity in the present context. This has to do with the broader process of the failure of the creation of a national identity in post colonial states as well as the restrictions in an identity based on caste, community or the family, especially for women. In the discussions on what constitutes the basis for an alternative cultural identity, feminists in South Asia have taken different stands.

Some have argued for religious, or on the basis of tactical reasons to reach out to the vast majority of women who are believers. Another view is to draw on the anti-brahmanical culture of the dalits and adivasis in India, to build an oppositional culture. All this requires a reassessment from a feminist perspective, of what has been the content of nationalism and the process by which each "nation state" was constituted in the region, the limitations of the present definition of secularism, the problems in trying to separate religion from culture and finally whether the women's movement, given its internal differentiation, can project an alternative culture for women in each country.

While these are crucial questions for future strategizing, at a practical level a significant development in the last few years is the linkage and exchange between feminists in South Asia. These exchanges have had a tremendous emotional impact as women shared their common problems even as their governments prepared for war against each other.

This process of the sharing of common experiential situation, the questioning of "national" borders and restrictions on travel and visits and the identification of similar issues and struggles is creating the basis for the emergence of a regional perspective. Such a perspective is crucial since the link between the state and religious fundamentalism in each country is closely tied to the political dynamics of the South Asian region as a whole. The strengthening of such initiatives provides hope for a process of democratisation and a redefinition of man-woman relations within the region.

6

Women and Living Spaces

ACCELERATING ADVANCEMENT OF RURAL WOMEN IN ASIA

A review of the situation of rural women and the regional trends relevant to agriculture and the rural economy that affect their situation across Asia and the Pacific region highlights a few realities. Although the contribution of agriculture as a proportion of national economies has declined, the role of rural women in farm and family economies has increased significantly. Yet despite this substantial increase in their responsibilities and workload, the enormous contribution of rural women to agriculture and rural economies is neither widely nor formally recognized at the local or national level.

Because of this lack of awareness and appreciation of their contribution and roles, efforts to support agricultural development and food security tend to ignore women's resource needs, as well as the barriers and constraints they face in fulfilling their productive roles both on farm and at home. At the same time, new regional trends and external forces are fundamentally changing the context in which rural women operate, and presenting opportunities and threats to their livelihoods.

Across Asia and the Pacific region the development community has embraced an agenda for the advancement of women and there also are emerging opportunities for the integration of rural women to improve agriculture productivity. The social and economic progress of rural women, however, is still inequitable. In the current milieu it is important to identify strategies to refocus attention on the situation of rural women in agricultural development and food security and their rights for resources and to strengthen policy and programme interventions that accelerate the advancement of rural women.

INFORMATION ON RURAL WOMEN

Efforts should be made to collect sex-disaggregated data and gender-differentiated information for all aspects of agriculture and rural development in the region. Such information would

a. Enable a fact based understanding of regional rural women's contributions, resource deprivations and powerlessness,
b. Advance the development of gender-specific rural human assets and labour resource and activity databases, which could be analysed and compared within and across countries and
c. Provide reliable information to guide policies and programme formulation for the advancement of rural women.

There is an urgent need to improve awareness among national governments of the importance of sector specific sex-disaggregated data, and of building the capacity of national agencies to collect, manage and analyse such data. In countries where national sample surveys or other periodic surveys already collect sex-disaggregated information, action should be taken to systematically analyse the data in order to develop a comprehensive understanding of the situation of rural women.

Advances in information technology and sophisticated data management systems should be exploited in order to compile relevant, needs-based and user-friendly information resources about the situation of rural women, and this should be made available to policy makers, programme managers and advocacy groups. It is important to develop strategies to improve the national census and agricultural census data to include sex-disaggregated information. Such macro data sets are an important basis for international comparison required by UN agencies. In the long run, a standardized data base would be most helpful to asses the progress made on the status of rural women.

It is also absolutely essential to develop country specific special studies that address women's and men's situations in agriculture and the rural economies. These studies should have household level data disaggregated by sex and should be all inclusive, that is they should go beyond activity analysis to include information on access, ownership and control of assets and resources and also gender specific constraints and limitations. Such databases should be maintained at the decentralized governance level. The decentralized governance officers should be trained to understand and use the sex-disaggregated information in local development planning.

With the assistance of donors and international agencies in many countries in the region, living levels data, including sex-disaggregated data on time use, have been collected. But these have not been analysed in depth to create sex-disaggregated information and a rural profile of the status of women. It would be helpful to mobilise external financial and technical assistance to analyse and utilize the existing data sets to create useful information for gender responsive planning and programme interventions to assist rural women.

Gender Empowerment Measures that really measure rural gender inequality should be developed. Though they can be modelled on the UN GEM, the indicators should reflect the realities of rural women. An example would be instead of women's participation in parliament, it could measure women's participation in local governance and leadership in community based organizations. Furthermore, the per capita income share indicator could be substituted with income value for time use data for unpaid family work in farm and home production.

Such RURAL GEM (RGEM) would focus on rural women's advances or lack thereof compared to men in the respective countries and help monitor gaps in achieving rural gender equality. As a monitoring and evaluation tool RGEM could provide information for guiding policy directives and resource allocation for the advancement of rural women. The local governance authorities could use the RGEM information in local planning for gender responsive development.

GENDER PLANNING IN AGRICULTURAL AND RURAL DEVELOPMENT

In Asia and the Pacific region the processes and benefits of using available sex-disaggregated data and gender-differentiated information in agricultural and rural development planning are still not widely understood. Inadequate efforts to use available data in planning processes highlight the necessity for capacity building within agencies that are involved in the formulation of agricultural and rural development policies and programmes. Organization wide efforts should focus on the integration of gender considerations and gender-differentiated indicators throughout the sequential phases of the policy formulation process as well as of the programme and project cycle.

In part, the prevailing confusion can be attributed to a situation where the planners are not effectively linking gender analysis outcomes to gender planning processes. It is also suggested that gender mainstreaming has come to represent a narrow set of analytical tools and training in applying these tools for gender analysis rather than the process of designing strategies to improve opportunities for rural women. Hence, a progressive process is needed to improve generations (current and future) of planners and macro economists in various agencies in developing counties to gain a comprehensive knowledge of gender biases impeding the improvement in the status of rural women as associated with increasing productivity in agriculture and rural economies.

A communication gap between gender advocates and the policy makers; the former presents the issues as part of the social equality agenda, whereas the latter views development as chiefly concerning economic productivity. Such a communication gap should be narrowed by cross learning on the value of gender equality in achieving economic development objectives, particularly poverty alleviation. It is crucial to support a gender responsive and women inclusive curriculum for agriculture and rural development students within the national agriculture education system.

It would be most appropriate for such knowledge to be acquired as part of their formal learning so that it becomes internalized professional knowledge with the long term and sustainable impact of creating a professional commitment to considering women as farmers and producers in the national planning process. On the other hand, the advocates of gender equality and gender specialists should make an effort to contextualize gender concerns within the realities of agriculture and rural development.

VALUATION OF UNPAID WORK

The importance of women's unpaid work in the home and farm production systems should be clearly recognized by national governments, bilateral and multilateral development organizations and academic institutions so that an appropriate technique to value this work is found and agreed upon. The household production model for farm family production offers one approach to quantify unpaid work inputs in terms of food security. Concerted efforts will be required to convince different stakeholders, including rural women, to recognize and reward unpaid work in agricultural and rural production.

Though there are UN discussions on including unpaid work in national accounting systems to systematically recognize women's contribution, it is important to improve the social valuation of women's work in household and community contexts. The local level development and governance agencies should be targeted to increase their awareness and skills to include women's unpaid work in their planning processes. Local knowledge, needs and constraints assessments among both men and women in rural areas should become internalized and integral components of the process of local planning.

EMPOWERING RURAL WOMEN WITH EDUCATION AND INFORMATION

Many countries in the region have focused on girls' education as an important process to equalize the gender gap and make investments in women's futures. Such educational interventions are beginning to pay off with incremental gains in female educational attainment. Still, poor access to schools and learning centres and the relatively high cost of education continue to be barriers for poor rural families to support girls' education. In addition, unrelenting social prejudice against female education continues to cause the gender gap in rural education. The generation of adults that were denied education contribute to high female illiteracy in rural areas and they are becoming the primary farmers.

Rural girls continue to face economic and social barriers to formal education and thus may not achieve their full potential as adults. Hence, the situation calls for increased resources and intensified efforts at the national level to substantially improve formal education for rural girls as well as enhance female adult literacy in rural areas and empower rural women with technical information and knowledge to improve their health and participation in the increasingly complex world. The potential of new information and communication technologies to reduce the educational disadvantages faced by older rural women through the development and dissemination of needs-based information in appropriate formats and accessible mediums should be leveraged.

REDUCTION IN HOUSEHOLD DRUDGERY FOR PRODUCTIVITY AND EMPOWERMENT

Persisting traditional perceptions on the worthlessness of women's unpaid work must be challenged if drudgery is to be reduced. At the same time, efforts should be made to expand basic services in rural areas in order to ease women's multitasking demands in the home and on the farm, and to develop appropriate technologies that reduce the amount of time women spend on daily household tasks. The time gained by reducing household drudgery could be invested in improving women's health and productivity. But investment in interventions to reduce women's drudgery is not seen as a productive investment by planners and considered as domestication and a home economics approach by the feminists.

Hence, a change in approach is required, namely one based on the view that reducing women's drudgery has health and time management outcomes that could be both empowering and productive. The provision of services and goods to reduce drudgery could directly improve rural women's ability to participate in a diversified economic enterprise system and social and political activities in the community.

TECHNOLOGIES AND TRAINING FOR RURAL WOMEN

Given their local knowledge and multiple roles, rural women should be fully involved throughout the development of women's work oriented technologies. In-depth assessments of the roles and constraints faced by rural women in different circumstances should be undertaken in order to guide the development and application of appropriate technologies. Training should build the capacity of rural women according to their multisegment production tasks, and new information and communication technologies should be harnessed to improve rural women's access to technical information and public sector support services.

The existing models of farmer field school and farmer-to-farmer learning approaches may have ignored gender biases that prevent women from taking advantage of such technology transfer approaches. It is important to explore the concept of increasing rural women's skills as technology trainers and knowledge providers in the rural areas. The technical experts in the extension, outreach and agriculture centres could ably support rural women's local efforts if the traditions of ignoring women's technology needs could be changed.

SYSTEMATIC STUDY OF RURAL GENDER DIMENSIONS

A few recent case studies and empirical findings have assessed the rural impact of recent trends in globalization, technology advances, HIV/AIDS and the like in the region, but the overall effect of these developments on rural households and in particular on women has not yet been studied systematically. Hence, systematic studies should be carried out to identify and evaluate the effects of significant regional development trends and critical incidents on rural women's roles, work, access to resources and livelihoods.

The findings of these studies should be widely disseminated targeting the policy makers in the development sector who influence policies and programmes so that new opportunities available to rural women can be leveraged and potential negative effects minimized. It is essential that future analysis of gender in rural areas be anchored in the context of these macro trends in order to develop effective interventions that support rural women to effectively manage these forces of change. Recent developments in the social, economic and technological arenas have important effects on rural women across Asia and the Pacific region.

The relevant trends are globalization, regional economic integration and accelerated commercialisation, urbanization, advances in agriculture and information technologies, political instability, civil war, HIV/AIDS, livestock epidemics and natural disasters. The multiple impacts on rural women bring significant implications for agricultural productivity, rural production and economic vitality, household food security, family health, family economic security and welfare. Few systematic studies have examined how these trends affect rural women.

Nonetheless, it seems reasonable to hypothesize that economic integration and advances in agriculture and information technologies present both opportunities and threats for rural women's livelihoods and work, whereas political instability, natural disasters and HIV/AIDS exert considerable additional pressure on rural women's access to resources and their work as farmers and producers.

ECONOMIC TRANSFORMATION AND AGRICULTURE'S CONTRIBUTION

Regional economic transformation was accompanied by a steady reduction in the relative share of agriculture to the Gross Domestic Product (GDP) across the region. While this reduction was striking in some countries - for instance in Thailand the contribution of agriculture to GDP dropped from 23.2 per cent in 1980 to 9.1 per cent in 2000 - it was not uniform throughout the region. Indeed, although the relative share of agriculture in the economy decreased in Asia and the Pacific region as a whole, agriculture continues to make an important contribution to the economy and by extension to food security and rural poverty alleviation in many countries. In 2000, agriculture accounted for 59.9 per cent of the GDP of Myanmar.

Bhutan, Cambodia, Lao PDR, Mongolia, Nepal and Uzbekistan each derived more than a third of their GDP from agriculture, whereas in Pakistan, Tajikistan, Vietnam, Papua New Guinea and Tonga agriculture contributed a quarter or more to the GDP. It is noteworthy that China and India - the two most populous countries in the region - continue to derive a significant portion of their GDP (15.9 per cent and 25.3 per cent respectively) from agriculture. In the region, most countries with substantial dependence on agriculture also are low-income food deficit countries (LIFDCs). The paradox seems to be that countries that depend on agriculture also lag in achieving improvements in food security.

An alternative view could be that the countries that are competing to serve the world agriculture market with cheap food to meet global consumer preferences confront food insecurity struggle at home. These data suggest that in countries with a high reliance on the agriculture sector, the rural populations - including women - could face the highest risk of food insecurity and low incomes. Consistent neglect of the agriculture sector in many countries throughout Asia and the Pacific region has made it a career of last choice for men and women with other more profitable options.

Economic structural transformation marked by decreasing reliance on agriculture has several implications for the economic role of rural women in the sector and consequently for food security. Firstly, fundamental changes in national economic systems and the agricultural sector result in a loss of livelihood opportunities. Secondly, subsistence food production to satisfy household food needs can become unsustainable and households become increasingly dependent on the cash economy to access food. Thirdly, opportunities are lacking for displaced rural women to find viable livelihood alternatives within the rural production system to give an economic return on their labour.

Finally, as agriculture production is transformed to become competitive amidst increased global economic linkages, rural women with limited skills and low education are likely to face greater risk of economic vulnerability. With the agriculture sector being organized for export driven production, land resources are being consolidated leaving subsistence farmers to sell the land; thus women may become agricultural labourers instead of farmers of family holdings. As women usually receive lower wages than men, their ability to ensure access to food will be adversely affected.

In this context it is important to address the issue of rural poverty in the region. The per cent age of the population below the poverty line declined in the region from 32 per cent in 1990 to 22 per cent in 2000. Yet the region is still home to 720 million poor people or two thirds of the world's poor (ADB, 2005). In Asia and the Pacific region poverty is basically a rural problem, and the gap between rural and urban poverty is widening over time in spite of impressive progress in the last three decades in economic growth and poverty reduction.

Two thirds of the world's poor live in this region and the majority of the poor are women. Most live in rural areas. Thus it can be inferred that rural women are the poorest among the poor. The increasing representation of women among the poor is referred as the "feminization of poverty". In many rural areas of Asia, more women than men are among the "working poor" than among the poor as a whole. Women also are disproportionately concentrated in the lowest remunerated categories of self-employment and casual labour (IFAD, 2002). The reinforcing causal link between the "feminization of poverty" and the "feminization of agriculture" is a key rural gender equality concern in the region with considerable importance to rural poverty eradication programmes.

GLOBAL ECONOMIC INTEGRATION

Initial unbridled enthusiasm for globalization across the region was gradually tempered by the realities of internal vulnerabilities, notably the lack of safety nets for the working poor and rural poor at times of economic crisis. In spite of the economic crisis that rocked the region in the 1990s, there remains a pragmatic realization that globalization cannot be circumvented, and that it must be properly managed for the benefit of the larger population rather than the enrichment of a few. The current reality is that regional economic integration - formal as well as informal - continues to affect household food security in Asia and the Pacific region.

The households' access to "food basket" commodities depends on economic and social circumstances beyond their local farming system. For example, labour migration for employment and overseas remittances have a positive effect on household food security in many Asian and Pacific rural communities. Similarly, aid and remittances play a major role in the relatively small economies of the South Pacific. In several Pacific Island countries per capita aid is amongst the highest in the world, and in many cases remittances exceeds export earnings.

The economic crisis in Southeast Asia brought a significant increase in urban poverty. Although the effects on rural areas and agriculture were not as great as initially feared, they were nevertheless considerable. Indeed, given the significant variations between and within countries, some rural areas suffered seriously. In general, the rural poor were adversely affected by crisis-induced cutbacks in rural expenditures by governments, reduced remittances and the return of unemployed urban workers that increased demands on rural households' incomes.

Very few systematic studies analysed the impact of the Asian economic crisis on rural women, largely because the crisis was seen as an urban phenomenon. At the global level, the failure to consider important aspects of gender relations (including women's unpaid reproductive work and intrahousehold allocation) leads to an inaccurate evaluation of the effect of economic liberalization on women both inside and outside the labour market. This begs the question of whether and how rural women's livelihood strategies might have mitigated the effect of the economic crisis in rural Asia.

"The effectiveness of rural women's livelihood strategies to support families and reduce adverse family financial impacts during the Asian financial crisis and other urban economic shocks remains poorly understood."

Economic integration can occur within national boundaries as well as among countries. These two distinct forms of integration may or may not be linked to the trend of accelerated economic globalization. Rural production can move from subsistence agriculture to the cash economy with or without access to global markets. The demand for agricultural commodities in the global market acts as a force that can influence production and affect rural women's situation, albeit with differences dependant on the scale and type of the farming enterprise.

Demand for cash can drive the commercialisation process of subsistence production as women take steps to sell their home-grown produce, small livestock and home-produced foodstuffs in local markets and urban centres. Such home-grown enterprises are likely to face competition from larger scale, industrially processed food products. For those fortunate groups with land holdings of a sufficient scale to be devoted to contract farming (either undertaken by farm households themselves or by agriculture processing enterprises), and the advantageous attainment of education and skills, it would be easy to trace the direct effect of the global market demand for agricultural produce.

In these production systems, which aim to capture a share of the global agricultural market, women with basic skills and education seem to find opportunities to expand their economic options. However, an inadequate understanding of formal labour contract processes and rules places women at risk of exploitation. At the same time, global consumer shifts in taste and demand have increased the economic risks to rural women involved in these kinds of contract agriculture enterprises. In Pacific small island countries, the intensive competition to export similar products such as papaya to the bigger countries within the region presents problems, and the trade restrictions in the importing countries present uncertainties to the local small producers where women are highly represented.

RURAL DEVELOPMENT SERVICE GAP AMIDST REGIONAL PROSPERITY

Uneven development in the region - largely at the expense of rural areas - has amplified the difficulties facing most rural men and women who continue to act as rural producers in family farms and subsistence agriculture and who also play a vital role in export-driven agriculture production. Although parts of rural Asia and the Pacific have experienced unprecedented technological and economic transformation in recent decades, the resulting economic growth has not translated into improved welfare for most rural residents.

The main reasons for the lack of improved welfare are the general lack of supportive institutions (particularly health and education services) and the inadequate attention to improvements in rural infrastructure. At the macro policy level the significant contributions of women to rural production and food security have generally been ignored, and poorly, if at all, considered in agriculture and rural development sector reform strategies and budgetary allocations. Although development in Asia and the Pacific region has tended to focus attention on fast-growing urban population centres, recent reports estimate that the number of rural Asians will not likely decline any time soon.

The Asian Development Bank estimates that there likely will be 2.2 billion rural Asians by the year 2020, and that this rural population will have much lower access to health and education and an overall lower level of general well being. In most countries of Asia and the Pacific region, the proportion of people who do not have access to proper shelter, clean and reliable water, and adequate sanitation in rural areas is higher than in cites and towns.

Uneven economic development has resulted in imbalances between rural and urban areas, and between agricultural and industrial areas both in economic opportunities and service infrastructure including education. Lack of basic services such as health care, clean water supply and sanitation makes it particularly difficult for rural women to fulfil their domestic and care giving activities. Lack of schools within close proximity to the villages is an impediment to rural girls' access to education.

DEMOGRAPHIC SHIFTS AND POPULATION DYNAMICS

Much of Asia has entered the final phase of the demographic transition: human fertility is gradually declining to match the decline in mortality that began during the 1960s. The three facets of the demographic scenario are declining fertility, an increasing population of elderly and an increasing population of youth. When the world's population reaches about 2,000 million in 2050, half of it will reside in Asia. Two other significant characteristics observed in the region are the ageing of the elderly and the feminization of ageing.

A considerable proportion of the elderly is living in rural areas where social and welfare services are underdeveloped. Another striking feature in the Asian region is the substantially higher labour force participation compared to the West because of Asia's higher concentration in agriculture and in the informal sector, both of which do not have a compulsory retirement age. Hence the "greying" of agriculture and rural communities is a certainty in Asia. The demographic changes in China that contribute to the greying of farming and the economic hardship for the ageing farmers are illustrated in the example below.

The increasing mobility of rural youth in highly populated countries contributes to the growing migrant population in urban centres. Ageing and a changing gender balance in rural areas - intensified as men and the young men are pulled to urban centres in search of better opportunities - are likely to further complicate rural demographics. Consequently, people with fewer options - generally poor, illiterate rural women have been compelled to assume a major role in the agriculture sector, resulting in the "feminization of farming". Such a demographic composition in rural areas may lead to neglect of this rural population group by planners, thus presenting a worrisome possibility of further marginalization of the rural sector.

As countries like Bangladesh, China and India seek to generate employment in small scale rural industries, microenterprises and town and village enterprises, the capable young women and men are lured away from agriculture, thus intensifying the demographic trends. Internal migration acts as a pull factor, drawing younger people to urban areas in search of more lucrative opportunities and leaving the elderly, particularly older women, behind as the principal farmers. Such a transformation of the rural population structure, along with the longer life span for women in Asia, contributes to the "feminization of the rural community".

Population pressures seriously affect rural households in many parts of Asia and the Pacific region, with particular implications for women's work, livelihood strategies and care-giving activities. For instance, the population of the Pacific Islands doubles every 30 years, placing considerable stress on natural resources and food security.

Rapid urban drift - predominantly of young men resulting in an acute shortage of agricultural labour - results in rising population densities such as in the Marshall Islands where 8,000 people live on Ebeye atoll less than 0.5 km^2in size. Very high densities also exist in the urban centres of South Tarawa (Kiribati), Majuro (Marshall Islands) and Funafuti (Tuvalu), thus intensifying pressures on availability of land for home gardens and clean water supply, and resulting in very high unemployment levels and increased vulnerability to poverty.

HIV/AIDS POSED THREATS TO RURAL COMMUNITIES

Asia and the Pacific region now accounts for one in every five new HIV infections worldwide. Over 8 million people in the region were living with the virus at the end of 2002, of whom 2.6 million were young people aged 14 to 24 (ESCAP, 2003). The effect of HIV/AIDS on rural populations and food security is a growing concern in many parts of the region, not least in the Mekong Basin countries. HIV/AIDS is highly prevalent throughout the Mekong countries, particularly in Myanmar and Thailand.

The spread of HIV/AIDS has been linked to an increasingly mobile population, moving in search of new work opportunities created by increased economic integration, unprecedented growth, and the shift from a centrally planned to a market economy. It is at the subnational level that the effect of HIV/AIDS on the economic output is likely to be hardest, especially in a region where more than 800 million people live on less than one US dollar a day. In rural parts of Cambodia, the high cost of medicine and the rural credit system combine to make HIV/AIDS a significant cause of landlessness. In Thailand it was found that among affected households one popular financial management strategy adopted was disposing of productive assets such as land, animals and equipment.

In the health sector, the spread of HIV/AIDS in many parts of rural Asia has served as a wakeup call for action, overtaking the traditional stance of silence and denial. A few countries in the region, particularly Thailand, enacted place measures in the past decade to combat HIV/AIDS. Such early commitment is paying off, but many regional countries still struggle to find a cohesive action strategy.

Anecdotal and observational information further indicates that the movement of urban immigrants infected with HIV/AIDS back to their rural villages likely will increase the demands on rural women's support as income-earners and caregivers. The rural women in HIV/AIDS high incidence countries will face additional economic and work burdens as the family structure changes because of the attrition of family members.

REGIONAL POLITICAL REALTIES AND GOVERNANCE DYNAMICS

The regional trends in political realities that affect the rural livelihoods of women highlighted here are civil conflict and the movement towards decentralized governance.

CIVIL CONFLICTS

Rising levels of political instability and the increased occurrence of civil conflict throughout Asia and the Pacific region have intensified pressures on rural producers, both women and men. The dire impact of war on agriculture and food production in countries like Afghanistan, Timor-Leste and Sri Lanka is widely known. Less, however, has been written about the effects of civil war and ethnic tensions in places like Nepal, Aceh, Bougainville and the Solomon Islands in the Pacific.

For women, political instability and conflict tend to result in increased agricultural work as men have been drawn away to wage war. Even in countries that apparently are peaceful today, the legacy of conflict lingers. Landmines in cultivated fields are an enduring reminder of past conflicts and constitute a real danger to rural communities. In countries such as Cambodia and Lao PDR, the number of abandoned ordinances is so great that farmers are forced to abandon productive land.

DECENTRALIZED GOVERNANCE

Within the governance arena, the push for decentralization in the region presents opportunities for taking action for the advancement of rural women at the local community milieu. In countries such as Bangladesh, India and Pakistan national efforts have been made to expand the participation of women in local governance councils and organizations through specific numerical quotas. Though women are becoming increasingly visible in the local governance bodies, their informed participation is yet to become a reality.

Many countries in the region promote decentralized governance and thus development responsibilities are shifted to local authorities. This has created disassociation between the national commitment to the global gender equality agenda and the local commitment to its implementation. Most importantly, there is a widespread lack of understanding of the national commitment and inadequate resources to support a social agenda promoting gender equality.

Traditional gender biases and power dynamics in the local communities do not support transformation towards gender equality; local elites, both men and women, are unwilling to support gender equality approaches and women's empowerment strategies in development interventions. Local governance structures may have decentralized responsibility for development, but not the authority for revenue generation and the provision of adequate funds to develop and implement programmes for the advancement of rural women.

POLICY AND INSTITUTIONAL CONSTRAINTS IMPEDING RURAL WOMEN'S ADVANCEMENT

National governments in the region have embraced CEDAW, though with differences in levels of commitment and progress in terms of achievement. Since 1979, countries in the region also implemented agencies such as the National Commission on Women, civil society organization coalitions and national ministries for the advancement of women, as well as units under the regional economic organizations (ASEAN, APEC and SAARC) to promote the advancement of women.

Following declaration of the Beijing Platform for Action, regional governments responded by creating new agencies and expanding the national institutions for the advancement of women. These institutions have become specialized agencies within national governments with a mandate to focus on the agenda for gender equality and the advancement of women. The regional responsibility of working with these national ministries falls under the Economic and Social Commission for Asia and the Pacific. Countries in the region also developed national plans of action for women, reflecting the national commitments to the Beijing Platform for Action that serve as blueprints for achieving gender mainstreaming and women's empowerment objectives.

Nonetheless, an inherent weakness of inadequate attention to the concerns of rural women in these institutions and policy instruments remains. In part, the foundation of these inherent weakness and invisibility of rural women can be traced to UN measures for women's empowerment and the indicators of Millennium Development Goals (MDGs). Gender Empowerment Measure (GEM) indicators used by the UN to measure women's advancement include urban biased indicators and do not reflect the current realities of rural women. GEM indicators include the relative per cent age share of women in parliament, in administrative and management positions and professional and technical jobs, and in adjusted GDP per capita (UNDP, 2004).

It is essential to examine objectively whether these indicators measure the advancement of rural women in the unpaid family work sector and facing social restrictions and resource constraints to provide for the household economy. An MDG indicator for measuring advancement of women is the changes over time in women's participation in non-agriculture sector employment (UNDP, 2004). Though the limitations of these indicators can be explained by data limitations in the rural sector, they also illustrate the lack of an articulate lobby and collective action to address the persisting rural gender inequality.

Most often the national ministries for gender mainstreaming and advancement of women are not adequately funded to undertake macropolicy and structural changes. They lack fundamental understanding of technical aspects related to agriculture and rural development sectors. In a few countries such as Fiji, Philippines and Sri Lanka and in some states in India a gender budgeting approach is being introduced. As one report explained:

Budgetary policies can ignore gender-specific needs and have differential impacts on men and women because of the systematic differences between the sexes in relation to the economy. Gender responsive budgeting applies a gender lens to budgetary resource allocation, providing more visibility to women's unpaid work.

In the Philippines, gender budgeting policy continues to serve as a key element in implementing gender mainstreaming, but there is need for budget literacy and defining accountability. There is some urgency to ensure that the GAD budget policy survives the current austerity measures amid the raging financial crisis in the Philippines.

In the region, diverse technical line ministries serve as agencies of change to address the concerns of rural women as actors in agriculture and the rural economy, and as stakeholders in rural communities. Ministries of agriculture, livestock, fisheries, environment and irrigation and rural development are examples of technical line ministries. The trend has been to create focal units or focal persons for gender or women within these technical line ministries, though with limited interaction among the various focal persons in the discrete line ministries. Consequently, the institutional situation remains with parallel structures to achieve objectives associated with the advancement of women and development in rural areas.

Agencies focused on gender equality and women follow the agenda for gender equality, women's empowerment and advancement of women. The technical ministries vested with responsibilities for the development of agriculture, rural communities and the rural economy function on their own fulfilling their technical objectives. Hence, these two parallel paths for development seldom cross unless explicit efforts are made to bring an integrated approach that would fulfil the agenda for the promotion of rural women. It is crucial that policy dialogue and interagency interaction for programme development to promote rural women should cut across many technical areas. Because of these institutional constraints and policy limitations, however, national efforts remain insufficient to respond to the real resource and service requirements of rural women.

"In Asia and the Pacific region a cohesive macro policy approach or framework for integration of rural women's concerns and effective strategies to transform the agriculture sector by taking advantage of the human resource potential vested among rural women has not emerged."

SOCIAL PROGRAMMES FOR EMPOWERMENT OF RURAL WOMEN

The Asia and Pacific Islands region is dynamic in social experiments focusing on assistance to rural women. Most frequently the programmes to assist rural women are funded by international development agencies. Though the trend in countries like Bangladesh, China, Malaysia, Thailand and India seems to move towards identifying national resources to achieve social equities for rural development, in general social programmes in many countries are mostly driven by donor assistance targeting rural women.

A common trend of promoting a gender equality agenda driven mostly by external resources raises the issue of sustainability of economic and social empowerment activities directed to rural women. India enacted a complex social programme delivery structure and involvement of multiple ministries serving rural women. There, the challenge is to make effective use of the assistance with accountability to the community stakeholders, timeliness of delivery and achieving positive effects. In contrast, many countries face the challenge of finding resources - both financial and human to support the national plans of action for gender equality and advancement of women. In resource poor policy environments, the agenda for advancement of rural women does not rank high when allocation priorities are set.

Monitoring at the local community level will become increasingly important to ensure rural gender equality. However, to date gender differentiated indicators, and processes to monitor and evaluate gender equality and the advancement of women in rural situations, have not been satisfactory. The region also witnessed the tremendous growth of non-government organizations (NGOs) in developing programmes for rural women.

These non-government agencies have become implementing agencies for the donor driven projects to assist rural women. Though some NGOs have done remarkable work, those that act as a mediating agency between funding sources and rural women tend to create dependency among rural women on the NGO. Asian rural women still have not mastered the art of dealing with public institutions in their own right because of limited knowledge of the complex process and bureaucratic rules and procedures in accessing public resources.

SELF-HELP GROUPS AND MICROCREDIT FINANCE PROGRAMMES

Asia and the Pacific region pioneered participatory rural appraisal and mobilization of rural women, and consequently witnessed the remarkable growth in women's groups focused on economic empowerment. A popular mode of social capital mobilization is through organizing women's groups in rural communities. Self-help groups in India, for example, mobilise the human potential of rural women, often by using microcredit as an entry point to mobilise them and to organize the community based groups.

Throughout Asia and the Pacific region, microcredit frequently is the central component of development strategies aimed to improve the economic empowerment of rural women. Although rural women's savings have contributed to capital mobilization in the region, women themselves have not recognized the significance of their contribution to fund accumulation in national banks and thus to affect macroeconomic capital market dynamics. In recent times, a pragmatic understanding of the role of microcredit/finance is emerging in the region, with the recognition that credit alone cannot contribute to economic and social empowerment of rural women. Historically in Asia and the Pacific region, microcredit programmes have not addressed the credit needs of small and marginal farmers.

The perceived problems in extending microcredit to farmers include the risk of investing in agriculture; seasonality of agricultural production; poor loan repayment performance of agricultural lending and the technical nature of the agriculture production system. Agriculture communities' microcredit needs should be addressed more thoroughly. From another perspective, in countries such as Cambodia, government regulations monitor the flow of funds and microcredit delivery.

Though such regulations are necessary to ensure accountability, some measures have made women's access to credit relatively more complicated and difficult to process. Yet another trend, found in India, is for commercial banks to join forces with traditional microfinance providers to serve women's credit needs. Restrictions on microcredit loans set by global financing agencies often pose additional problems for rural women. As financial markets integrate at the global level and formal credit organizations are promoted as primary funding sources to improve agricultural productivity and rural enterprises, it becomes urgent to investigate the constraints that the associated stringent measures and competitive processes place on rural women's access to microcredit programmes.

ENVIRONMENTAL DESTRUCTION AND NATURAL DISASTERS

The 1999 UNDP Human Development Report identifies the importance of the environment for human development. The report states, Human development also depends on unpaid work by men and women in the household or community, providing "care" so essential to human survival. And it also depends on the natural environment, another essential resource for all, particularly for poor people who derive their livelihood from natural resources. It recognizes seven threats to human security, differing for individuals at different times, and included among these are economic insecurity, food insecurity and environmental insecurity.

This care aspect could be expanded to include care for the environment as the base for livelihood, most often accomplished through the unpaid work of men and women living in agriculture and rural communities. There is a growing concern that destruction of the environment to support economic growth and new life styles comes with negative consequences for rural livelihoods. The UNDP report identifies two types of environmental emergencies: the "silent emergency" of chronic environmental degradation, and the "loud emergency" associated with such things as wild swings in temperature and rainfall (UNDP, 1999). Irrespective of underlying causes, Asia and the Pacific region experiences its fair share of natural disasters and repeated cycles of disaster recovery with dire consequences for livelihood stability.

ENVIRONMENTAL DEGRADATION AND VULNERABILITY

Documented evidence substantiates that the loss of environmental resources in Asia and the Pacific region threatens human livelihoods. In the report, *State of the environment in Asia and the Pacific,* the situation related to forest use and livelihood options is explained as follows:

Among the tropical regions of the world, Asia and the Pacific have the fastest rate of deforestation (1.2 per cent per year), the fastest rate of commercial logging, the highest volume of fuel wood removals, and the fastest rate of species extinction. Among the subregions, Southeast Asia has the highest deforestation rate followed by South Asia. The large and rapidly growing populations and high economic growth in many countries are placing exceptional demands on the region's forest resources. The two major causes of forest destruction in the region are clearing for agriculture (including shifting cultivation) and excessive cutting of industrial timber and fuel wood. Fuel wood collection, an important source of livelihood for millions of poor people in the region, also accelerates the rate of deforestation.

The Word Bank identifies eight major global environmental issues that contribute to environmental instability: Global climate change; loss of biodiversity; stratospheric ozone depletion; freshwater degradation; desertification and land degradation; deforestation and unsustainable use of forests; marine environment and resource degradation and persistent organic pollutants. In each category various social and economic factors are recognized; none is positive, and all adversely affect the livelihood security of people dependent on natural resources. Though the effects of forest resource loss on women's lives are well articulated in the development literature the impact of desertification, land degradation and the loss of biodiversity on rural livelihoods, particularly those of women, are not well documented.

DISASTERS AND VULNERABILITY

Asia and the Pacific region has suffered repeatedly from natural disasters such as flooding, drought, typhoons and earthquakes and rare but catastrophic tsunami have created hardship for rural communities as a result of considerable damage to livelihood assets and loss of human lives. An increasing incidence of natural disasters in recent times has resulted in a serious loss of property and agricultural assets, which has threatened agricultural production and intensified vulnerability leading to food shocks and food insecurity.

The region witnessed famine in *Democratic People's Republic of Korea* because of drought, and the dire situation in Mongolia that brought the threat of a food security disaster in a community dependent on livestock and land for its livelihood. The example of arsenic poisoning of rivers in Papua New Guinea illustrates a man made environmental emergency that ruined the livelihoods of fisher folks. Floods in Bangladesh and drought in the southern Indian states are becoming common occurrences that lead to the immediate loss of livelihoods and threaten the long-term economic viability of households and the community as a result losing the asset base.

Evidence confirms that prolonged drought causes migration of rural households seeking alternative livelihoods in urban centres, usually low wage work, and of farm household members becoming casual agricultural labourers. In the Asian region, particularly in East Asia two major disasters have affected the national economy and the health of the population. The first is the human epidemic of Severe Acute Respiratory Syndrome (SARS) that affected the general economy. So far, the effect of SARS on rural households has not been well documented.

The second disaster, the Avian Influenza epidemic, directly affected agriculture households in East Asia. Avian Influenza is potentially dangerous for human lives in the region and could become a global human health hazard. It is documented that the economic impact of the Avian Influenza varied depending on the type and scale of poultry production systems. The direct impact was caused by the death of sick animals on farms, stamping out the virus, cleaning the farms and the associated costs and other implications for farmers, their families and workers.

"Because of the crisis in Vietnam, the poultry sector has decreased in size. Poultry production in the surveyed households before the outbreak was the main economic activity for 68 per cent of the male headed poultry farms and 32 per cent of female-headed, whereas in July 2004 the survey found these rates to be 30 per cent and 12 per cent respectively. Households with few assets and no other animals than poultry have experienced Avian Influenza as a shock, leading to reduction in assets."

Women are more vulnerable during disasters because they have less access to resources, are victims of the gendered division of labour and are the primary caregivers to children, the elderly and the disabled. According to OXFAM, more women than men were killed by the Asian tsunami, as figures from India, Indonesia and Sri Lanka suggest. In some areas the disaster claimed four times as many women as men. The report states that women were worse hit because they were waiting on beaches for fishermen to return, or at home looking after children at the time.

Various case studies and local narratives suggest that gender is a highly significant factor in the construction of social vulnerability to risk, and in the responses to hazards and disasters. Men and women clearly have different coping strategies during the disaster cycle. For instance, during the cyclone of 1991 in Bangladesh, a greater number of casualties were reported among women, who failed to receive warning signals largely because of socially imposed constraints on female mobility and their responsibilities to care for children and livestock. Similarly, women suffered more during the post disaster period, experiencing a sharp increase in workloads because of their multiples roles.

At the same time, although many of their traditional income-generating activities disappeared (home gardens and livestock), women (unlike men) were unable to look for work outside the home (UN Economic and Social Council, 2002). In this context, gender-responsive institutional changes and collective action strategies are needed in disaster management to balance women's vulnerability to disaster with their proven capabilities to cope under difficult conditions.

EMERGING TECHNOLOGIES: PRODUCTION AND COMMUNICATION

In Asia and the Pacific region the focus on emerging technologies considered here fall under two general categories, namely the technologies associated with agriculture and rural production and the information and communication technologies.

AGRICULTURE TECHNOLOGIES

Agriculture technologies can be grouped into two broad categories, namely the mainstream agriculture technologies and alternative agriculture technologies. Mainstream agriculture technologies are defined here as those technologies that are promoted by the agriculture research, education and extension organizations to improve productivity and that depend on high external inputs. Alternative agriculture technologies are defined as technologies that promote local control in production systems, empower local communities, restore the environment and use low external inputs (Savant, not dated).

The proponents of mainstream agriculture promote productivity. The promoters of alternative agriculture emphasize sustainability. Though it should be obligatory for those working on improving the situation of rural women to assess current and potential gender specific impacts of technologies promoted by competing paradigms, in reality very limited attention has been paid to addressing such women specific impacts of competing technologies. For example, a Cambodia-IRRI-Australia Project documented that women's labour requirements intensified when the farm adopted high yielding rice varieties and other new varieties.

More work was also involved with extra fertilizer applications, improved seed storage techniques and knowledge intensive activities like Integrated Pest Management (IPM). Demand for women's labour decreased by land levelling and direct seeding. New technologies for agriculture are generally knowledge intensive and thus demand improved resource management practices.

It is imperative to weigh both the benefits and disadvantages of these advanced technologies for rural women as well as the implications for their economic opportunities in such a changing technological milieu. Knowledge intensive technological development favours the educated and skilled in the developing countries of the region. Given the regional situation where rural women record less formal educational attainment, it is important to anticipate and counter the adverse impact of these knowledge-intensive technologies on the work and livelihood strategies of rural women workers.

INTEGRATED PEST MANAGEMENT

The Asian region has pioneered both the green revolution and Integrated Pest Management as technologies for improving food production and resource management. The green revolution approach in the last century was promoted to improve agriculture productivity. IPM is promoted as a technology to improve resource management and contribute to sustainability. The concept and practice of IPM has been widely adopted first beginning with rice, then to cotton and vegetable production. IPM from a crop-based approach to a community-based approach is promoted in the region.

In Pakistan, FAO implemented Cotton-IPM Project focused on the health risk concerns of farm women and their families in intensive pesticide dependent cotton production and developed programmes to train women facilitators to train farm women on cotton-IPM practices. To date, there has been limited well-researched documentation on the role of women in IPM, its relevance to women's crops and the impact on their workload and the contribution of their unpaid labour for the economic efficiency of the IPM based production systems.

BIOTECHNOLOGY

Biotechnology has emerged as a significant technology in Asia and the Pacific to expand agriculture production gains. Marked by strong ideological differences between the non-governmental sector (mostly against) and the scientific community and private sector (in favour), the debate about the benefits and hazards of biotechnology continues unabated. The extent to which modern biotechnology will contribute to the achievement of food security for all is still an open question.

In this context, most governments in the region appear to be following a "watch, wait and see" approach. There is general lack of information about the extent to which women farmers in the region know about and understand the potential opportunities and risks of a new agricultural revolution driven by biotechnology. Yet given the low educational attainments of women throughout the region, and the highly sophisticated organization of production likely to be required in biotechnology-based agriculture, it seems reasonable to speculate that the majority of rural women would be further marginalized by such developments.

LIVESTOCK REVOLUTION

Livestock technologies for expanding production to meet the regional growth in demand for livestock products will also present challenges to rural women's role in this sector. According to Delgado *et al.* (1999), The Livestock Revolution is a structural phenomenon that is here to stay. As in the case of the green revolution, the stakes for the poor in developing countries are enormous. How good or bad the livestock revolution will be for the people of the developing countries, depends on how these countries choose to approach it. Lack of policy will not stop the Livestock Revolution, but will ensure that the form it takes is less favourable for growth, poverty alleviation and sustainability in developing countries.

Women play a crucial role in livestock production on homesteads or in backyards, but "[i]n rural areas, far from cities and markets, the predominant system is one of scavenging with very few inputs provided by the owner, who will typically be a woman". Thus it would be important to identify strategies to improve rural women's livestock based livelihood as the livestock revolution pervades the region. Asian lessons learnt from the green revolution in the cereal crops sector and the white revolution of the dairy sector should guide the planners in devising livelihood strategies for women in the livestock sector.

FARMER FIELD SCHOOL

The Farmer Field School (FFS) approach is an innovative communication modality developed for effective transfer of IPM technology (FAO, not dated). Limited research information and anecdotal notes have begun to appear on women's participation in FFS for IPM, especially in East Asia. In Indonesia it was observed that many development programmes have had an adverse effect on female farmers, including within the IPM work. In order to overcome this limitation, alternatives such as intensive participatory approaches and Gender Field School experiments have been encouraged.

There was a difference in women's participation in IPM FFS training programmes in Nepal because of cultural factors that supported or negated their participation. In one area where men were involved in non-farm activities to generate income there was not much competition for women from the local men to take part in IPM farmer field schools. But in another location, where the dominant ethnic group restricted women's movement outside their home, their participation in IPM Farmer Field Schools was very limited (FAO, 2000).

The study in Vietnam presents the differential participation of women in IPM in FFS. Four years after the start of the programme female participation nationally was 19 per cent or one in every five participants in a FFS is female. Between 1994 and 1996 female participation increased from 13 to 19 per cent. However, it still does not reflect the importance of women in agriculture. Especially in the south and centre the participation of women is low, less than 10 per cent. In the north, female participation is over 35 per cent. For women it was more difficult to arrange their time to go to FFS since they have many responsibilities at home and work. If women want to attend a FFS they need to get support from their family to do so. For men whether to join the FFS or not is more an individual decision.

Additionally, women's heavy workload and their responsibilities in on-farm, off-farm and household production deter their participation. Moreover, limited technical content or monocrop oriented training may not interest them. Thus, the current modality of Farmer Life School (FLS) for covering wide ranging topics may have greater potential to attract the women in rice based systems.

The FLS is a tool that helps farmers to develop their critical thinking on their livelihood. Later FFS approaches have been applied to provide an integrated knowledge package to agriculture communities. But the content development in the

FFS/FLS falls short in fulfilling the technology information needs of rural women who perform multiple roles in response to production demands of rural economies both on the farm and in the home.

INFORMATION AND COMMUNICATION TECHNOLOGIES

Recent debates on overcoming the digital divide are indicative of increasing interest among international agencies and investors in promoting the use of information and communication technologies (ICTs) in development.

According to one report, In the rural context, the ICTs usually provide very little employment or direct income unlike labour-intensive manufacturing and the Green Revolution, both of which created substantial employment. ICTs then need to be evaluated mainly in terms of their effect on productivity of other sectors (agriculture, farming or other rural, non-farm economic activities) and especially on agency development, including that resulting from sharing experiences of mobilization and innovations.

Many countries in Asia and the Pacific region recognize the potential of Information and Communication Technologies to improve women's access to information and knowledge, enhance education and learning, and accelerate technology transfer. Radio and television are used extensively in several countries to inform and educate rural women about topics such as health, nutrition and agriculture. The most often quoted cases found in websites on ICTs potential benefits for rural women's rural livelihoods are: Bangladesh Grameen Communications' venture of rural women's cell phone enterprises; M.S. Swminathan Research Foundation supported Pondicherry Village Information Shops; e-Chaupal for market information; SEWA's programme on skills development to support women's work in the informal sector; Sri Lankan Kotmale project and information kiosks and telecentres in the region.

Despite the potential, however, the threat of an increased "digital divide" that would widen information, education and knowledge inequality between urban and rural communities is real. "Access to ICTs is still a distant reality for the vast majority of people. The countries in the South, particularly rural populations, have been left out of the information revolution. In many of these countries there is a lack of basic infrastructure, resulting in high costs for installing and running ICTs".

Indeed, already evident is the wide variations in Internet access and in the availability and quality of relevant language content both between and within countries in the region. In the Pacific Islands, for instance, women's access to, and use of information technology, is largely confined to urban areas and generally limited compared to most Asian countries. A number of barriers to the increased use of ICTs for the empowerment of rural women include inadequate infrastructure, high costs and limited capacity, all of which are more acute in rural areas (Aitkin, 1998).

More importantly the content relevancy presents the greatest challenge to the use of ICTs for the advancement of rural women. Indeed, according to Green and Trevor-Deutsch (2002), The major barrier to the use of ICTs for women is its lack of relevancy to their lives. Women encounter barriers to the use of ICTs when the learning content is not directly relevant to their livelihood, and when it does not value their knowledge, wisdom and experience.

Certainly, there are opportunities to use ICTs to educate and empower a large number of rural women and men provided that user-friendly and gender-responsive content and applications are developed, and the agents of development are well trained and gender-sensitive. One such application is on the education front. With appropriate and adequate investment in content and learning resources a distance education modality could reach women in the rural areas. ICT applications can be either directed to women as primary users of ICTs and/or for capacity building among service providers and social agents who serve the women's programmes. In the rural context, women as primary users of ICTs are still a social curiosity rather than a common occurrence.

The opportunities for using ICT applications for improving livelihood skills for rural clients are currently mediated through development service providers (government and non-government) and hence they must be trained in ICT applications to improve women's livelihood. It would be important to distinguish the potential of ICTs to improve the livelihood of women to ensure economic empowerment and their prospects to improve access to information and knowledge to improve their quality of life and informed participation in various spheres of society.

7

Marriage

In today's rapidly globalizing world, marriage as a contract between two individuals based on love and commitment to each other is increasingly considered a norm. The degree of women's control over their marital decisions and choice of mate, based on individual traits rather than the family's socio-economic status, is seen as a measure of whether a society has embraced modernity. In reality, marriage involves many actors with complex decision-making processes and multiple considerations.

In many Asian societies, being and staying married, for both men and women, is a social and family obligation and a criterion of social standing. Kin members, the state, marriage intermediaries (institutional or individual) and commercial sectors are all involved in decision-making. This is particularly the case of cross-border marriages, with the state deciding and controlling who is allowed to marry, whether spouses are allowed to enter or reside in the receiving societies, as well as their naturalization and assimilation process.

As well as a rapidly increasing intra-Asian flow of marriage migration, there is a continued growth of Asian women marrying and migrating to the West and 'in between' diaspora communities. For the most part, it is women marrying (and 'marrying up') and migrating to wealthier countries. The dominant view is that women enter cross-border marriages for economic gains, and generally in order to extricate themselves (and their families) from poverty. Scholarship on cross-border marriages in Asia has been vigorous in recent years.

Two terms indicating rather different conceptual emphases are used: cross-border and transnational marriage. These two terms are used interchangeably but often not defined clearly. To make it more confusing, both terms can be used to refer to cross- ethnic/cultural or same-cultural marriages. The term *cross-border marriage* emphasizes geographical, national, racial, class and gender and cultural borders constructed in the hosting societies. These borders are mainly mediated by the states as well as other social actors in order to differentiate the 'we' and 'the others'.

This stream of scholarship concerns the impact of marriage migration on the host societies in terms of population pressure and social security, the political and social citizenship of marriage migrants and their integration and acculturation. Particular attention is paid to studying how to empower migrant wives in exploitative situations, such as domestic violence and commodified marriage brokerage. There is also a growing scholarship on the actors' strategies of crossing these borders.

The term *transnational marriage* emphasizes a transnational network and space created by the actors themselves; as well as the transactions of economic resources, symbols and political and cultural practices between the sending and receiving communities and how these transactions influence local development, social practices and cultural norms in both sending and receiving societies. The term 'transnationalism' by no means suggests the end of the nation-state; instead, it focuses on how actors' opportunities and choices are mediated by the state and other transnational actors.

The articles in this theme issue follow this framework on transnationalism. They address diverse aspects of transnational marriages and challenge assumptions made by earlier scholarship, particularly the social actors other than the state. Lenore Lyons and Michele Ford's article tells of couples comprised of Singaporean men and Indonesian wives in the Riau Islands. The men choose to live in Singapore; however they do establish a base in the Riau Islands and make regular visits to their wives.

On the one hand, their choice of residency is shaped by the restriction of immigration policies imposed by both the Singaporean and Indonesian governments. The immigration polices of both governments are tied up with labour policy and class status. The husbands of cross-border marriages have to prove to the state that they are of sufficient means to support their wives and thus will not become a welfare burden. On the other hand, the state's intervention does not seem to matter much for the couples in their daily experiences. For them, the choice of residency is clearly a lifestyle choice.

As well as benefiting from an immediate improvement in their economic situation, Indonesian wives also experience class mobility. Their marriage to Singaporean men allows them to move into the lower-middle class. Equally, the working-class Singaporean husbands who are marginalized in Singaporean society can enjoy a comfortable middle-class lifestyle in the Riau islands. Lyons and Ford make the point that the wives do not wish to live in Singapore, a place they consider to be stressful and isolated.

Like Lyons and Ford's article, Shuko Takeshita's essay on transnational families of Pakistani men and Japanese women shows that aside from the economic motivation (job opportunities or wealth) and cultural practice (patrilocality), there are other factors affecting the transnational families' decisions and choices of residency. In this case children's education and the transmission of cultural and religious values. Takeshita studies the importance of religion in children's education and socialization.

The United Arab Emirates (UAE) are chosen as the migration destination of Japanese wives and their children instead of the couples' countries of origin. Pakistani men establish a transnational, kin-based business network trading used vehicles between Japan, UAE and Pakistan. Japanese women favour a home in the UAE over Pakistan because of the modern lifestyle and less control from their husband's family, yet they can still enjoy the social support of some kin members. The transnational kinship network therefore provides business opportunities, social support and helps maintain religious and cultural identities.

Japanese women are active agents in this multiple migration process by choosing the destination, forming a support network among themselves, and developing educational strategies for their children who learn English and Japanese while being socialised in an Islamic environment. Panitee Suksomboon's article gives a nuanced picture of Thai women who marry Dutch men and live in the Netherlands. These women actively maintain social ties with their home communities, and by doing so, they create a transnational space.

This transnational space is important for Thai women not only in terms of social support, but also because their class mobility only exists in their home community and not in the host society. To maintain their new-found social status Thai women transfer economic resources to their natal families either by economic remittance or via cultural practices such as gift- giving or paying for holidays for the whole family.

They also disguise their economic and emotional hardships, creating an image of a happy life in Europe. This image, together with the socio-economic disparity between families with and without women marrying foreign men, fuels the desire of more women to marry abroad, thus triggering a chained migration. Suksomboon shows the linkage between the movement of people, transaction of economic resources as well as the cultural ideas and practices flowing in between this transnational space.

All three articles give pictures of marriage migrants as active agents in the migration process. Their choices challenge the assumption that marriage migrants marry either for economic gains, citizenship and welfare or lifestyle in an affluent society. However, as Lyons and Ford warn us, their choices are limited by the existing gender ideologies and their dependency on their husbands, which is strengthened by the economic disparity between the host and sending countries.

While marriage migrants actively create a transnational space, not all of them can engage their husbands in it.

While Singaporean and Pakistani men enjoy the advantages of the transnational space, Dutch men appear to have greater difficulty in appreciating the cultural practices of the wives' community and do not enjoy the social status and respect that their wives 'win' for them. Parents in many Asian societies are heavily involved in the marital decision and mate choice of their children. This is also the case in cross-border marriages.

Hsing-Miao Chi's article addresses an understudied aspect of transnational marriages in the current literature - the inter-generational relations. This generation of mothers-in-law in Taiwan is 'caught in-between', in the sense that when they were young they were expected to fulfil the role of obedient daughters-in-law; now that they are old they are expected to do domestic work and care for young grandchildren when their Taiwanese daughters-in-law enter the job market.

Previous research shows that one of the motivations for Taiwanese parents to choose a foreign wife (mainly from Southeast Asia) for their sons is that Southeast Asian women are considered to have 'traditional virtue' of gender roles and to be more obedient. Despite such expectations, Chi's study shows that the Taiwanese mothers-in-law of local marriages and those of cross-border marriages may have the same experiences. Having a foreign daughter-in-law does not necessarily increase the power of the mother-in-law.

On the contrary, the unfamiliarity of the language and cultural practices of their foreign daughters-in-law makes them suspicious of daughters-in-law's intentions and creates what Chi calls 'emotional burden'. A large number of intra-Asia cross-border marriages are intermediated either by institutions or individual matchmakers within the actors' kin and social network. These marriages are termed 'commodified marriages' and at times equated to trafficking. Michiel Baas's article problematises the dichotomy between 'love' and 'arranged' marriage in the context of India's IT industry.

IT professionals in Bangalore tend to choose their marriage partners within the industry, regardless of their caste. On the one hand this is due to the fact that the transnational business practice of the industry is based on meritocracy - the IT companies deliberately discourage employees from following the cultural practices of the caste system. On the other hand, migration experiences, both internal and international, uproot IT professionals from their social and kin networks and place them in an isolated working environment that demands long working hours and flexibility.

The IT professionals are able to break away from the practices of arranged marriage within the same caste and choose their marriage partners with the families' permission (what Baas calls 'arranged love marriage') due to the economic benefits and social prestige associated with the industry. However, rather than based on romantic love, their mate choice is a result of practical considerations such as maintaining the lifestyle the transnational business practice requires.

8

Nutrition and Discrimination

"When you grow up, you can be whatever you want to be." Little girls in the United States hear this all the time, from their mothers to teachers to "Sesame Street" characters. Almost everywhere they go, they are encouraged to believe that girls can be just as smart, athletic, and successful as boys. Even the pictures of spunky women on magazine covers at the checkout stand tell them that when you're a girl, anything is possible. But for little girls in developing countries, the message is just the opposite. From the day they are born, they are constantly reminded of the things they are not allowed to do.

Eliminating hunger and malnutrition is one of the most fundamental challenges facing humanity. Malnutrition and its associated disease conditions can be caused by eating too little, eating too much, or eating an unbalanced diet that lacks necessary nutrients. Under nutrition, defined as failure to consume adequate energy, protein, and micronutrients to meet basic requirements for body maintenance, growth, and development. Malnutrition is one of the most devastating problems worldwide and is inextricably linked with poverty. The scale of under nutrition has also been studied among other populations and age groups, such as pregnant and lactating women.

This chapter mainly focuses on malnutrition in women. The oppression of women socially and culturally means they have less access to everything, including food, resources, health care, community support and information. The problems arise from cultural, political and economic realities that must be addressed in tandem. However, one significant step should be taken to educate and to make them aware contribute to struggle against terrible problem of malnutrition. Malnutrition among women has long been recognized as a serious problem in India, but national-level data on levels and causes of malnutrition have been scarce.

The present epidemiological and biochemical study has been undertaken in the district Sangrur, Punjab (India). The samples survey has been undertaken from the area covered and 1000 subjects were selected randomly for questioning regarding the different aspects of epidemiology. Out of these 1000 samples, 500 are from urban population and 500 from rural population On the basis of WHO criteria for body mass index categories malnutrition among subjects can also calculated.

In 19th century, Mathematician Lamber Adolphe Jacques Quetelet described the body mass index as a relation between body weight and stature in human. Body mass index (BMI) is used to estimate your best weight range for your health. The body mass index is a useful tool in both clinical and public health practice for assessing the nutritional status. In this chapter, only malnutrition in women is discussed.

In the present study 20.2% males and 25.2% females were malnourished in the Sangrur district of Punjab, India. Value for BMI >30 kg/m 2 is 8.31% in females and 5.04% in males. Most of the women were illiterate and house- wives. Malnutrition refers to any disorder of nutrition-whether it is due to dietary deficiency, called under-nutrition, or to excess diet, called over-nutrition. Malnutrition worldwide includes a spectrum of nutrient-related disorders, deficiencies, and conditions such as intrauterine growth retardation, protein-energy malnutrition, iodine deficiency disorders, vitamin A deficiency, iron-deficiency anemia, and overweight/ obesity and other diet-related non communicable diseases.

Risks of being underweight (BMI less than 20) may be malnourishment, compromised immune function, respiratory disease, tuberculosis (an infection of the lung), digestive (stomach) disease, cancer, osteoporosis etc. Many factors have been associated with both forms of malnutrition of women in the literature. These include the socioeconomic (e.g., occupation, educational background and the standard of living); cultural (e.g., religion and caste); the demographic (e.g., age and marital status) and dietary characteristics.

Body mass index is an accepted measure of chronic energy deficiency malnutrition. Under- nutrition remains the nutrition problem of greatest concern in developing countries. The prevalence of malnutrition (includes both under- nutrition and over-nutrition) among women in Kerala is quite high. Under nutrition remains the nutrition problem of greatest concern which is an important determinant of health and an important outcome of ill health.

Differential treatment of girls and boys in terms of feeding practices and access to health care is among the factors responsible for higher female mortality. As a consequence of their lower status overall, women experience discrimination in the allocation of household resources including food and access to health services. Under nutrition and anemia among pregnant women and adolescent pregnancies are the main contributory factors for low birth weight babies. Intrauterine growth retardation (IUGR) during pregnancy is the main cause of low birth weight and nutritional anemia during pregnancy which is a major determinant of IUGR.

An adolescent girl, who is not yet fully developed, gives birth to a low birth weight infant. Compared to a well nourished child, a mildly malnourished child has twice the risk of dying from common childhood diseases; moderately malnourished child has eight times at risk. In developing countries indicates that malnourished individuals, that is, women with a Body Mass Index ss(BMI) below 18.5 kg/m, show a progressive increase in mortality rates as well as increasedin1995, about one million adult deaths resulted from health problems exacerbated by over-nutrition, while half of it were associated with under-nutrition. For social and biological reasons, women of the reproductive age are amongst the most vulnerable to malnutrition.

While malnutrition in India is prevalent among all segments of the population but poor nutrition among women begins in infancy and continues throughout their lifetimes. Women and girls are typically the last to eat in a family; thus, if there is not enough food they are the ones to suffer most. Children of illiterate mothers are three times as likely to be severely undernourished as children of mothers with at least a high school education. The BMI can also be applied to define chronic energy deficiency/ underweight and overweight/obesity.

Underweight/CED is usually indicated by a BMI of less than 18.5 kg/ m^2 and overweight and obese indicated by a BMI of more than 25.0 kg/. In the present study value of value of BMI >25 kg/is 30.8% in females and 22.5% in males. There are several studies on nutrition transition in Asia and the Pacific, as well as the developing world, in general. In India, which is typically known for large incidence of undernutrition, significant proportions of overweight and obese now coexist with the undernourished (IIPS and ORC Macro 2000) and there is some evidence of even emerging nutrition transition also.

Traditional foods meant for children, pregnant and lactating mothers are being forgotten and biscuits, bread, noodles, instant infant foods of very high cost are getting more popular. The value of traditional foods including coarse grains, sattu, khichadi, idli, dalia, matharies, ladoos etc need to be revived. These foods contribute fibre, antioxidant vitamins, Beta carotene, vitamin C and Folic acid, which help in preventing diet related chronic disorders like diabetes, hypertension and cancer etc. Adult malnutrition has received much less attention than that of child.

It, therefore, can be concluded that the present study becomes representative study which shows the prevalence of gender difference in nutrition in the population of District Sangrur (Punjab). India has a long history of activism for women's welfare and rights, which has increasingly focused on women's economic rights. A range of government programs have been launched to increase economic opportunity for women, although there appear to be no existing programs to address the cultural and traditional discrimination against women that leads to her hopeless conditions.

Despite the magnitude of the problem, programs to improve their nutritional status did not receive a high priority. Only a few organizations have effective programs that address their nutritional and health needs. In addition to expanding the coverage of the healthcare system, less-traditional avenues need to be tapped to help the women to improve their nutritional status in the future. The findings of this study suggest that wide-ranging programs are needed to tackle malnourishment in women.

GIRLS: HOUSEHOLD SERVANTS

When a boy is born in most developing countries, friends and relatives exclaim congratulations. A son means insurance. He will inherit his father's property and get a job to help support the family. When a girl is born, the reaction is very different. Some women weep when they find out their baby is a girl because, to them, a daughter is just another expense. Her place is in the home, not in the world of men. In some parts of India, it's traditional to greet a family with a newborn girl by saying, "The servant of your household has been born."

A girl can't help but feel inferior when everything around her tells her that she is worthless than a boy. Her identity is forged as soon as her family and society limit her opportunities and declare her to be second-rate. A combination of extreme poverty and deep biases against women creates a remorseless cycle of discrimination that keeps girls in developing countries from living up to their full potential. It also leaves them vulnerable to severe physical and emotional abuse. These "servants of the household" come to accept that life will never be any different.

GREATEST OBSTACLES AFFECTING GIRLS

Discrimination against girls and women in the developing world is a devastating reality. It results in millions of individual tragedies, which add up to lost potential for entire countries. Studies show there is a direct link between a country's attitude toward women and its progress socially and economically. The status of women is central to the health of a society. If one part suffers, so does the whole. Tragically, female children are most defenseless against the trauma of gender discrimination. The following obstacles are stark examples of what girls worldwide face. But the good news is that new generations of girls represent the most promising source of change for women—and men—in the developing world today.

DOWRY

In developing countries, the birth of a girl causes great upheaval for poor families. When there is barely enough food to survive, any child puts a strain on a family's resources. But the monetary drain of a daughter feels even more severe, especially in regions where dowry is practiced. Dowry is goods and money a bride's family pays to the husband's family. Originally intended to help with marriage expenses, dowry came to be seen as payment to the groom's family for taking on the burden of another woman.

In some countries, dowries are extravagant, costing years' worth of wages, and often throwing a woman's family into debt. The dowry practice makes the prospect of having a girl even more distasteful to poor families. It also puts young women in danger: A new bride is at the mercy of her in-laws should they decide her dowry is too small. UNICEF estimates that around 5,000 Indian women are killed in dowry-related incidents each year.

NEGLECT

The developing world is full of poverty-stricken families who see their daughters as an economic predicament. That attitude has resulted in the widespread neglect of baby girls in Africa, Asia, and South America. In many communities, it's a regular practice to breastfeed girls for a shorter time than boys so that women can try to get pregnant again with a boy as soon as possible.

As a result, girls miss out on life-giving nutrition during a crucial window of their development, which stunts their growth and weakens their resistance to disease. Statistics show that the neglect continues as they grow up. Young girls receive less food, healthcare and fewer vaccinations overall than boys. Not much changes as they become women. Tradition calls for women to eat last, often reduced to picking over the leftovers from the men and boys.

INFANTICIDE AND SEX-SELECTIVE ABORTION

In extreme cases, parents make the horrific choice to end their baby girl's life. One woman named Lakshmi from Tamil Nadu, an impoverished region of India, fed her baby soap from an oleander bush mixed with castor oil until the girl bled from the nose and died. "A daughter is always liabilities. How can I bring up a second?" said Lakshmi to explain why she chose to end her baby's life. "Instead of her suffering the way I do, I thought it was better to get rid of her."

Sex-selective abortions are even more common than infanticides in India. They are growing ever more frequent as technology makes it simple and cheap to determine a fetus' gender. In Jaipur, a Western Indian city of 2 million people, 3,500 sex-determined abortions are carried out every year. The gender ratio across India has dropped to an unnatural low of 927 females to 1,000 males due to infanticide and sex-based abortions. China has its own long legacy of female infanticide.

In the last two decades, the government's infamous one-child policy has weakened the country's track record even more. By restricting household size to limit the population, the policy gives parents just one chance to produce a coveted son before being forced to pay heavy fines for additional children. In 1997, the World Health Organization declared, "...more than 50 million women were estimated to be 'missing' in China because of the institutionalized killing and neglect of girls due to Beijing's population control program." The Chinese government says that sex-selective abortion is one major explanation for the staggering number of Chinese girls who have simply vanished from the population in the last 20 years.

ABUSE

Even after infancy, the threat of physical harm follows girls throughout their lives. Women in every society are vulnerable to abuse. But the threat is more severe for girls and women who live in societies where women's rights mean practically nothing. Mothers who lack their own rights have little protection to offer their daughters, much less themselves, from male relatives and other authority figures. The frequency of rape and violent attacks against women in the developing world is alarming. Forty-five per cent of Ethiopian women say that they have been assaulted in their lifetimes. In 1998, 48 per cent of Palestinian women admitted to being abused by an intimate partner within the past year.

In some cultures, the physical and psychological trauma of rape is compounded by an additional stigma. In cultures that maintain strict sexual codes for women, if a woman steps out of bounds—by choosing her own husband, flirting in public, or seeking divorce from an abusive partner—she has brought dishonor to her family and must be disciplined. Often, discipline means execution. Families commit "honor killings" to salvage their reputation tainted by disobedient women.

Appallingly, this "disobedience" includes rape. In 1999, a 16-year-old mentally handicapped girl in Pakistan who had been raped was brought before her tribe's judicial counsel. Although she was the victim and her attacker had been arrested, the counsel decided she had brought shame to the tribe and ordered her public execution. This case, which received a lot of publicity at the time, is not unusual. Three women fall victim to honor killings in Pakistan every day—including victims of rape. In areas of Asia, the Middle East, and even Europe, all responsibility for sexual misconduct falls, by default, to women.

LABOR

For the young girls who escape these pitfalls and grow up relatively safely, daily life is still incredibly hard. School might be an option for a few years, but most girls are pulled out at age 9 or 10 when they're useful enough to work all day at home. Nine million more girls than boys miss out on school every year, according to UNICEF. While their brothers continue to go to classes or pursue their hobbies and play, they join the women to do the bulk of the housework. Housework in developing countries consists of continuous, difficult physical labor. A girl is likely to work from before daybreak until the light drains away. She walks barefoot long distances several times a day carrying heavy buckets of water, most likely polluted, just to keep her family alive.

She cleans, grinds corn, gathers fuel, tends to the fields, bathes her younger siblings, and prepares meals until she sits down to her own after all the men in the family have eaten. Most families can't afford modern appliances, so her tasks must be done by hand—crushing corn into meal with heavy rocks, scrubbing laundry against rough stones, kneading bread and cooking gruel over a blistering open fire. There is no time left in the day to learn to read and write or to play with friends. She collapses exhausted each night, ready to wake up the next morning to start another long workday.

Most of this labor is performed without recognition or reward. UN statistics show that although women produce half the world's food, they own only 1 per cent of its farmland. In most African and Asian countries, women's work isn't even considered real labor. Should a woman take a job, she is expected to keep up all her responsibilities at home in addition to her new ones, with no extra help. Women's labor goes overlooked, even though it is crucial to the survival of each family.

SEX TRAFFICKING

Some families decide it's more lucrative to send their daughters to a nearby town or city to get jobs that usually involve hard labor and little pay. That desperate need for income leaves girls easy prey to sex traffickers, particularly in Southeast Asia, where international tourism gorges the illegal industry. In Thailand, the sex trade has swelled without check into a main sector of the national economy. Families in small villages along the Chinese border are regularly approached by recruiters called "aunties" who ask for their daughters in exchange for six years' wages. Most Thai farmers earn only $150 a year. The offer can be too tempting to refuse.

The girls who are forced into prostitution to support their families often feel their burden deeply. "When I was at work, 50 per cent of me hated what I was doing," said one 14-year-old girl, who felt conflicted about being taken out of a brothel in Chiang Mai, Thailand. "But the other 50 per cent wanted to stay so that I could earn money for my parents. My father cannot work. He is very old and I must support the family. It is my job." It's estimated that 1 million children around the world are involved in the sex trade; a third of all sex workers in Southeast Asia are between the ages of 12 and 17.

GIRLS' EDUCATION: BREAKING THE PATTERN OF GENDER DISCRIMINATION

Education is the tool that can help break the pattern of gender discrimination and bring lasting change for women in developing countries. Educated women are essential to ending gender bias, starting by reducing the poverty that makes discrimination even worse in the developing world. The most basic skills in literacy and arithmetic open up opportunities for better-paying jobs for women. Uneducated women in rural areas of Zambia, for instance, are twice as likely to live in poverty as those who have had eight or more years of education.

The longer a girl is able to stay in school, the greater her chances to pursue worthwhile employment, higher education, and a life without the hazards of extreme poverty. Women who have had some schooling are more likely to get married later, survive childbirth, have fewer and healthier children, and make sure their own children complete school. They also understand hygiene and nutrition better and are more likely to prevent disease by visiting health care facilities. The UN estimates that for every year a woman spends in primary school, the risk of her child dying prematurely is reduced by 8 per cent.

Girls' education also means comprehensive change for a society. As women get the opportunity to go to school and obtain higher-level jobs, they gain status in their communities. Status translates into the power to influence their families and societies. Even bigger changes become possible as girls' education becomes the cultural norm. Women can't defend themselves against physical and sexual abuse until they have the authority to speak against it without fear. Knowledge gives that authority.

Women who have been educated are half as likely to undergo harmful cultural practices such as female genital mutilation (FGM) and four times as likely to protect their daughters from it. The Global Campaign for Education also states that a primary education defends women against HIV/ AIDS infection—disproportionately high for women in developing countries—by giving "the most marginalized groups in society—notably young women—the status and confidence needed to act on information and refuse unsafe sex."

FGM and HIV/AIDS are too large to adequately address in this chapter, but they represent desperate challenges to the basic health and well-being of women in developing countries. You can help pull down the barriers that keep girls from attending school and begin to bring change for women in developing countries. The most direct way is by easing the financial need that forces families to take their children out of school in the first place.

Dozens of international organizations are working to improve the livelihood of impoverished people. By building infrastructure and providing aid, vocational training, and education programs, they give families in developing countries resources to create healthy and stable lives. That takes the burden of mere survival off young women and gives them the time to get an education. With practical help and encouragement, girls are more likely to enroll and stay in school.

UNICEF is encouraging all international organizations to come up with strategies for girls' education as part of their initial development plans. It has also started a movement to monitor school materials, facilities, and teachers to ensure that girls get a quality education that promotes appropriate perceptions of women, and that female students are given the same privileges as male students. All UNICEF and other reputable organizations need now are the resources to fund their efforts.

Malnutrition affects one out of every three pre-school age children living in developing countries. This disturbing, yet preventable, state of affairs causes' untold suffering and, given its wide scale, presents a major obstacle to the development process. Volumes have been written about the causes of child malnutrition and the means of reducing it. But the role of women's social status in determining their children's nutritional health has gone largely unnoticed until recently. This study explores the relationship between women's status and children's nutrition in three developing regions: South Asia, Sub-Saharan Africa (SSA), and Latin America and the Caribbean (LAC).

The study defines women's status as *women's power relative to men*. Women with low status tend to have weaker control over household resources, tighter time constraints, less access to information and health services, poorer mental health, and lower self-esteem. These factors are thought to be closely tied to women's own nutritional status and the quality of care they receive, and, in turn, to children's birth weights and the quality of care they receive. The study sets out to answer three main questions: First, is women's status an important determinant of child nutritional status in the three study regions? Second, if so, what are the pathways through which it operates? And finally, why is South Asia's child malnutrition rate so much higher than SSA's?

To answer these questions, this report brings together Demographic and Health Survey data on 117,242 children under three years of age from 36 developing countries. It uses two measures of women's status: women's decision making power relative to that of their male partners and the degree of equality between women and men in their communities. The empirical results leave no doubt that higher women's status has a significant, positive effect on children's nutritional status in all three regions.

Further, they confirm that women's status impacts child nutrition because women with higher status have better nutritional status themselves, are better cared for, and provide higher quality care to their children. However, the strength of influence of women's status and the pathways through which it influences child nutrition differ considerably across regions. In South Asia, increases in women's status have a strong influence on both the long-and short-term nutritional status of children, leading to reductions in both stunting and wasting.

The human costs of women's lower status in the region are high. The study estimates that if women and men had equal status, the under-three child underweight rate would drop by approximately 13 per cent age points, meaning 13.4 million fewer malnourished children in this age group alone. As women's status improves in the region, so does the quality of the pathways through which it influences child nutrition.

The pathways identified by the study are women's nutritional status (as measured by body mass index [BMI]), prenatal and birthing care for women, complementary feeding practices for children, treatment of illness and immunization of children, and the quality of substitute child caretakers. In Sub-Saharan Africa too, women's status and the long-and short-term nutritional status of children are linked. If women and men enjoyed equal status, child malnutrition in the region would decrease by nearly 3 per cent age points—a reduction of 1.7 million malnourishedschildren under three.

The pathways to this judicious outcome are largely the same as those in South Asia, except that higher women's status improves child nutrition only for women with very little relative decision making power and has no influence on treatment of child illness. LAC exhibits a different pattern from that of South Asia and SSA. Women's status has a positive effect only on children's short-term nutritional status and only in those households in which women's relative decision making power is very low. Women's status has a distinctly *negative* influence on their BMI in this region, where weight gain is an emerging public health problem.

The effect probably reflects the greater tendency among higher status women to "weight watch" and likely does not threaten children's nutritional status. The pathways connecting women's status and children's nutrition include prenatal and birthing care for women, feeding frequency, immunization, and quality of substitute caretakers. Among the developing-country regions, South Asia's particularly high child malnutrition rate has remained a puzzle. South Asia trails even SSA, despite surpassing that region's record on many of the determinants of child nutritional status—national income, democracy, food supplies, health services, and education.

The study indicates that three broad socioeconomic factors help explain this "Asian Enigma": women's status, sanitation, and urbanization. Women's status makes by far the greatest contribution to the regional gap in children's nutritional status. It plays this role not only because it is lower in South Asia than in SSA, but mainly because its positive impact is stronger in South Asia—making its costs in terms of child malnutrition far higher in that region. The implication of the study's empirical results is clear: in the interest of sustainably improving the nutritional status of children, women's status should be improved in all regions. Doing so is especially urgent for South Asia, followed by SSA.

Accomplishing this task requires policies that eradicate gender discrimination and policies that reduce power inequalities between women and men by proactively promoting catch-up for women. Examples include enabling women to gain access to new resources, implementing cash transfer programs that promote girls' education and health care, introducing technologies that save household labor, subsidizing child care for working parents, and initiating programs to improve the nutritional status of adolescent girls and young women.

In communities that resist shifts in the power balance between genders, policies can mitigate the negative effects of the imbalance, rather than addressing it directly. Targeting health services to communities where women's status is low is one example of this indirect approach. The study also warns that improving women's status can lead to reduced breastfeeding, which is harmful to child nutrition. Efforts to improve women's status, therefore, must be accompanied by efforts to protect, support, and promote breastfeeding.

This research shows unequivocally that making a decision at the policy level to improve women's status produces significant benefits. Not only does a woman's own nutritional status improve, but so too does the nutritional status of her young children. Raising women's status today is a powerful force for improving the health, longevity, mental and physical capacity, and productivity of the next generation of young adults.

The indicators of social empowerment of women include the base of gender inequality, sex ratios, life expectancy rates and fertility rates which shows the general status of women in terms of literacy, economic growth, availability of health care and birth control facilities, educational status of women, age at marriage, literacy rates and participation of women outside the home. Gender inequality is a worldwide phenomenon and leaving aside some Nordic nations, gender inequality base reflects very poorly for almost all major countries in the world.

Sex ratio is against women in Asia and even though life expectancy has gone up around the world including in Asia it has not improved the overall status of women in much of the world. Same is the case with fertility rates which have declined in some regions including Asia but the positive impact of this change on women around the world is not as much as that was desired. Glaring gender gap exists in terms of literacy rates though it is narrowing across Asia. The figures for female literacy rates are not at all encouraging in the developing world. Now let's focus on various issues that are closely associated with the social empowerment of women

SOCIAL EMPOWERMENT OF WOMEN

Violence against women is a real fact and we need to acknowledge the real tragedy behind this crime. It totally shatters the women from the core psychologically as well as physically. It is time that community development and feminist values are made an integral aspect of empowerment of women. Women need to be educated and made aware of their rights and they should be encouraged to stand united against the biased and discriminating social environment which directly and indirectly affects their psychological and physical self. Education and awareness would be a big step towards the fight against gender based violence.

Only through education and awareness we can connect with the vast majority of women living in various parts of the world and prevent them from falling pray to the numerous forms of possible violence in their life. We have to accept the fact that women are constantly under the threat of violence from various sides. The oppressive structures of the society need to be changed and oppression of women need to be stopped but it won't happen through some quick fix solutions. The change can be only possible through social empowerment of women at the grass root level with education and awareness.

ISSUES RELATED TO SOCIAL EMPOWERMENT OF WOMEN

When we talk of social empowerment of women then we are actually addressing various issues which might be applicable to different parts of the world for improving the overall status of women. Among them the prominent issues relate to education for women, health for women, nutrition for women, drinking water and sanitation for women and their family, housing and shelter for women and their family, environment and the connection with women, participation of women in the field of science and technology, care for women under difficult circumstances, fighting the violence against women and rights of the girl child.

EDUCATION FOR WOMEN

We need to accept the fact that gender inequality and discrimination has been the norm of the society and in this regard it touches all aspects of the life of women. Education and training for women is one of the major goals of social empowerment of women which need to be universally made applicable to all parts of the world. This will definitely enhance the awareness in women which in turn will increase her confidence. A confident and well aware woman would be able to tackle inequality and discrimination in a far better way than an ill-equipped and ill-trained woman. But on the other hand we have to accept the fact that women and girls never had equal access to education as men and boys have. Illiteracy is the highest among the female of the population.

Women are far behind in terms of having gainful occupation or vocation because of lack of skills and education. There is an enormous gender gap in secondary and higher education. Moreover religious and caste equations have made things worse in many parts of the world. The work has to start at the grass root levels. The educational systems need to be made more accessible to women at grass root levels and they need to be revamped to include gender sensitive educational system which prevents sex stereotyping and discrimination. Social organizations can play a major role in universalizing education at the basic ground level. This can be achieved through increasing the enrollment and retention rates of girl child in the primary schools and offering quality education and skills to them so that they can stand up on their feet and live a dignified life.

HEALTHCARE FOR WOMEN

Coming to the health of women we need to understand that women are facing very difficult times at all stages of their life cycle. It is sad to note that a section of our society is highly prejudiced against the girl child and in fact can be labelled as criminals of the highest order as they practice the heinous crime of female feticide. Then we have the problem of high infant mortality and maternal mortality and one of the major reasons for this being the early child marriages. Quality health care for women is not available in many parts of the world. Women's right to informed choice regarding her reproductive rights is another area which needs attention.

Talking of reproductive rights women even don't have affordable choice of family planning methods. Education and awareness in this regard is nonexistent and absent. Women are vulnerable to sexually transmitted diseases and other endemic, infectious and communicable diseases. HIV/AIDS is another major problem. Women's traditional knowledge of health care and nutrition, alternative systems of medicine are actually underutilised and not recognized. It is necessary to recognize these alternative systems and integrate them with the main stream health care systems to make it work in tandem. This shall help in providing reasonable and quality health care for women.

NUTRITION, DRINKING WATER, SANITATION AND HOUSING

For women, from the stage of infancy and childhood to the stage of adolescent and reproductive phase the risk of malnutrition is the highest. There is a close link between the health of an adolescent girl who becomes a pregnant and lactating woman latter and the health of the infant child. Macro and micro nutrients are needed for these special conditions but they are not available to the vast majority of women. In house the women and girl child face great discrimination as regards to good nutritious food. This happens in the early growth period of a child as well as to a pregnant and lactating woman.

Other major issues are drinking water and sanitation especially in rural areas and urban slums. Housing and shelter are also area of attention including adequate and safe accommodation for single women, heads of the households, working women, students, apprentices and trainees. These are very real issues of the very real world that we live in. Without addressing these basic needs we cannot think about any meaningful step towards social empowerment of women.

WOMEN AND ENVIRONMENT CONSERVATION

Social empowerment of women and environment is closely linked. Women can play a major role in conservation and restoration of the environment. Rural women use unconventional and nature friendly source of energy in the form of animal dung, crop waste and fuel wood. Using of solar energy, biogas, and smokeless stoves can really help the rural women as they can act as environmental friendly tools.

PARTICIPATION OF WOMEN IN DEVELOPMENT OF SCIENCE AND TECHNOLOGY

Women's empowerment cannot be complete without their equitable participation in science and technology. Women have special role to play in the area of science and technology. They can bring a wave of creative and generative energy in the field of science and technology. Today their participation is restricted and limited to very less numbers because of widespread discrimination at the basic education levels and lack of opportunities for pursuing higher studies. Reducing drudgery with the help of science and technology is another major area of importance for freeing women from the never ending domestic chores and making her contribute to the mainstream of the society.

HELPING WOMEN IN DIFFICULT TIMES

Women in difficult circumstances need special attention. These include women in extreme poverty, destitute women, women in conflict situations, women affected by natural calamities, women in less developed regions, disabled widows, elderly women, single women in difficult circumstances, women heading households, women who are displaced from employment, migrant women who are victims of marital violence, deserted women and prostitutes.

These women are in difficult circumstances which are not of their own making. They are the victims of the selfish streak of society. It is ironical to note that women become the primary pray for all the malice and sins of the society. It is time to reverse this phenomenon. Organizations especially the grass root level social organizations should come in large numbers to help these women who are at the receiving end for a sin which is not of their making.

FIGHTING AGAINST VIOLENCE AND DISCRIMINATION

Violence against women is heinous crime against humanity. Violence can be both physical and psychological and it happens at the domestic front as well as at other levels of the society. It is in fact openly practiced in many societies through various forms which include customs and traditions. Sexual harassment at work, dowry related violence and trafficking of women and girls are different types of violence against women. Discrimination against women starts when they are just children. Girl child discrimination is the most prevalent form of harassment seen from the early age of a child.

Parental sex selection, female foeticide, female infanticide, child marriage, child abuse including sexual and psychological abuse and child prostitution are the many kinds of violence and discrimination against the girl child that is seen within the home as well as the society. Special awareness and education programmes needs to be formulated and implemented at every level to fight the violence against women. Strict laws need to be formulated to fight the crime of violence against women. More than formulating the laws the priority should be to implement and enforce these laws so that we can root out violence against women. This is necessary for any meaningful social empowerment of women.

India is a country of rich natural resources and talented human resources and yet its dream of becoming self- sufficient and considered a 'developed country' rather than a 'developing country' seems a distant reality due to the complexity of its problems. India, the second most populous country in the world, has no more than 2.5% of global land but is the home of 1/6th of the world's population. Its high population density makes it appear as a resource poor country despite its significant achievements in the fields of medicine, agriculture, industry, literature, nuclear physics and information technology.

One of the reasons is that 36% of its population still lives below the poverty line. Majority of Indian population lives in rural areas. (72% rural as compared to 28% urban population) where the pace of progress in literacy, education, employment and technology is slow; urban areas get the maximum benefits of the progress. The patriarchal system prevalent in India (except in one state) makes women the worst victims of poverty as their multifaceted responsibilities include that of a carer, giver and a protector.

Women are socialized to be self- sacrificing from childhood onwards to give first and take only if somebody chooses to give or if there is something extra to give. Women work more at home as well as at the work place, to take care of the families particularly men and children, but they earn much less than men because majority of them are engaged in self-employed, unprotected work with no social security benefits. This is more true among those women belong to the low socio-economic groups in urban slums and rural areas.

Women receive the minimum benefits of health care, nutrition and economic gains which is evident from the fact that level of anaemia among women ranges from 50-80% which is a major contributor of the high maternal morbidity and mortality in India. Although India has made considerable progress in the economic sphere, it is one of the few countries where men significantly outnumber women. Maternal mortality rate in rural areas figures among the world's highest, and communicable diseases and malnutrition account for majority of the disease burden.

Women and girls, particularly the poor, are more susceptible to and trapped in the cycle of disease and illness primarily due to their nutritional status being affected by unequal access to food, health care and heavy work demands. To add to this, very often, they do not receive medical treatment before the illness is well advanced. In India the nutrition and health status of women is abysmally low. The

National Nutrition Monitoring Bureau (NNMB) survey (1990) done in India shows that women's calorie requirement after the age of 10 years is not adequately met.

This itself indicates whether women are victims or decision-makers. The poor health status of women in India is mainly due to patriarchy and other socio-cultural constraints leading to her secondary status at home and poor health. It is a bitter reality that in India women's health and nutrition is inextricably linked to social, cultural and economic factors. In India when the food intake of the "privileged" and "underprivileged" males and females was compared it was realized that 24% of the females were malnourished in the privileged group, while 74% were malnourished among the underprivileged.

The per cent age for males was lower in both cases; 14% among the privileged and 67% in the underprivileged. In some cultural and social contexts in India, women are prohibited from eating essential quality food particularly during menstruation, pregnancy and lactation such as milk and green leafy vegetables. In India parents who wish to postpone the marriage of their daughters often limit their food intake because they fear that girls who are well nourished will mature at a younger age, and this will place them at a vulnerability of early marriage. Let us have a look at the present scenario, to get a picture of how women are treated in community and families all over South Asia.

WOMEN AS VICTIMS OF RELIGION, CULTURE AND SOCIETY

Indian social customs and traditions dictates differential attitudes, behaviour and practices related to their food entitlements - girl babies tend to be breast fed for shorter periods of time and as they get older receive smaller portions of food, particularly quality foods, e.g. milk, fruits and vegetables, than that of boys. From a very early age itself, girls are taught to deny themselves of their own needs. When serving food, women serve larger portions to their husbands and male children first only then do they feed their female children and they tend to ignore the importance of their own food requirements. In the Indian context, due to the patriarchal set up.

Women are also expected to follow several social and religious rituals, which limit their food intake without reducing her work load. In addition, Indian women are socialized to eat less, last, the least and leftovers. This gender discrimination begins in childhood itself, which is further compounded by food taboos, and religious beliefs. Indian girls and women also fast on several days of the week for social and religious reasons. While some amount of fasting may be good for the body, this is generally practiced by girls and women looking for a good husband, for the long life of their husband or for bearing a male child.

Though fasting itself may not be harmful, but when undertaken by underfed, undernourished girls and women, it could have disastrous effects on women's health. Who decides to fast? On the surface it seems like these decisions are made by the girls and women themselves, but on deeper probing it will be realized that it is the socialization family, norms and peer pressure, which is responsible.

Regular fasting without reducing the work load depletes the already undernourished women of critical micro nutrients which not only affects her physical health, and well being but also affects her future storage. The high morbidity among Indian older women is a cause for concern in India. Indian women particularly in rural and tribal areas start looking old and haggard at an early age and suffer from osteoporosis and arthritis in later life. This depletion affects the health of women making them more prone to infectious and other fatal illnesses in later life.

COOKING FOOD "ARE WOMEN DECISION MAKERS OR VICTIMS"

In India it is commonly believed that since women generally cook the food at home they are the decision- makers on what to cook and what to eat. In some families they are also called "Queen of the kitchen". However on deeper probing, we realize that while women are only doing the labour of cooking, the decision of what to cook is generally made by the choices of their husbands or families.

This is amplified by the women who report that *"when my husband is away, I feel tired to cook, and do not cook a full meal"*. This clearly indicates that the food choices are male dominated and the women do not exercise their right of cooking food of her choice. This is true of women from all classes, caste and creed. In some Indian communities, the men also purchase the food thereby ensuring that whatever food is cooked at home is of their choice.

WOMEN AS VICTIMS OF OVERWORK

Women are continuously working in villages in fields often to grow and cook the food, which is consumed by the entire family. Even though they are working tirelessly, travelling long distances for fetching water and firewood required for cooking, however at the end of the day she rarely gets to eat a balanced meal, as a result of socialization and poverty at home. Over work has the severest consequence in women during the child-bearing years. Typically women work until late in their pregnancy depriving them of adequate food and rest, at a time when their nutritional requirements are the highest.

This leads to a situation in which most women become anaemic, placing them at high risk of unsafe delivery. If the women do survive the childbirth, she has to immediately start her domestic and productive tasks, before she has adequate time to rest and recuperate. In addition several restrictions are put on women as a result of food taboos which grossly affect women's decision about food intake particularly during menstruation, pregnancy and lactation. Some existing food taboos and myths are given below.

In a study conducted by CHETNA on perceptions of men on violence, 40% men revealed that they beat their wives because they did not like the quality and the kind of food served and 14% violence took place when it was not served on time. This also lead to lot of physical and mental torture of women. So whenever women do make a choice of food recipes themselves, or are delayed in serving food, they paid a heavy price for it. In some joint families young brides feel shy to eat or cook food of their liking and live continuously in the mental fear whether the food that is cooked would be appreciated as they are aware of the consequences.

This is because cash crops (Tobacco, sugar and cotton) have replaced the coarse cereals and pulses in several instances. This affects women and children the most because women have to manage households on a limited amount of money which is given to them. Nutritious food has become more expensive due to its unavailability in the villages. In case of use of milk powder for infants and children, the dilution of milk was found to be far beyond the recommended level on the tin because they felt that since the tin was expensive it would last for longer period if they diluted it as a result of which, children particularly girls received less nutrition. Whenever, there is food shortage at the household level and it is the women who suffer the most, as they feed the children and husband first, then the other family members, and have to remain herself be satisfied by eating the last, the least and leftovers.

WOMEN AS VICTIMS OF THE POOR IMPLEMENTATION OF PUBLIC DISTRIBUTION SYSTEM (PDS)

In order to address poverty, a variety of cereals, pulses and sugar are sold at low cost through the Public Distribution System (PDS). However often these are sold by the fair price shops in the open market, thereby depriving the poor communities, particularly women and children of the essential micro nutrients. However, it has been observed that whenever women from the village level monitor the distribution of food grains through these fair price shops, women's health and nutritional status does improve.

Women as Victims of Disasters

In disaster conditions like famines, floods, war, drought etc. women and children's nutritional status is the most severely affected. This again is related to the quality and quantity of food available at the family and the community level, of which the women gets the least share.

Women as Victims of Media

Even in families where women can afford to buy food, women particularly young girls choices are affected by media which portrays beautiful images of thin/slim girls, prompting many teenagers to eat less food, in order to remain slim. From young age itself this leads to a deficiency of iron, proteins, calories and calcium. In an urban survey area located in University 27% of girls were found to have multiple nutritional deficiencies like iron, protein, etc., which may not show any disastrous effect in the youth, however it can result in particularly dangerous effects in older age, particularly during the child-bearing phase. Indian girls/women begin with a nutrition disadvantage of being underfed from infancy onwards leading to small height for weight.

Height and weight of Indian women in comparison with their counter parts in other countries is much less. Average weight of an adult woman should be 58 kgs. In Gujarat State of India, the average weight of adult woman is 49 and height is 157 cms. which indicates their poor intake of nutritional food in the life cycle. This is not only observed in poor families but also in the economically better off communities. While some of this may be genetic, a large majority of it is affected by cultural and social myths including food taboos etc. The effects of these are enhanced during pregnancy and child bearing years.

Women as Victims of Superstitions and Beliefs

The illiteracy in India is extremely high. It ranges from 20-70% in different States. The exposure of women to the outside world is also limited. This affects her choice of food and its adequate consumption. Though fruits and vegetables are grown in some villages, women do not consume them mainly due to economic reasons (since they are expensive), however sometimes it is also due to misconceptions and lack of information. Many locally grown fruits and vegetables are nutritious both when consumed as food or as traditional medicine.

Ironically it is the very women who work tirelessly in the fields for growing of these vegetables, cereals, pulses, that do not consume them leading to malnutrition and ill health. Women also spend a lot of time and energy in caring and mulching cows, however the milk that is produced is sold to co-operative/dairies, rather then being consumed at home particularly by the women herself or the girl children.

Even the fruit of her labour in terms of money does not come back to her as the money is spent often by the husband on alcohol and other material products. Decision-making particularly to make her domestic tasks easier are also ignored or hampered by her lack of choice or control on the money.

Looking after the needs of her family particularly the men and children and the older persons first, women often sleep hungry and has also been observed to consume just water and a piece of bread in the night. Is this is an indication of her being the decision-maker? So we can see from the above that the women are victims not decision makers at the family, community, societal level and lack critical decision making power on what to cook, how to cook and what to eat, which results in depriving women's prime nutrition which she rightfully deserves.

9

Gender and Education

EMPOWERING EDUCATION

The Empowering Education (EE) Program, which began in Ukraine, has operated as a network program since 1999. EE is coordinated jointly by the Women's Information and Consultative Center (WICC) and the NWP. EE is an innovative grassroots popular education program that develops awareness and sensitivity of gender and human rights and builds self-esteem, conflict transformation, and critical thinking skills. The largest target audience for training sessions is still secondary school students, but the program also works with many other diverse groups, such as disabled people, journalists, lesbian youth, rural families, ethnic minorities, refugees, religious leaders, "pregnant parents," HIV positive people, and IV drug users.

The program has a network of trainers who conduct trainings in schools, some universities, and non-formal settings in Ukraine, Azerbaijan, Georgia, Kazakhstan, Kyrgyzstan, Lithuania, Moldova, Tajikistan, and Uzbekistan. In 2002 and 2003, trainings were also conducted with Burmese diaspora working in Thai border areas, and with Indonesian activists and Afghani educators. Participants from Armenia, Mongolia, and Russia have also taken part in some network events in the past. As the coordinating body of the program, WICC provides advanced training of trainers and technical assistance to individual countries in order to strengthen the local training capacity, and hopes to create a cadre of global trainers.

GENDER EQUITY IN EDUCATION

In 2003, the NWP and OSI's Education Support Program (ESP) collaborated to produce Open Minds: Opportunities for Gender Equity in Education in Central/South Eastern Europe and the Former Soviet Union, a regional overview on gender equity in education in Central Europe, South Eastern Europe, and the former Soviet Union. Filling a major gap in current educational reform debates, Open Minds provides policymakers, administrators, teachers, parents, and advocates with a useful tool to influence policy change. The report provides specific recommendations for advocacy and practical interventions at both the policy and school levels, such as calls for increased gender balance in texts, teachers' practices, and in school leadership positions.

It outlines necessary changes in the education policy-making, implementation, and monitoring processes, including increased analysis of education statistics and augmented roles for teacher-training institutions, international organizations and NGOs in generating new education policy and practices. Open Minds argues that while there are significant challenges to gender-sensitive educational reform, there are also resources within the region on which to build. These resources include a strong commitment to educational reform, a focus on critical thinking, and a body of knowledge on curriculum development and innovative pedagogy developed within gender studies programs and women's NGOs in the last decade.

GENDER STUDIES

The NWP believes that gender/women's studies programs instill critical thinking skills, serve as an analytic resource for the women's movement, and help promote women's perspectives in emerging democracies. In partnership with many of the Soros foundations, the NWP has supported the development, introduction, institutionalization, and networking of such programs in Central and Eastern Europe and the former Soviet Union since 1997. In 1998, the NWP organized the inaugural conference on gender studies for countries in transition, bringing together 140 women from 30 countries, and also created a Library Core Collections program and a Translations project.

The three-year library program awarded more than 100 collections of approximately 50 books each to gender studies programs, libraries, and NGOs. The four-year Translations project awarded more than 80 grants to translate classic texts each year into local languages, focusing on such themes as advanced gender studies works, women at risk, ethnic/minority women, women in Muslim societies, and globalization. In 1999, the NWP collaborated with Central European University's Gender and Culture Program to produce the region's first Gender Studies Directory and also convened the first regional women's history conference in Minsk, Belarus, which resulted in the publication of the anthology *Gendered Histories from Eastern Europe*.

The NWP also co-funded grants to seed gender studies programs, and awarded women's studies fellowships to 36 scholars from Albania, Azerbaijan, Croatia, Moldova, Mongolia, Russia, Ukraine, Slovenia, and Serbia to recognized women's studies centers in nine cities, including Kharkov, Prague, Moscow, Bucharest, and Budapest. Mainstreaming gender studies into higher education has been a priority, both for sustainability and the transformation of educational systems in reform. In 2003, the NWP supported the launch of two regional gender studies efforts: (1) the South Eastern European Network for Gender Studies in collaboration with the Research Center for Gender Studies (Macedonia) and the Belgrade Center for Women's Studies (Serbia); and (2) a gender studies network focused primarily on Central Asia and the Caucuses in development with the Institute for Gender and Social Policy (IGSP-Russia) and the Women's Program of Open Society Institute Assistance Foundation-Uzbekistan (OSIAF-Uzbekistan).

In collaboration with IGSP and OSIAF-Uzbekistan, the NWP sponsored the "Gender Education: Theory and Practice" conference in November 2003. Over 100 participants attended the two-day conference, which engaged gender studies and Empowering Education scholars/practitioners in examining the next stages of development for gender education in Central Asia and the Caucuses, Mongolia, Moldova, Russia, and Ukraine. Among the priorities identified were: regional summer schools; cross-border collaborations; databases of experts, trainers, and literature; translation of texts; Internet and information resources; curriculum development on women in Muslim societies and women in post-conflict zones; regional networking and exchange, among others. For the upcoming years, the NWP's primary focus in gender studies will be on institutionalizing high quality programs in two regions—South Eastern Europe and Central Asia/the Caucuses/Mongolia.

WOMEN'S ORAL HISTORIES

Central to the NWP's mission and programs on gender and education is the belief that open societies cannot fully develop without the contribution of women's critical thinking and perspectives. The Women's Oral History Program in Central Asia, the Caucasus, Russia and Ukraine supports national and regional women's oral-history projects to preserve the "unofficial" realities and experiences of women in post-Soviet regions. Women's oral history work often allows women to speak about difficult realities that are impossible to articulate in other contexts, and it is an accessible and empowering tool for preserving and presenting women's realities to their own communities, to international academic and politically informed audiences interested in the region, and to global women's networks.

The process is empowering for both the interviewer and interviewee. In addition to supporting oral history workshops since 2000, the NWP includes an ongoing mentorship component, linking researchers with workshop faculty. The NWP and the national women's programs have supported over

10 research projects/publications, including a methodological reader, a nine-volume multi-ethnic study of women in Georgia, and a compendium of original research. In 2003, the national Central Asia/Caucasus/Russia/Ukraine women's oral history research projects were published and distributed in local languages. The NWP produced a booklet, *To Look at Life through Women's Eyes*, which provided a small sampling of these projects. In addition, the NWP and the Women's Program of the Soros Foundation-Kyrgyzstan published and distributed the sub-regional women's oral history reader.

In 2004, the NWP will disseminate Volume II of the Women's Oral History Reader, including country research results (in Russian and some English translations). The publication will be organized around key themes that emerged in many of the interviews: women as members of ethnic minority groups; women in conflict and post-conflict situations; the impact of transition on women; violence against women; rural women; and women's memory and history. Priorities for the upcoming years include integrating oral history research into gender studies curriculum development and teaching in established gender studies centers and programs; supporting seed grants for projects that focus on minority women and women's cross-ethnic experiences; adding new regions and promoting cross-cultural women's oral history action research projects.

The current development policy emphasis on human resource development in general, and female education in particular, is couched largely in terms of economic efficiency and social welfare arguments. The rationale for investment in education tends to be based on economic arguments about rates of return and efficient allocation of resources, using neo-classical models of household decision-making, where rational, maximising investment and consumption decisions are made on the basis of quantifiable costs and benefits.

An extension of this argument, but still from a mainstream economic perspective, is that investment in education provides social benefits which are not captured by individuals or households, and which therefore justify state subsidies to education. This argument is used particularly to justify greater subsidies to female education, since, it is held that social benefits to female education (e.g. reduced fertility, improved health etc.) are greater than those to male education.

PRIVATE RETURNS TO EDUCATION

Private returns are those which accrue to individuals or households from investment in education. These are generally held to be similar for boys and girls, and are usually measured by increased earnings as a result of higher levels of education. If rates of return to education are similar for boys and girls, this then begs the question as to why parents appear to under-invest in girls' education. There are several possible reasons which have been put forward to explain this:

- The costs of educating girls are higher than those of educating boys;
- Boys are themselves more able to contribute to their own education through market earnings;
- The returns to educational investment do not accrue directly to parents, who make the investment decision, but are only accessed by parents through inter-generational transfers - it is argued that girls are less likely to support their parents in old age or contribute to the household, because they marry into other households, at least in patrilineal systems;
- Parents have imperfect information about the returns to female education, and/or regard the risks associated with investment in female education as greater (this also relates to the above point);

There are other, non-economic, constraints which prevent parents from investing in female education - usually represented as variables such as 'culture' or 'religion'. Girls' education is sometimes argued to be more costly than boys' because of higher:

- Direct costs (e.g. for uniforms - especially where seclusion is required - or provision for safe transport);

- Indirect or opportunity costs because girl children do more labour in the household than boy children.

Direct private costs of education vary according to educational level, generally rising at secondary and tertiary levels, such that the disincentives to female education may be higher, further up the educational system. Schultz (1991) has argued, on the basis of evidence from a number of countries, that when appropriate methodologies are used, private returns "tend to be at least as high for women as they are for men, varying from 30 to 10 per cent in the less and more developed countries respectively'.

Schultz gives the following reasons to explain why, given these high returns, investment in female education is low: "the structure of aggregated demand for labour... economic constraints such as per capita income, the costs of delivering school services and the structure of regulations and incentives in public (and private) education systems, and the preferences of parents who may fail to value increased productivity of females as highly as that of males, or to appreciate the enhanced non-market productivity of better educated women).

This places the policy emphasis on reducing the costs of and changing the structures of delivery of schooling services, on the one hand, and interventions to change parental attitudes and household behaviour on the other. Herz *et al* (1991), whilst using the same basic framework, have a somewhat different emphasis: they argue that the returns to female education may be lower than those to male education for reasons which have not been accounted for in many estimates to date, i.e. because of labour market conditions, biases in allocations of resources, macro-economic policy distortions, or higher direct costs of girls' schooling or opportunity costs of girls' labour.

They argue that a vicious circle ensues whereby: 'men earn more, making the returns to male schooling higher, so boys are sent to school more often than girls. Girls then grow up lacking the education they need to compete. Cultural traditions may reflect and reinforce economics, especially in poor rural settings. This suggests the need for action at the level of macro-economic policy and the labour market, as well as directly in education policy.

SOCIAL RETURNS

Beyond the private gains to education through increased earnings and improved productivity, there are social benefits (externalities) which are not captured at the individual level, and thus, according to conventional welfare economic reasoning, justify state subsidies. The social payoff of female education is, it is widely argued, higher than that of male education - through the improved health and education of children and reduced fertility.

Social rates of return to female education are generally thought to be highest at primary level, and lower at secondary and particularly tertiary levels. There is some more recent evidence, however, that social rates of return at secondary level may be higher than previously thought. Herz *et al* (1991) present considerable evidence of the links between female educations and, for example, child health, child education and family size, to support their claim of higher social returns to female education.

However, the difficulty of quantifying health and other social benefits means that these wider externalities are often not included in calculations, thus tending to lower estimates of social rates of return to female education. However, not all commentators are as enthusiastic about the externalities to female education. Behrman (1991) holds that they are not as great as often claimed and, in fact, are realised mainly as private benefits.

Furthermore, to the extent that there are externalities, he argues that these might be gained in a more cost-effective way by spending directly on child health or family planning, rather than female education. The social benefits to female education, whether privately captured or seen as externalities, tend to be narrowly defined in terms of child health and welfare and fertility reduction. Improvements in women's decision-making capacity and ability to participate in social and economic life, for example, are rarely direct considerations in such discussions.

EFFICIENCY, EQUITY OR EMPOWERMENT

Efficiency and welfare focused approaches lead to an instrumental view of education in general, and female education in particular, usually seeing female education as a means to increasing child welfare and reducing fertility. Relying on such arguments as a rationale for female education may prove problematic, if, as some researchers claim, the external benefits to female education are limited, or if they are less apparent at higher levels of education. This may ultimately weaken the rationale for female education - particularly beyond certain levels.

There is insufficient emphasis on the need for female education to increase women's social and political participation, or raise their aspirations, for example. Economic approaches to investment in education also tend to focus heavily on the need for skills and knowledge acquisition for employment, or on the enhancement of productivity brought about through increased education, rather than education as a developmental process in itself, aimed at nurturing critical thinking or creativity. A narrow focus on education for employment may, in the longer-term, serve to reinforce women's concentration in particular areas of employment, since this approach will lead to the selection of women for areas of skills training relevant to existing employment opportunities.

Consideration should also be given to strategies for tackling patterns of gender segregation and discrimination in the labour market and in access to other productive resources such as credit, land, and other inputs. There are also equity arguments for promoting female education. Here, attention is focused on ensuring equal access by gender to educational opportunities. Beyond this, there is some attention to issues of gender stereotyping in curricula and fields of study, and on women's participation in decision-making about education (i.e. in educational administration and management). This approach implies that once equal access to existing forms of education provision is assured for girls, the problem will be more or less solved.

Mazumdar, however, contends that: the critical issue in analysing the inter-relationship between education and women's status is not only the question of access but that of content, values and structures of educational systems. Mazumdar (1989) characterises the current education system in Asia as a compromise between indigenous knowledge systems, western imposed scientific-rational education values and control systems; and movements arising out of reactions to imperialism, which include liberal democratic, secular and socialist as well as religious, cultural revivalist and fundamentalist movements.

Projections of appropriate gender roles, are, she argues, central to this compromise. Radical approaches to development have questioned the elitist, hierarchical systems and western-based scientific-rational values which are promoted through formal education structures in much of the developing world, and have stressed an alternative approach to education based on popular participation, self-development and empowerment or in the Freirian tradition 'conscientisation'.

Feminist critiques of mainstream education provision have also stressed its promotion of patriarchal values and western capitalist development models, its negation of indigenous knowledge bases (particularly those of rural women) and consequent perpetuation of unsustainable development patterns (e.g. Jain, cited in Mazumdar, 1989).

Asia and the Pacific in the Global Context

As discussed in the previous section, returns to girls education may be greater than those to boys', yet paradoxically, many countries invest less in girls education. The gender gap is worst in Africa, Middle East and South Asia and particularly worrying at secondary level. Once countries reach a certain per capita income, the gender gap tends to close. However, below $2000 per capita GNI (Gross National Income), variation in education provision for and attainment of women is considerable.

In both cases, whilst Asia as a whole is second only to Latin America, this is primarily because of the positive experience of East Asia. When South Asia is considered separately, it fares worst of all the regions shown, particularly at secondary level. Moreover, the graphs show that, whilst considerable progress has been made towards gender parity since 1970, this progress slowed in the period 1980-7. Discussion of Asia and the Pacific as a region is problematic, given the wide variation in levels of economic development, overall levels of educational enrolment and gender parity in enrolment. South Asia is clearly the sub-region with the poorest performance, with the exceptions of Sri Lanka and the Maldives.

East Asia fares best, with the NICs (i.e. Taiwan, Korea, Hong Kong, Singapore) reaching levels of education on a par with western industrialised market economies. In Southeast Asia, general education levels are also relatively high in most countries and gender disparity not wide. With the exceptions of Papua New Guinea and the Solomon Islands, primary enrolment ratios and literacy rates are high in the Pacific. However, there is very little consolidated information about gender differentials in education in the Pacific region and detailed data is scarce. Similarly, detailed information was lacking on Laos, Mongolia, and Cambodia. No enrolment data could be found on Cambodia. National participation rates, even when broken down by gender, obscure regional and other differentials.

For example, female participation rates in education in India in the mid-1980s, ranged from nine per cent in Rajasthan to 80 per cent in Kerala. Elsewhere, regional and rural-urban differentials are also striking. Within urban areas, slum neighbourhoods also experience poor access to education. In rural areas, tribal groups or those working on plantations may be particularly disadvantaged. Ethnicity is another factor which often differentiates access to education, often strongly related to regional differentials, and which interplays with gender biases.

SOUTH ASIA

South Asia is the region where, apart from Sub-Saharan Africa, girls education lags most severely behind boys'. Gender differences in primary level enrolment range from 15 to 50 per cent age points. There has been considerable expansion of enrolments between 1960 and 1987 (from 51 to 78 per cent at primary level) but progress has been slower than in most regions and educational expenditure in the region remains low. At post-primary level South Asia has the widest gender gap of any third world region.

One third of boys but only one fifth of girls attend secondary school - this is the cumulative effect of disadvantage at primary level and of high drop out rates of girls - although data in this area are scanty. Poor education indicators and wide gender disparities in South Asian countries in part reflects their low per capita incomes, agrarian based economies and relatively low female labour force participation rates in most South Asian countries, but are also a function of low educational spending, and pervasive patterns of sex segregation and gender discrimination.

Low female life expectancy (compared to male - the only region in the world where this is the case) and imbalance in sex ratios in the population have been widely documented in the region, reflecting patterns of gender discrimination in the allocation of food and spending on health. Socio-cultural factors restricting women's mobility and autonomy (e.g. purdah, dowry, early marriage) are also major constraints to women's participation in education in the region.

EAST ASIA

East Asia has the fastest economic growth rate and highest education level of any third world region. Most countries in the region fall into the middle income category (excluding Cambodia China, Laos and Vietnam, which are low income countries). However, within the region, there is a wide range of income levels, from US $200 (1992 estimate) in Cambodia (EIU, 1993) to US $7410 in Singapore (1987).

The fast economic and technological growth in East Asian countries is in part a result of their relatively high levels of education and growing pool of post-primary educated workers. In this region, there is near universal primary education and two thirds literacy on average. The mean level of education of the labour force is high, ranging between 4.5 (China) and 8.8 years (Hong Kong) in the early 1980s. Spending on education as per cent age of GNP is generally high, at over two per cent, reaching as high as 7.8 for Malaysia (1986/7).

However, per cent age expenditure appears to bear little direct relation to progress made in extending educational opportunity. For example, the Philippines, with an expenditure of two per cent of GNP, has done better than Malaysia at nearly eight per cent of GNP. East Asian countries are, on the whole, highly patriarchal societies. However, some indicators of gender inequality are less marked than elsewhere in Asia. Women have a high and rising life expectancy, in some cases several years higher than men's.

The education gender gap is relatively low and women comprise larger share of labour force than in any other third world region, ranging from 31 per cent of the total labour force in Indonesia to 47 per cent in Vietnam. On average, women's literacy rates in East Asia are well over 50 per cent, and in several countries, they are over 80 per cent. The stock of educated adults still contains more educated males than females, however. In all countries, in East Asia, at all educational levels, there are more educated men than women.

In East Asia, the gender gap at primary level closed by 1987. About half of school age boys and almost half of school age girls attend secondary school. By the mid-late 1980s, women's share of secondary enrolment was over 40 per cent in all East Asian countries. In some countries in East Asia, there are more girls than boys at secondary (e.g. Philippines, Sri Lanka) and even tertiary (Malaysia and the Philippines) levels.

In East Asia, whilst gender equality of access to education remains an issue at secondary and particularly tertiary levels in some countries, gender constraints in education relate increasingly to curriculum bias and gender differentials in fields of study at secondary and higher levels, and to subsequent labour market opportunities. Despite significant progress, gender differences in education [in East Asia] persist, particularly in the distribution of male and females by field of study at the secondary and higher levels. For example, girls tend to take traditionally female dominated courses such as nutrition, nursing, and teacher training. In the Philippines, more than 90 per cent of the students in each of these fields were women. Males tend to dominate in engineering, law, agriculture and technology.

TRENDS IN ENROLMENT AND LITERACY IN ASIA

PRIMARY ENROLMENT

There may be inconsistencies in the data across both countries and time periods, due to different sources or methods of data collection. For this reason, it is difficult to make more than the broadest of comparisons. Gross enrolment ratios are given in most cases; net figures are given in brackets where available, but as noted above, these are limited and thus cannot be used as a basis for comparison. These are: China, Hong Kong, Indonesia, Republic of Korea, Mongolia, the Philippines, Singapore, Sri Lanka, and Vietnam.

There are also several countries with GERs approaching 100, with gender parity, e.g. Thailand and Malaysia. India, Laos and Nepal have GERs of over 100 for males, but a considerable gender gap (over 25 per cent age points for India and Laos and over 50 per cent age points for Nepal). In the case of India, there has been a narrowing of the gender gap since 1970, whilst for Laos it has remained more or less the same, even showing some widening after 1985. The gender gap in education in Nepal remains the widest of any country in Asia at both primary and secondary levels.

In some countries in Asia, GERs of 100 and gender parity (or near gender parity) had already been achieved by 1970, e.g. Hong Kong, Republic of Korea, Mongolia, the Philippines,

Singapore, and Sri Lanka, and have since maintained similar levels of education. In other countries, e.g. Indonesia, Thailand, UPE with gender parity was achieved by 1980, although in the latter case, more recent data cast some doubt on this. Similarly, for Malaysia, while 1985 data show UPE with gender parity, 1990 data show lower GERs.

For other countries (China, Vietnam), data is not available before 1980, and thus trends are difficult to establish. Recent transition to market-based economies in both these cases may be leading to pressures on access to education, particularly for women. In Laos, similarly, data for the 1980s show a slight fall off in attendance, particularly for girls, following considerable progress in the 1970s. In India and Bangladesh, considerable progress has been made, from a low base in 1970, both in increasing overall enrolment and in moving towards gender parity, although there is still a long way to go on this. In Nepal, which has the lowest ratio of females to males in Asia at both primary and secondary levels, although overall enrolments have increased considerably, there has been little improvement in gender gaps.

In some countries - Pakistan, Afghanistan and Bhutan - limited progress seems to have been made in expanding access to primary education, particularly to girls. They still have enrolment ratios of around 50 per cent or under for both sexes and a wide gender gap, with almost twice as many of the eligible boys as girls attending school.

One worrying tendency is that, in a few countries - e.g. Nepal and Pakistan - the rate of progress in addressing gender inequality appears to have slowed considerably since 1980. These are also the countries together with Bhutan and Afghanistan with the worst record on gender equality in education in Asia and the Pacific. Average enrolment rates and gender parity are only loosely related, at primary level. Some countries achieve gender parity at overall enrolment rates of about 60 per cent, whereas in others enrolment rates may be as high as 80 per cent but still conceal a wide gender gap.

SECONDARY ENROLMENT

The caveats raised above about the comparability of data also apply here. Only one country - Mongolia - had high (over 80 per cent) levels of both male and female enrolment in secondary education in 1970. All other countries in the region have increased enrolments from a low base, although at varying rates. Some countries already had one third to a half secondary enrolment in 1970 (the Philippines, Sri Lanka, Singapore, Malaysia, Republic of Korea, Hong Kong), whereas in others, enrolment in secondary education served less than one quarter of the population at this time, among whom very few were female (Bhutan, Laos, Nepal, Pakistan, Thailand, Indonesia).

Interestingly, Mongolia has consistently higher female than male enrolment ratios at secondary level. Based on 1990 data, the Philippines, Sri Lanka and Singapore, all have two thirds or more enrolment of both males and females, with a slightly higher enrolment ratio of females in each case. Korea also has high levels of secondary enrolment, but with a slightly higher enrolment of males than females (88 per cent compared to 87). Malaysia is approaching 60 per cent enrolment of both males and females, the latter being slightly higher (58 per cent compared to 55 per cent).

China, India, Indonesia, Nepal and Vietnam have 40-55 per cent enrolment of males enrolled at secondary levels, but there is a considerable gender gap in all cases except Vietnam, ranging from eight per cent age points in Indonesia, to twenty six points in Nepal. For those countries where male GERs at secondary level are less than 40 per cent, (Thailand, Pakistan, Laos, Bhutan, Bangladesh, Afghanistan), all except Thailand have wide gender disparities.

On the Pacific, again, data is patchy. Overseas scholarships and private education become features of the education system at this stage, as well as a highly competitive, exam based system for the award of places and scholarships. Because of these factors, gender constraints may be of a different kind to elsewhere. Fiji has over 50 per cent enrolment at secondary level, with gender parity, having made considerable progress in the

1970s. By contrast, in Papua New Guinea, only 15 per cent of males and 10 per cent of females are enrolled at secondary level.

Bhutan, Nepal, Pakistan and Bangladesh have over twice as many boys as girls in secondary school; India and Papua New Guinea have only slightly over half as many girls as boys. Increases in participation rates at secondary level and improvements in gender parity are even more loosely related than at primary level.

TERTIARY ENROLMENT

Access to higher education is generally much more restricted than to primary or secondary education and is predicated on already having passed through lower levels of the system. Where women are under-represented at lower levels, there is thus a cumulative bias against women. This may be reinforced by competitive exam selection for places at higher levels, which can act against women's representation at higher levels. Direct costs of education are higher at tertiary level, which limits its affordability to low income households.

Even in East Asia, where there is limited gender bias at primary and secondary levels, strong biases in access emerge at tertiary level. Gender biases in access to tertiary education, and more specifically in distribution by gender across fields of study, may be based on different constraints to access at lower levels, and more closely tied to labour market conditions. In South Asian countries, female graduates often have much higher unemployment rates than male graduates.

For example, in Bangladesh, 17 per cent of female graduates are unemployed compared with 2.3 per cent of male graduates. General unemployment data for East Asia also show higher unemployment for women than men in China, the Philippines and Taiwan. In South Asia particularly, given the high private costs of tertiary education, the relocation usually involved and the perception of girls' limited prospects in the employment market, parents are unlikely to favour higher education for girls, where resources are constrained. Studies have found that, in rural areas, parents may favour sending boys to college but not girls.

Some rural households adopt strategies where one son is sent to college in order to get a white collar job, for example in Nepal (*ibid.*). Notwithstanding these factors, there may be a class factor at tertiary level which to some extent counteracts these gender biases. Middle class families may favour education of daughters, partly because of their own educational and occupational background and partly because of expectations of marriage into a similar or higher social strata. Moreover, middle class women are increasingly expected to contribute to household income.

On the whole, women in higher education are more likely than men at this level to be middle class. Data coverage is limited, particularly for more recent years. Of the sixteen countries for which recent data is available, over ten per cent of women are enrolled at tertiary level in three cases; between five and ten per cent in two cases, between two and five per cent in five cases and under two per cent in six cases. The Republic of Korea stands out, with over 50 per cent enrolment of males and over 25 per cent enrolment of females at this level in 1990.

Mongolia and the Philippines also have high enrolment ratios at tertiary level - 17 per cent of males and 26 per cent of females; and 23 per cent of males compared to 33 per cent of females respectively, showing a greater proportion of females than males in higher education in both cases. Hong Kong has tertiary enrolment ratios of 17 per cent for males and 9 per cent for females. All other countries for which data is available have enrolment ratios below ten per cent for both sexes at tertiary level and - with the exception of Malaysia - a considerable gender gap. In most cases, twice or more as many males as females are enrolled at this level. China, Laos and Papua New Guinea have particularly low enrolment at tertiary level.

Education science and teacher training, humanities, fine and applied arts and commerce and business administration are areas where women tend to have higher than average representation at tertiary level; moreover, the majority of women in higher education are in one of these areas. In countries where sex segregation is the norm, women may have higher than average representation in medical courses. Mazumdar (1989) argues that too much emphasis is placed on women's lack of representation in agricultural courses (which she sees as often irrelevant to women's needs), rather than on their under-representation in areas such as law, through which women may have direct influence on policy and the political process.

In only a few countries in Asia do women form more than 10 per cent of those enrolled on vocational courses and only in Mongolia do women outnumber men in vocational education. In technical training courses, women are found primarily in areas such as garments; embroidery; clerical work; nutrition; and food processing. Men, by contrast, are concentrated in mechanical disciplines. There are considerable social pressures on women to enter employment fields which are less remunerative, and this influences their choice of subjects at tertiary level. Women tend to choose subjects which relate to non-market as well as market work, foreseeing considerable periods of time when they will withdraw from the labour force for child-rearing purposes.

Women also lack access to professional jobs - in many East Asian countries, less than five per cent of the female labour force are in professional occupations. Within marriage, when men's uptake of education and training to enhance career and earnings prospects increases, women's tends to decline. This form of inequality, it is suggested, may be resistant to policy reform. In the Pacific, gender biases are most evident at tertiary level. In Papua New Guinea, enrolment is low, at tertiary level, at around two per cent overall - of which only 35 per cent are female.

Whilst women form 50 per cent of the intake at teachers college, they are only 20 per cent of university entrants. In Fiji, where only 3.1 per cent of females compared to 5.4 per cent of males are in higher education, there are clear gender differentials in subject selection with women forming 97 per cent of general and secretarial students, 47 per cent of teacher trainees and only 17 per cent of agricultural students. Women received a relatively high proportion of university scholarships - 43 per cent - but only 10 per cent went to Indo-Fijian women.

By contrast, in the Cook Islands, women form the majority of those attending university (61 per cent) and doing degrees, whereas men tend to follow technical courses. The proportion of scholarships going to women has increased from 30 per cent in 1987 to 46 per cent in 1991. Given the small size of many Pacific populations and the scattered geography of the region, distance education or overseas scholarships are major means of accessing higher education. Overseas scholarships are highly competitive and whilst girls may perform well at lower secondary levels, their attainment drops higher up the school system, as in Tuvalu, possibly limiting access to tertiary education. In Tuvalu, 59 per cent of students abroad are male (this includes secondary level as well as tertiary students); Kiribati provides only 20 overseas degree scholarships to 200 possible candidates.

Given a tight labour market and high population growth rates, there is high unemployment of young people in the Pacific, and particularly of women. Currently, there is emphasis on expanding vocational education to make education more relevant to labour market requirements and on providing support to self-employment opportunities. At present, there are considerable gender biases in access to and take up of vocational training opportunities. Women are concentrated in teacher training, nursing, secretarial skills and home economics, and have low representation in technical and scientific courses, or agriculture, in spite of their major role in the agricultural economy. Curricula specifically aimed at women (e.g. home economics) also lack relevance to their daily lives.

There is a need to provide better information about training to girls, and to encourage more women to enter previously male preserves. One encouraging trend at tertiary level over recent years in Asia and the Pacific has been the burgeoning of women's studies and research centres, which are enabling women to redefine their own experiences, and review theoretical concepts and historical events from a feminist perspective.

Literacy rates and trends; Whilst considerable progress has been made in some countries in Asia and the Pacific in increasing enrolment in formal education and reducing or eradicating the gender gap in enrolment ratios, overall levels of literacy, and gender differentials in these, reflect the historical legacy of lack of education provision, particularly for females. These gender differentials persist in spite of the fact that female illiteracy has been falling, in some cases faster than male illiteracy, since 1970. Over three quarters of women are illiterate in: Afghanistan, Bangladesh, Cambodia, Nepal and Pakistan, which all have male illiteracy between 50 and 60 per cent. Two thirds of women in India are illiterate compared to around 40 per cent of men.

In Indonesia, Malaysia, Myanmar and Laos, between one quarter and one third of women are illiterate, compared to rates for men between 8 and 15 per cent. Ten to twenty per cent of women are illiterate in Vietnam and Singapore (21.4) and Sri Lanka, where rates for men are 10 per cent or less in all cases. Under 10 per cent illiteracy of women is found in Mongolia, Korea, the Maldives, the Philippines and Thailand. Illiteracy in South Asia has fallen over the last two decades, but overall illiteracy remains high in most countries and gender differentials remain wide. For example, in Bangladesh, male and female illiteracy rates were 53 per cent and 78 per cent respectively in 1990.

The figures for India were 38 per cent and 66 per cent ; for Nepal 62 per cent and 87 per cent ; and for Pakistan, 53 per cent and 79 per cent. This shows a gap of at least 25 per cent age points in illiteracy rates by gender in each case. Sri Lanka and the Maldives are the only two countries in the region with relatively low illiteracy, at 6.6 per cent and 16.5 per cent for men and women in Sri Lanka respectively; and 8.8 per cent for men and 8.5 per cent for women in the Maldives.

These data are from about 1980, and so the picture will have improved since then. Nevertheless, they show, strikingly, that in India, Pakistan and Bangladesh over 80 per cent of females had no schooling, compared to around 60 per cent of men. In Bangladesh, rural men were better schooled than urban women. In the Solomon Islands, with the worst literacy record in the region, 44 per cent of women are literate compared to 69 per cent of men.

In Vanuatu, the overall literacy rate is also low by Pacific standards, at 64 per cent, but no gender breakdown is available. However, other sources demonstrate an inherited imbalance in educational attainment, In the 35-39 age group, only 31 per cent of women compared to 46 per cent of men have more than six years schooling in Vanuatu.

CONSTRAINTS ON FEMALE EDUCATION IN ASIA

As seen above, there remains a considerable gender gap in education in Asia and the Pacific, but with great variation between countries. Broadly speaking, the gender gap is least pronounced in East Asia and worst in South Asia (with one or two exceptions). There are numerous factors which underlie both the continued existence of a gender gap in education and also its variation between countries and regions.

These include historical, economic (both macro- and micro-), and socio-cultural factors, as well as factors related to educational policy and the nature of school provision. Some of these are reviewed below, using evidence from Asia and the Pacific, but the account is by no means exhaustive. Although discussed separately, these factors cannot be easily categorised into independent variables, since the nature of educational provision will be largely determined by historical and macro-economic factors, micro-economic decisions will respond to wider economic conditions, and socio-cultural norms, or at least the extent of adherence to these, are susceptible to change under economic pressures.

Many of the countries in the Asia region have experienced direct colonial rule and/or other forms of external intervention, which have had a major impact on their societies, not least through the creation of new education systems. The effect of this may have been the provision of education for elite groups, or particular ethnic groups, whilst excluding lower classes, other ethnic groups and the majority of women, for example, thus creating a legacy of educational differentials. Thus, the relative educational privilege of Indo-Fijians in Fiji, or of Tamils in Sri Lanka, can be partly explained by colonial policies.

On the other hand, colonial intervention or missionary activity may have been instrumental in creating wider access to education. Nevertheless, in part because of this historical legacy, the Philippines has one of the best records in the region on education provision in general and, particularly, female access to education. Where access to education was extended to women through colonial policies or missionary activity, it also exposed women to new sets of patriarchal values, through the curriculum and education system, rooted in the western nuclear family model, and often limited women's participation to fields which were in keeping with these values. This legacy also remains today.

ECONOMIC FACTORS

As described above, on the whole, low income countries are more likely than middle or high income countries to have low overall enrolment ratios and also low gender parity in enrolments. Schultz (1991), using cross-national data, finds that the income elasticity of girls' education is higher than that of boys'. However, when the relationship between per capita gross national income and enrolment ratios is explored through regression analysis, for a range of countries, including some in Asia, although positive, the association is not strong.

The same applies also for gender parity and per capita income. Herz *et al* (1991: 10) concluded that: Firstly, neither high levels of per capita GNI [gross national income] nor economic growth ensures improved female enrolment with gender parity. Higher female enrolment and gender parity do not occur automatically as development proceeds. So waiting for per capita GNI to grow enough to fix the gender gap in education and raise female enrolment is not a promising strategy for most poor countries. Second, several countries with low per capita income and limited economic growth achieved remarkable improvements in female education with gender parity. In these countries, deliberate public policy choices evidently made a difference, and it was not simply a matter of increasing public spending on education.

Other standard macro-level indicators of development, such as the level of urbanisation, are also not good predictors of gender parity in education, particularly at low levels of urbanisation, where there is great variation in enrolment ratios. High population growth rates are often associated with low levels of educational provision, and particularly lack of gender parity. Low levels of education of women are often associated with high fertility. The corollary to this is that higher levels of education, especially for women, may reduce fertility.

At the same time, high population growth rates undermine educational provision because they reduce the amount of available expenditure per child. However, the countries in Asia where population growth has been reduced, e.g. China, India, Sri Lanka, are not always those which perform best on educational indicators. In East Asia, with, in aggregate, the best record of gender parity in education, whilst population growth rates have slowed considerably in some countries, to under two per cent per annum, in others they remain relatively high, e.g. Vietnam, Malaysia, Taiwan and the Philippines.

EMPLOYMENT, UNEMPLOYMENT, WAGES AND RETURNS TO EDUCATION

Other economic issues relating to employment have been raised to explain continuing gender differentials in education, such as low levels of female participation in the labour force, high female unemployment rates, and wage discrimination faced by women, leading to low returns to educational investment. There is a clear positive relationship between participation in education and probability of being in the labour force, for women. Thus, as indicated above, countries in East Asia with high female participation in education also tend to have high rates of female labour force participation.

However, it is unclear as to what impact participation in the labour market has on participation in education, though one might assume it motivates both women and their parents to increase investment in education. Wage discrimination according to gender is a feature of labour markets world-wide, to varying degrees. This acts against female participation in education in two ways: by reducing the possibilities for women of supporting their own education through earnings and by lowering the returns to educational investment for women and/or their families. However, the relationship between wage discrimination and participation in education is not clear-cut.

In East Asia, for example, where there is relative equity in education, wage discrimination is quite marked. For example, ILO data show that, in 1991, female earnings were only 69 per cent of male earnings in manufacturing in Hong Kong, 51 per cent in Korea and 56 per cent in Singapore. In Sri Lanka (in 1990) female manufacturing earnings were 90 per cent of male earnings and in Burma (now Myanmar) in 1986, female manufacturing earnings were 86 per cent of male earnings.

Even in government jobs, where pay is nominally equal, full earnings data (taking account of fringe benefits) would probably show a gender differential Parents and female children may perceive limited opportunities in the labour market and low wages as obstacles to realising the returns to educational investment, or at least as increasing the risks attached to this investment. The less it is perceived that education will lead to increased future earnings, the less likely women are to continue in school. The reverse effect, whereby wage discrimination forces women to get more education to increase their earnings relative to men, is apparently not prevalent.

Unemployment may tend to put downward pressure on female participation in education in the short term, as girls and/or women are pushed back into a secondary earner role under recessionary conditions and girls are taken out of education as a result. Boys may also be removed from school to earn income, but are less likely to be substituted for female labour in the home.

Increased unemployment may also lower investment in education in the longer term, since it will decrease the perceived likelihood of returns being realised in the form of earnings. However, it may, at the same time, reduce the opportunity costs of education and thus encourage greater participation - this is more likely to be true of boys, than girls, however. Where there are gender differentials in unemployment at particular levels of education, such that women's unemployment is higher, this will clearly reduce the expected returns to female education.

In many East Asian countries, women have lower unemployment rates than men but in some countries with high female participation in education, (e.g. the Philippines) female unemployment rates are relatively high, compared to others, e.g. Thailand, with relatively low female enrolment at secondary and higher levels, but relatively low female unemployment.

In Bangladesh, unemployment rates of female graduates are much higher than those of male graduates. In order to analyse more precisely the linkages between macro trends in employment, unemployment and wages, and gender biases in education, education specific data by gender and employment status are required. Beyond this, there is a need for more attention to the economic impact of female education on activities outside formal sector labour markets, i.e. in informal sector activities; small farming; home based production etc.

The impact of female education may be limited where women's access to employment or resources which would enable them to be more productive is constrained. Floro and Wolf (1990) suggest that it is the combination of independent income and the skills and attitude changes generated by education, which leads to greater decision-making power and autonomy for women.

INTRA-HOUSEHOLD RESOURCE ALLOCATION

There has been considerable work done, from an economic perspective, on household decisions about investment in children's education, as part of a wider literature on the economics of the family and the household. Some of this work highlights the importance of remittances or inter- generational transfers of income from children to parents, and also, gender differentials in allocation of resources such as food, health care and education, to children.

The broad argument advanced from a neo-classical economic perspective is that parents invest less in daughters because they expect lower returns (either because daughters will get lower paid jobs, spend less time in the labour force, and/or because they will leave the family and get married), or because their tastes and attitudes, which are given, prejudice them against female education. However, this assumes that parents make joint decisions and have the same interests in their children education which may not be the case.

Alternative analyses, based on bargaining power approaches to the household, have stressed the need to look at gender relations within the household as a factor in determining how resources are allocated. Whilst it is often argued that parents' will not realise the benefits from educating daughters, in fact, parents may be able to access earnings of young female members of the household more easily, at least in the short-term before they marry and have children.

In the patriarchal family structure, daughters incomes may be more easily appropriated by the household, or daughters may feel more obliged to meet expectations to provide income to the household. It is well documented that men retain a larger portion of their income for own consumption than women. It has already been shown that in Taiwan, for example, daughters incomes are often used to finance sons education.

It is not clear how decisions to invest in children's' education are related to (a) expectations of financial returns by parents, or (b) actual returns to parents from educational investment, for sons' compared to daughters' education. Although it is often argued that men support parents because women marry out, once sons are earning, and particularly when they have their own families, they may be unwilling and/or unable to give money to parents.

Moreover, in some kinship systems, social obligations are such that women, rather than men, are expected to support their parents. This is the case, for example, in Thailand and is sometimes used as an explanation for relative gender parity in education there. Given pervasive patterns of gender discrimination in the labour market, parents may see the possibilities of their daughters earning a decent income as limited. Nevertheless, numerous examples can be found where parents do realise the earning power of daughters - at least in particular kinds of jobs - or the value of educating daughters as a strategy for marrying into more wealthy, or well-connected families.

In South India, families are said to educate daughters as a strategy against famine, intending to marry them to white collar employees with a greater degree of security. In Bangladesh, and elsewhere, women who work in manufacturing industry, with relatively high education levels and wages, are often sought after marriage partners. Beyond the broad generalisations about the costs and benefits underlying household decisions about education, more detailed analysis is needed about how considerations of social mobility and economic security interact with kinship structures and obligations, to influence gendered decisions about investment in girls education in particular contexts.

Gender Bias in Allocation of Food and Health Care

It is well documented for at least parts of South Asia, that there is at least selective discrimination against some girls within households through unequal allocation of food and health care resources, compared to boys. Such biases in household resource allocation may act to reinforce any biases in educational expenditure, since undernourished or sick girls are likely to perform less well at school and have more regular absences. School feeding and health care programmes may be one approach to addressing this problem, although some analysts would argue that this will simply lead to a re-allocation of resources away from girls within the household.

Opportunity Cost of Child Labour

Various studies in Asia have looked at the relative involvement of girls and boys in domestic and market labour, to assess the opportunity cost of schooling. For example: In Nepal, studies have documented that the demand for girls labour exceeds the demand for boys labour by half. In India and Bangladesh, and Nepal, by the age of 5 many girls are involved in such household responsibilities as collecting water and fuel and managing younger siblings and farm activities. Between the ages of 10 and 15, girls may work 8 to 10 hours a day on productive activities inside and outside the home.

Time use studies in India have shown that younger girls worked 5.5 hours and older girls 7.7 hours a day in adult household and agricultural tasks, whereas younger boys spent only 1.8 hours and older boys 3.6 hours on such tasks. Although boys also perform some household chores, they are more likely than girls to work in the market, possibly contributing some of their own income to school costs. Girls are more likely to be assigned domestic responsibilities at young age. A recent study in Indonesia found that families rely much more on older girls than on older boys to care for younger siblings' and that girls are much more likely than boys to drop out of school to look after sick siblings, for example.

In some situations, boys labour may (e.g. in herding) may also carry a high opportunity costs, on the whole: Sons do fewer chores at home and do not liberate either parent to earn more. The full opportunity cost of educating girls may thus be higher than that for boys, especially for poor families. This difference may help explain why poor parents often invest less in their daughters schooling than in their son's.

HOUSEHOLD CHARACTERISTICS

Various household characteristics, such as level of education of parents, occupation of parents, family size and income group, have been put forward to explain variations in female enrolment. *Education* Studies show that as parents' level of education increases, so does the likelihood of female enrolment, but there are variation in studies as to whether mother's or father's education has the greatest impact on daughters' education. One study in Lahore, Pakistan, found that father's education had a much greater influence over daughters than sons schooling.

Mother's education was less important, except in upper middle class families. Elsewhere, studies have shown that mother's education level has a major effect on attitudes to daughter's education and in some cases, a significant impact on education of both sons and daughters. In some cases, mother's education affects daughters but not sons. The literacy rate of the community as a whole, as well as within particular households, has a significant impact on female participation rates in education, suggesting a demonstration effect within communities, even socially very conservative ones.

Literacy (especially of women) was also found to be a significant predictor of both total enrolment and gender parity, at the national level, lending analytical weight to the saying "When you educate the women, you educate the nation'.

Occupation

Similarly, parents in white collar occupations are more likely to support daughters'education than those in blue collar occupations. It is not clear how mother's occupation, separately, might influence daughters, since most such studies focus on the occupation of head of household (presumed to be male). Where mothers are working, they may be more motivated to send daughters to school, because they perceive the connection between education and increased earnings and, possibly, because they can financially assist in supporting their daughters'education.

On the other hand, female employment, and increased female wages, may increase the likelihood of dropout or non-attendance of girls, due to substitution of labour. According to one study on India, a 10 per cent increase in female wages was said to cause a five per cent drop in girl's school attendance. The overall impact of mothers occupation depends on the relative strength of substitution and income effects. It may be necessary to combine labour market initiatives with counter measures to offset the increase in opportunity cost of daughters labour in the home, when mothers engage in market activity.

Family size

Whilst there is some micro-study evidence that girls in larger families are less likely to go to school and/or perform less well, in aggregate, this is not necessarily borne out in all cases - e.g. the Philippines, with average family size of 5.9, has better female enrolment than other countries with smaller average family size. Thailand, on the other hand, has the second highest aggregate family size in the (East Asia) region (5.7) and one of the lowest female participation rates in secondary and tertiary education.

Income

At the micro-level, poverty may be critical in decisions on female education. Income (or other measures of wealth, such as land-holding) has more affect on girls than on boys education. In higher income strata, girls are considerably more likely to be enrolled in school than in low income groups. This may reflect a strategy favouring boys where parents cannot finance all children to attend school, and also higher opportunity costs of girls'labour in poorer households.

Opportunity costs of child labour may be particularly hard for low income households to bear - in poorer households; girls are less likely to attend school, since their labour is more essential to the household, where mothers are more likely to be working. The per cent age of direct costs of education in average household income varies across countries but is similar for boys and girls, reaching as much as ten per cent of household income.

Poorer households in particular will find it harder to meet the direct costs, as these will represent a higher proportion of household income. Data on the proportion of household expenditure spent on education do not, however, reveal the division of responsibility within the household for paying for schooling costs for different children. If, for example, mothers are generally responsible for school fees, then there is little basis for assessing affordability on total household income.

SOCIO-CULTURAL FACTORS

Religious, ethnic and other socio-cultural factors are not static constraints on female education, but interplay with other factors, and are susceptible to change.

RELIGION

The evidence on the impact of religion on girls' enrolment is inconclusive, suggesting that it is too simplistic to associate low participation of girls with particular religious affiliations. Whilst examples can be found which appear to link, for example, the predominance of Islam with low female enrolment and wide gender gaps in education, there are also counter examples. The two predominantly Muslim countries in East Asia - Malaysia and Indonesia - have the lowest female literacy levels in the sub-region after China, but Malaysia has a relatively good record of gender parity in secondary and higher education.

In Sri Lanka, for example, Muslim communities lag behind other communities in terms of access to education. However, these associations are, on the whole, too simplistic - religious practice varies considerably between different countries and communities and class, income and other factors mediate the impact of religious attitudes.

South Asia is a culturally heterogeneous region, in terms of religion (encompassing Islam, Hinduism, and Buddhism as well as significant Christian and other religious minorities), so that no single doctrine can be isolated to explain low female enrolment in the region. However, certain socio-cultural practices associated primarily, but not exclusively, with Islam and Hinduism, such as purdah, early age at first marriage and dowry, may be particularly limiting in terms of girls' access to education.

AGE AT MARRIAGE AND MARITAL SYSTEMS

Marriage, particularly early marriage, may affect girls' educational achievement. Single women tend to have higher educational levels than married women, but the trade off is not simple; there may be common causes of both, rather than a clear causal link. In most countries, the legal minimum age at marriage, and actual average age at marriage, is lower for women than for men. Early marriage thus probably acts as more of a deterrent to female than to male education.

In South Asia, the legal minimum age at marriage in most countries is between 15 and 16 for women, and at least two years older for males. Actual average age at marriage in Pakistan, Bangladesh and India ranged between 17 and 22. In Sri Lanka, with better participation of women in education, over half of women were still unmarried at age 23.

The practice of dowry introduces further hidden costs of female education. Allowing girls to continue in education means that, where men expect to marry women less educated than themselves, parents will have to pay more dowry to marry their daughter to more educated men. Even university educated men do not show a preference for women of the same educational level (*Ibid.*).

The need to save up resources for a girl's dowry may take away resources which might otherwise be available for girl's education or oblige girls to enter the labour market to save towards marriage. Some researchers have suggested providing a dowry subsidy to parents as an incentive to promote female education. On the other hand, in some instances, education of daughter may be seen as a substitute for dowry, and therefore represent a good investment from parents' point of view, rather than a hidden cost. This may be more likely among urban and middle class families, however, where women are increasingly expected to be wage earners.

Ethnicity

Ethnicity may also impact on female education, partly due to cultural practices in particular communities and partly as a result of state policies. Where state policies positively discriminate in favour of one particular ethnic group, for example through scholarship or quota systems, e.g. Fijians in Fiji, rather than Indo-Fijians; Malays in Malaysia, rather than Chinese. This may either exacerbate or temper gender differentials in particular ethnic groups.

School Related Factors

The extent, quality and nature of available schooling can have a considerable influence over educational enrolment patterns, including by gender. In many instances, the ways in which schooling is delivered limits girls' access or performance. The quality of educational provision tends to affect attendance and performance. This may have a particular impact on girls, where, for example, there is a general tendency for teachers in large classes to pay less attention to girls.

Types of School

In some Asian countries, e.g. Malaysia, girls have much higher enrolment ratios in religious schools than boys. This may be because parents feel that such schools inculcate moral values which are not taught in state schools. Sex-segregated schools may also be preferred by parents for girls, and there is some evidence that girls, although not boys, perform better in these than in co-educational schools.

In the Pacific, there is considerable involvement of the private sector and churches in education provision, particularly at post-primary level where public supply is limited, as well as local community involvement, for example in pre-school education, but also in community colleges in Papua New Guinea and Tuvalu, for example. In Papua New Guinea, community schools are reportedly subject to temporary closures due to local conflicts.

No analyses have been found of the varying gendered conditions of access to these different institutions, nor indeed any information about the extent to which gender issues are under discussion in different institutional contexts. There is some indication that, in Papua New Guinea, girls have higher representation in church schools post-primary level, but elsewhere there was no strong evidence on greater or lesser biases in private or NGO provision. It is suggested, that parents prefer to send daughters to church schools in Papua New Guinea.

DISTANCE AND LOCATION OF SCHOOL FACILITIES

Distance of school facilities is used as a conventional measure of the adequacy of supply of school places. It is often argued that the greater the distance of the school, the more the gender gap in participation will be increased, because, for example, of parents' concern about girls' safety, or moral reputation (particularly in communities where female seclusion is the norm). Fall off of attendance tends to occur especially as girls' approach puberty, when family honour (*izzat*) in some predominantly Muslim societies becomes linked to concerns over daughters' sexual modesty.

Transport availability is a bigger issue for female students than male and may introduce other hidden costs of female education. Similarly, the need to provide girls with suitable clothing, where questions of moral reputation and seclusion are at stake, can prove a disincentive to female education. Where separate schools are the norm, shortage of places and distance of female facilities may be a particular issue. However, costs of duplicating facilities may be prohibitive and may lead to second rate institutions for girls.

Distance is more of a problem at secondary level, partly for reasons given above, and partly because facilities tend to be further away; moreover, enrolment at primary level may be affected if there is no nearby secondary school, or if the primary school facility is not complete. In fact, the evidence is not clear as to whether it is distance *per se*, or other factors, such as lack of separate facilities such as toilets, lack of walls around schools, lack of provision for transport, or other barriers are really responsible for lowering female attendance.

Some studies have shown that relatively short distances reduce female attendance, it is worry about females crossing a major river or road, or simply being exposed to public scrutiny, which prevents attendance. Issues of social, rather than simply physical, distance, may be constraints on attendance, e.g. where schools are located in upper caste areas of villages which lower caste children may not be able to enter, although there is no clear specifically gender bias arising from this. From a gender perspective, questions of distance take on a different slant.

The real barriers around distance, transport and secure facilities relate directly to questions of violence against women, or the pervasive threat of this. The threat, particularly of sexual violence, against young women, becomes a rationale for parents to keep daughters out of school. For example, in Papua New Guinea, which has a high incidence of violence against women, villagers in Pimanga, in the Southern Highlands, were: *most reluctant to allow a girls to attend high school and rationalised this response by saying that boys could walk home from school using back tracks but if girls' did this they might be raped.*

There is some evidence that female enrolment can be increased with a greater supply of school places and greater proximity, or accessibility of schools to communities. For example, in the Philippines, expansion of the school system has increased female enrolment considerably. Satellite schools have been successfully introduced in some villages in Bangladesh, to bring facilities closer to home. However, distance is no longer the major problem in some places; supply of school places is thought to be adequate overall, for example, in India.

Even in this case, however, supply may be a problem for particular sections of the community, such as tribals, living in remote areas. Supply may remain a more general problem in countries where terrain is difficult and/or populations scattered, such as Nepal, or some Pacific islands. Beyond the question of increased supply and accessibility of places, there is clearly a need to devise long-term strategies to tackle violence against and sexual harassment of young women, who may thus be prevented from getting an education. As well as making safer provisions for female students, there is a need for community based awareness raising and action.

CURRICULUM BIAS AND RELEVANCE

Curricula may project stereotyped and limited role models/ representations of girls and women. Gender-based conditioning which influences choices about subject areas in secondary and higher education and about employment begins early on. "Culturally conditioned perceptions of girls and the hidden curriculum in schools influence their educational and vocational aspirations, their subject choices and their options for further study and employment".

Another aspect of the curriculum is its perceived relevance, both by parents and by students, and the impact of this on attendance. This is a tricky area, since parents' perceptions of what subjects are appropriate and relevant for girls may be quite limiting. Parents tend to have an instrumental attitude towards education, seeing it principally as a route to employment, or transferring skills and values which will make girls better wives and mothers. Rural families particularly, may favour traditional skills such as childcare, cooking and handicrafts for girls.

Where increased local participation in school financing and management is being promoted, this may be leading to increased conservatism about appropriate curricula for girls. Where places at higher levels are rationed by a rigid examination policy, female access may suffer, or drop out may be higher. Domestic demands on girls may mean that they take more regular absences; they may also have less time for homework.

These can result in them doing less well in exams thus reinforcing parental bias towards investing more in boys. Where girls drop out and repeat years, performance will be affected - repeaters or those withdrawn for temporary periods and re-entering do less well than those with consistent attendance. One solution to this may be to enforce compulsory enrolment at prescribed ages, although this might have unintended negative effects.

FEMALE TEACHERS

Low representation of female teachers is thought to be a constraint on improving access of girls to education and quality of girls' education, due to

a. Parental worries about contact of adolescent girls with male teachers, particularly in highly sex-segregated societies;
b. Conversely, the lack of attention given by male teachers to female students; and
c. The need for female teachers as a role model for girls.

On the whole, representation of women among teachers' declines higher up the educational system, with lowest representation at tertiary levels. Those countries with a low representation of female teachers also tend to have low enrolment ratios of females in schools, and low gender parity, e.g. Afghanistan, Bhutan, Bangladesh, Nepal, and Pakistan. However, the relationship is not direct: India, for example, has higher female enrolment ratios than Pakistan or Afghanistan, but lower representation of female teachers (in the latter two cases, segregated schools may partly explain this).

Those countries with high representation of female teachers (Hong Kong, Mongolia, Philippines) tend also to be those with a longer history of high enrolment of girls. There is also a danger, however, of teaching (particularly at primary level) becoming a feminised profession (as for example in the Philippines), and consequently suffering from low status, pay and conditions, relative to other labour market opportunities. In aggregate, there is an association between low representation of female teachers and poor access/ performance of girls and conversely, between high representation and high female enrolment and gender parity.

However, it is not clear to what extent female teachers actually improve girls' educational prospects, since the representation of female teachers is itself a function of the representation of girls in the education system, particularly at secondary and higher levels and on teacher training courses. Although these broad patterns suggest that female teachers encourage female enrolment, there are very few micro-level studies which examine this hypothesis. Some of the constraints on increasing female representation in teaching are similar to those on increasing female enrolment generally, e.g. lack of separate facilities, lack of secure accommodation. Policies adopted to increase female representation in teaching will be examined in the next section.

POLICY AND PROGRAMMES

Three promising types of measures to increase girls' education have been identified, i.e.: increasing the economic returns of educating girls (through economic policies); lowering the costs to parents of educating girls; and providing direct incentives. Identifying appropriate policies depends on the context. There is wide variation by region and country, in the extent and nature of the gender gap and in the range of constraints limiting female education.

In poor agrarian societies, direct and opportunity costs, as well as socio-cultural factors, pose severe constraints and the gender gap is wide, as in much of South Asia. In these countries, progress in education requires policies addressing a number of constraints simultaneously, through economic, as well as educational approaches. At the same time, severe budgetary constraints mean that there is little if any additional expenditure available for education.

In the countries under transition in East Asia (China, Laos, Vietnam), there is a need to ensure that past progress in extending education and lowering gender inequalities are not sacrificed in the drive towards liberalisation. In middle income countries, the constraints on female education are less severe, particularly at primary level. Attention needs to be focused on secondary and tertiary education, and on widening fields of study and labour market opportunities for women.

ECONOMIC POLICIES

Policies to improve girls' access to education, reduce gender gaps and increase the quality of girls' education are not restricted to the education sector. As seen above, macro-economic and employment policies can directly impact on the returns to girls' education in terms of the possibilities of their labour market participation, self-employment and returns to economic activity. Macro-economic policies may cause distortions which create biases against women's economic activities, where, for example, women are concentrated in sectors which are discriminated against by pricing structures, availability of credit, access to markets etc. Such distortions may limit women's ability to realise the returns of educational investment in increased productivity or income.

In poor agrarian societies, where women have a very limited range of opportunities, policies which increase women's access to labour markets and improve their productivity and earnings will be particularly important. As well as measures to assist women in increasing productivity and earnings, measures are also needed to offset the increase in opportunity costs of girls' household labour arising through increased female labour force participation and wages, e.g. through improved childcare provision, water supply provision.

In rural Pakistan, for example, there are few employment opportunities for women with education, except for government jobs, e.g. in health and teaching, which require relatively high levels of education. The investment required and the risks involved are too high for most families, given the limited range of employment options for women in local communities. One response might be to lower employment requirements for women in government jobs in rural areas. Another would be to lower the costs of education to families. Better information and analysis is required about the potential interactions between macro- economic policies, employment policies and educational investments, in overcoming constraints to female education.

PUBLIC EXPENDITURE AND EDUCATIONAL FINANCING

The share of education in government expenditure and GNP is low in South Asia, particularly in Bangladesh and Pakistan (2.2 and 2.1 per cent of GNP respectively) compared to the low income developing country average of 3.3 per cent. Even Sri Lanka, with a previous record of high public spending on social programmes, has shrinking expenditure in this area since the 1970s, but particularly since 1987. Where military expenditure is rising, educational expenditure tends to fall; the reverse is also true.

In East Asia, on the other hand, educational expenditure is higher on average, with most countries spending at least three per cent of GNP and some much more (e.g. Malaysia). Similarly, in the Pacific region, educational expenditure is over four per cent of GNP for Papua New Guinea, Tonga, and Fiji. Where investments are currently low, increased education expenditure is a necessary but not sufficient pre-condition for expanding enrolment and tackling the gender gap. To this extent, a reorientation of government (and donor) expenditure priorities may be required. However, there is considerable variation in the efficiency of education systems, which mediates the effectiveness of increasing public expenditure.

Additionally, more money alone will not necessarily overcome gender-based constraints, without some restructuring of service delivery systems and simultaneous action in other areas. Decentralization of school management and financing has some positive aspects in introducing more flexibility in systems, enabling local solutions to gender constraints to be found, as reported for China. However, whilst such measures may allow increased flexibility which works in favour of increased girls' enrolment and also more rapid expansion of education provision, there may also be negative quality and equity impacts, such that those areas most in need of investment to improve the quality of education are those least able to afford to finance it.

Education policies

A wide variety of measures have been tried, within the education sector, to address gender constraints in education. These include: awareness campaigns; recruitment of female teachers; protection of girls' privacy (sanitation facilities etc.); separate schools for girls, of equal quality to boys' schools; more flexible schedules; retention of pregnant girls and mothers; child care provision; and special scholarships and other direct incentives. Other educational measures are not gender specific, but may help girls more than boys where parents are reluctant to send daughters to school, for example, smaller, closer schools; improved quality of schooling; reduction of direct costs of education for all children; deepening community involvement; making school compulsory.

LEGISLATIVE MEASURES

Legislation which makes education compulsory up to a certain age can be useful in promoting enrolment generally and particularly, enrolment of females. Some countries in Asia have a long history of compulsory education at primary level and/ or of legislation providing for equal access to education by sex. Thailand has such legislation dating back to 1921, the Philippines to 1901. There remain a number of countries in Asia and the Pacific which do not have compulsory education, e.g. Bhutan, Papua New Guinea and where enrolment rates are relatively low. However, enforcing compulsory education in a situation of inadequate supply of school places, may be counterproductive.

Awareness Campaigns

Parental literacy, especially mothers' literacy, was shown above to be related to improved educational opportunity of children, and particularly for girls. Awareness and enrolment campaigns linked to adult literacy or other non-formal education for adults may be particularly successful. The importance of conveying the practical benefits of female education to parents have been stressed. The involvement of community and/or religious leaders in promoting female education may be another potentially successful strategy.

China is cited as a country where awareness campaigns have had considerable success, but this may relate to the existence of social and political organisations at all levels of society, a legacy of communist policy which may now be weakening, and reducing the scope for community based activities of this kind. This may also be true of Vietnam, Laos and Cambodia. Little is known about the impact of such campaigns. Attitudinal change is difficult to assess or relate directly to interventions rather than other factors; moreover, during and immediately following campaigns, schools and campaign organisers are likely to inflate their enrolment figures more than usual.

INCENTIVES AND SUBSIDIES TO FEMALE EDUCATION

Subsidies to girls' education are justified on both efficiency (externalities) and equity grounds. Incentives are necessary to overcome the direct and opportunity costs of female education, where these may be higher than those for boys and/or where parents tend to favour educating boys in a situation of scarce resources. Numerous approaches to providing special incentives or subsidies to encourage girls to attend school have been adopted in Asian and Pacific countries in recent years.

These include: exemption from fees; subsidies for uniforms and textbooks, scholarships; and school feeding and health programmes, *inter alia*. Such policies have been implemented in India, for example, and also Bangladesh. The Bangladesh Secondary Education Scholarship Programme, which started in 1977, gave over 18,000 scholarships in grades 6-10 to cover secondary tuition and succeeded in expanding enrolments ratios of girls from 27 per cent to 43 per cent of the eligible population in the project area (it is not clear how this compares to increases in non-project areas) and in reducing drop-out of females, as well as having spin off benefits at primary level.

However, it was also found that: The decision to limit funding to a target group of girls from "poor" families... proved unwise as: a) the chosen indicator of poverty was too low; b) administrative costs increased and school places were left empty because of problems identifying suitable candidates and c) community support deteriorated when some girls were excluded.

The Bangladesh Fourth Primary Project (1980-86), which provided free uniforms to female students, found: No evidence that the distribution of uniforms contributed to a substantial increase in the enrolment of girls. There was a marginal increase in girls' enrolment at the start of the programme, but enrolment decreased when some girls, although not eligible for free uniforms, dropped out of school because they were excluded from the programme. Details of other experiences, and the numbers of students covered, were not found, but the above suggests that provision of direct incentives may have limited impact, in the absence of other measures, and that narrow targeting of such incentives undermines their effectiveness.

RECRUITING FEMALE TEACHERS

Increasing the proportion of female teachers, particularly at primary and secondary levels, is another major strategy which has been tried in order to reduce gender inequality in education. Various measures have been tried. Quotas for entry into teacher training and/or teaching jobs are one approach. However, in some cases, quotas can become ceilings such that women's recruitment does not advance beyond a certain level, particularly if they are set too low. It also may give the appearance of having dealt with the problem, when in fact quotas are not filled.

In come countries, female representation in teaching is very high - e.g. Philippines. However, above a certain level, increased representation of female teachers is liable to create a ghettoized profession, particularly at primary level. Thus, increased representation of female teachers should not be seen as a wholly positive development. Experience from elsewhere shows that, in the context of structural adjustment programmes, or more generally, restrictions on public expenditure, teachers real salaries may have been progressively eroded due to rising inflation, such that they either abandon the profession or take up other jobs or income earning activities concurrently.

Where there are pressures of this kind, training of new recruits to the profession will be of limited benefit unless they can be retained through improved pay and conditions, or other incentives. Such problems may be particularly pertinent to those Asian economies undergoing currently transition to the market (China, Laos, Vietnam), where private sector opportunities may be increasingly attractive relative to working in a low wage public sector.

Lowering the entry qualifications for women is another form of positive discrimination which could increase female representation in the profession, particularly where recruitment from local communities is being encouraged, often linked to the creation of community based facilities. Many such programmes have been implemented, often taking in girls at post-primary level and enrolling them in teacher training courses at secondary level. Adequate training and support, and possibilities for further training and promotion should be given in such instances, however, to ensure that a second class tier of female educators is not created.

In 1971, in Nepal, a programme was started to increase rural women's access to teacher training, through a variety of measures including awareness raising, community involvement, financial assistance, tutoring, home posting and in-service training. Over eight years the per cent age of females in the teaching force rose from three to ten per cent and girls' enrolment in schools also increased dramatically in schools affected by the project. A *mohalla* (home school) programme in Baldia, a large squatter settlement in Pakistan, recruited local women with a high school education and trained them as teachers, to work in homes, therefore avoiding issues of *purdah* and cutting costs on travel, uniforms, shoes etc.

The programme is reported to have had considerable initial success, enrolling some 1500 young women in the mid-1980s. Similarly, Bangladesh Rural Advancement Committee (BRAC), a large NGO in Bangladesh have, as part of their Non-formal Education Programme, required communities to supply a local female secondary school graduate to be trained as a teacher, as well as to provide a one-roomed school building. Hours of teaching are arranged flexibly around domestic work demands and a more appropriate curriculum has been devised. These schools also require a two thirds enrolment of females as students.

Retention rates have been high, even in impoverished areas, countering claims that poverty is the main constraint to female education in the Bangladeshi context. Elsewhere in Bangladesh, problems have been reported with local recruitment of teachers - i.e. absenteeism, taking on students for private tutoring and favouritisms towards private tutees. For these reasons, villagers did not favour local teachers. Recruiting from outside the locality brings in another set of problems, however, since few women are willing to relocate to unfamiliar communities, particularly in remote rural areas.

Issues of isolation, physical security and vulnerability arise for female teachers posted to remote communities. Financial and other incentives may be required to encourage teachers to relocate to rural areas, e.g. provision of housing, relocation expenses, transportation etc. However, on their own, these will be insufficient. Allowing regular home leaves and creating networks of support may also be necessary. Encouraging re-entry of women into teaching after long breaks from the labour force may be another way of increasing female representation.

NON-FORMAL EDUCATION PROVISION

More flexible community based forms of education provision, with greater community participation, flexible hours, adapted curricula and other innovations, have had considerable success in increasing female enrolment and reducing drop out rates. BRAC's programme in Bangladesh described above is one such positive example. One scheme in Pune, Maharashtra (India) held classes in the evenings, between 7 and 9 p.m., when evening meals and domestic chores were completed, to make them accessible to girls.

Another project in Nepal, for low caste girls, held classes early in the morning, before household chores had begun, again with some success in reducing drop out. However, upper caste families were able to oppose the subsequent enrolment of these girls into local public schools. This underlines a concern that non-formal programmes may introduce a two tier system unless bridges are found into the formal system. Distance education has been seen as a solution to extending educational provision, particularly at tertiary level, in the Pacific, partly because of the geography and demography of the region.

There are sizeable extension programmes e.g. in University of Papua New Guinea. From a gender perspective, distance education may have some advantages: it increases access to wider range of people, has lower costs, and enables participants to combine study with work and/or childcare. It may also ease budgeting of educational costs for women. It has also been argued that it is better for women in that they are not exposed to the negative influences of discriminatory attitudes and behaviour of teachers and peer groups in the classroom.

On the other hand, distance education does not provide space for women to study separately from other responsibilities and they may thus have greater difficulties than men in maintaining their commitment. Where study skills are required to prepare people for distance education, women may be disadvantaged without additional support. Overall, data suggest that distance education is still dominated by men: In Papua New Guinea (in 1988) women represented less than a third of distance learners; in Tuvalu, there were more men (two thirds) than women enrolled for distance education courses at the University of the South Pacific extension centre.

One structural problem with all these examples of non-formal education provision is that, whilst they address the practical issue of how to make schooling accessible to women who are tied by their domestic responsibilities, they do so by working around these responsibilities, rather than reducing them. Other measures, such as childcare provision attached to schools, or attempts to involve men/boys more in domestic chores to allow women to study, might be more in women's strategic interests in the longer run.

In Andhra Pradesh, India, one study recommended that pre-school child-care centres (locally known as *anganwadi*) should be integrated with primary school provision and that this should be considered at the school mapping stage.

Provision of child care facilities as a means to reduce the opportunity cost of female labour will not be helpful unless it is provided at times and locations which relate to the availability of schooling.

CURRICULUM BIAS

Few initiatives are reported in Asia and the Pacific in the area of curriculum reform from a gender perspective. Whilst several surveys report findings that textbooks overwhelmingly present men or boys as leading actors, and under-represented women, or represent them in stereotyped roles and attitudes, little information is found about measures taken to address these biases. According to Jayaweera (1987: 465) Although studies have been carried out particularly in Bangladesh, India and Pakistan on gender role stereotypes in educational materials... only China, India and the Philippines have taken specific measures to introduce curriculum materials that may promote gender equality.

Educational materials are only one issue in curriculum bias, however. The attitudes of teachers, and others who influence decisions about subjects of study, and the allocation of girls and boys to particular subject areas, are equally, if not more important, as shown above. Improved teacher training, including gender awareness and equal opportunities training, and encouragement to girls to take up and pursue subjects like maths and science from early on are required.

One source recommends the increased involvement of village women who possess handicraft of domestic skills as assistants or demonstrators in local schools, as a positive measure in terms of girls' education. This may appear positive from the point of view of community participation and increasing the 'relevance' of the curriculum to everyday life, but raises questions about the maintenance of curricular standards and professionalism in teaching. From a gender perspective, bringing in older women to demonstrate traditional feminine skills would be of limited strategic value to improving girls' employment opportunities or widening their horizons.

ASSESSMENT OF INTERVENTIONS

The above range of policies and programmes illustrate some attempts to date to address gender biases in educational provision and also gender constraints to school enrolment, persistence and achievement. So far, there has been a tendency to act on quality of school provision rather than demand constraints which would reduce the costs of education to parents.

There is a need to devise policies which would reduce the reduce direct and indirect costs of education to parents. However, this is being advocated at a time when:

a. Budgets for education are being squeezed and cost-recovery in education promoted; and
b. Pressures on households, particularly poorer households, are increasing such that the opportunity costs of child, especially girls' labour may be increasing.

Quality of schooling has also suffered under restrictions in spending and this may have led to falling enrolment. Where the financing and management of schools is becoming more decentralised, and contributions from the community playing a larger role, this is leading to a variability in the quality (or even quantity) of provision according to the capacity of the community to pay. Increased local involvement in school management also brings in the danger of increased conservatism over appropriate curricula for girls.

Community participation needs to be more critically examined as a strategy for increasing female enrolment. Some of the most innovative approaches to overcoming constraints to female education have been through non-formal education programmes, which have succeeded, in many instances, in increasing female enrolment, even in impoverished areas. A key issue here, however, is the need to provide mechanisms for the reintegration of girls into the formal system, or the need to adapt the formal system along the lines of non-formal provision.

In the longer term, a more strategic approach is required to reducing girls' child care responsibilities and other domestic labour burdens, e.g. through the provision of school based child care. Across the range of measures which have been attempted, there is little clarity about which, in practice, are the most effective and which constraints are the most binding on female attendance and retention, although packages of two or three measures, rather than single measures, seem to work best. Thus, there is a need for project related research which looks at the impact and cost-effectiveness to different approaches to overcoming constraints.

Furthermore, there is a need for greater understanding regarding the interactions between economic policies and educational policies: A top priority should be research that would model and test more precisely how innovative education policies and other policies that improve women's productivity, can be combined to maximise female education at minimum cost. Education programmes with a gender perspective should also look beyond the issue of increasing women's productivity, or the conventionally defined social returns to female education, to initiatives which are geared, also, to increasing women's autonomy, decision- making capacity, and participation in civil and political institutions.

RECENT TRENDS IN FEMALE EDUCATION

The 1990 census indicates a long-term upward trend in male and female access to education over the last fifty years in China. In 1988 the overall ratio for net primary school enrolment was 97.2 per cent, as compared to 50 per cent in 1952, indicating near- universal attendance of primary-age children. The most significant periods of expansion of female education occurred between 1950 to 1958 following the establishment of the People's Republic of China (PRC) in 1949 and during the Cultural Revolution from 1966-1976.

During both these periods the Chinese government was committed to eliminating the various manifestations of social stratification. During the period 1977-1982 attempts to extend quality primary and secondary education to rural areas were put on hold. 'Schools in rural areas were now under- funded and under-staffed compared to schools in urban areas, especially those in cities of strategic importance to modernisation'. Reflecting the overall improvements in availability and accessibility of schooling since 1949, female access to education has improved markedly over the last 45 years. In 1951, females comprised only 28 per cent of primary school students; by 1973, their share had risen to 41 per cent.

More recently, female gross enrolment ratios (GERs) for primary education have risen from 103 per cent in 1980 to 115 per cent in 1985 and 120 per cent in 1990. The upward trend in female secondary enrolment was broken by a decline between 1980 and 1985 from 37 to 32 per cent, with a subsequent rise to 42 per cent in 1990 and 45 per cent in 1991. Female GERs for tertiary level education, although showing an increase between 1980 and 1990, from 0.6 per cent to 1.1 per cent, remain extremely low. Similar upward trends, bar the decline in secondary school GERs between 1980 and 1985, are apparent for males.

However, despite these improvements in enrolment ratios at all levels of education, women continue to face considerable inequality within the education sector. In 1987, the ratio of females to males in primary education was 88.6 per cent ; at secondary level the ratio was lower at 74 per cent. In 1991, GERs at primary level were 127 for males and 118 for females (net figures were 99 per cent and 94 per cent respectively); and for secondary level, 56 per cent for males and 45 per cent for females. Official government statistics indicate that the per cent age of illiterate females fell from 37.1 per cent in 1970 to 28.3 per cent in 1980 and 14.2 per cent in 1990.

Over the same period, men's illiteracy rates fell from 11.6 per cent to 4.0 per cent. However, other sources give significantly higher illiteracy rates for women of 32 per cent in 1990, compared to 13 per cent for men, making it difficult to assess trends. Reflecting recent improvements in the supply of educational facilities, younger cohorts have substantially higher literacy rates than older cohorts. These figures indicate a significant lessening of the gender gap between 1973 and 1975, particularly at primary and secondary levels.

The female proportion of total enrolment at primary school levelled off at approximately 45 per cent between 1975 and 1989. The 1990 Census indicates that the gender gap within recent age cohorts has diminished almost to non- existence at primary levels in both rural and urban areas. In the case of secondary education, the gender gap is wider than at primary level, although negligible within urban secondary schools (*ibid.*).

Around 41 per cent of secondary school pupils were female in 1989. Again, the most rapid narrowing of the gender gap happened between 1973 and 1975. Females are still highly under-represented compared to males at tertiary level education - females comprised only 33.7 per cent of students in 1989. Within this cohort, females from rural areas are heavily under-represented. Moreover, females entering higher education are far less likely than male students to graduate. In 1985, only 18.76 per cent of graduates were female.

The significant decline in the female proportion of total enrolment at secondary and tertiary levels between 1978 and 1983 coincided with a period when the government's 'goal of minimising social differentials [was] relinquished in favor (sic) of policies designed for a quick economic recovery. The overall provision of special education is low, although significant increases in provision have occurred since 1949. Facilities are available mainly for blind and/or deaf children. In 1987, 62 per cent of students in receipt of special education were boys, again indicating significant under-representation of girls in these schools (UNICEF, 1989:117).

REGIONAL AND ETHNIC DIFFERENTIALS BY GENDER

Aggregate figures tend to obscure regional, rural/urban and ethnic variations in access to education. However, all these variations are cross-cut by male/female differentials. The children remaining outside the formal primary education system are 'mostly girls, mostly from rural and remote mountainous areas, and from minority group. Data for 1988 show that economically deprived provinces and regions such as Guizhou, Tibet, Gansu and Ningxia revealed greater gender differentials in primary level enrolment ratios than urban centres such as Beijing, Tianjin, and Shanghai.

Likewise, the 1982 census indicates that, in general, provinces with below average literacy rates exhibited greater male/female differentials in literacy. Xinjiang province, despite being a non-Han Chinese border area, with a large Muslim population, has above average literacy rates and one of the lowest gender differentials in literacy of all provinces and regions (i.e. overall literacy of 69 per cent ; 64 per cent for women and 75 per cent for men).

The relatively high literacy in this region may be partly explained by in-migration of Han Chinese and attempts to 'sinicise' the population. Variations in literacy rates by ethnic group have also been identified. Several interesting features emerge from this data. Firstly, the majorities *Han* Chinese (who form about 95 per cent of the total population) are not the ethnic group with the highest literacy rate and the gender gap in literacy among the *Han* is comparatively wide.

Secondly, the most literate groups, which are also those with the smallest gender gaps in literacy, are concentrated in the North and North-east (one of the areas of China with a long history of economic development). The *Kazaks*, concentrated in the North-west border areas, also, surprisingly, have a very high literacy rate. Thirdly, the lowest literacy rates are found among minority groups in the South-west and, particularly, Tibet. For these groups, the gender gap in literacy is wide, ranging between 26 and 44 per cent age points.

ACADEMIC PERFORMANCE

Various studies of academic records within the tertiary sector have indicated that the performance of female students equals or surpasses that of male students. However, some studies have shown that female performance is perceived, by both sexes, to be due to hard work rather than intellectual gift. Information on performance by sex within the primary or secondary sectors is currently unavailable.

An increase in female drop out rates over the last decade, particularly in rural areas, has been reported and this has generated a great deal of debate within the Chinese press. However, these rates are difficult to determine accurately because of the way in which enrolment ratios have been exaggerated. The following sections examine, in turn, the supply and demand factors which have contributed to the persistent gender gaps in education and, more specifically, to the recent increase in female dropout.

CONSTRAINTS TO FEMALE PARTICIPATION

Supply Factors

Supply factors include the extent of provision of educational infrastructure, the quality of education and the availability of incentives for attendance. Supply factors may be of limited relevance in the primary and junior secondary sectors, where provision has been adequate to meet demand since the 1950s, such that: "the parental decision whether to educate a son or a daughter is governed by patterns of social, demographic, and economic incentives rather than by accessibility of schooling.

However, quality of provision at these levels, and in some areas, availability of schooling, is emerging as major concerns. The demand for tertiary education currently exceeds availability and thus supply factors are important in this instance. Although actual numbers of university places have grown over the last three decades, demand for these places has grown at a greater rate, thereby dramatically increasing competition for places. There is evidence to suggest that when competition for places increases, males tend to be privileged over females.

Increasing Costs of Education

A major economic barrier to girls' education is the resurgence of fees and other costs for education, especially during the period of high inflation in the mid to late 1980s. Although in theory tuition fees are not charged for education, other miscellaneous costs such as registration fees, graduation and examination fees, levies for burglary prevention and school repairs can add up to a significant sum. It is common for families to pay between one and ten yuan per term at primary level and higher rates at secondary and tertiary levels.

Within urban areas, these costs are sometimes borne by a parent's workplace. However, rural farming families do not have the option of transferring costs in this manner and so the impact of the growing private cost of education has fallen more heavily within rural areas. Again, this may act as a major disincentive to female education. Within the university system tuition and lodging are provided free and students pay only for maintenance.

A survey undertaken by the National Women's Federation found that 38 per cent of females studying at five universities received either minimal or no support from their families and were forced to rely on special subsidies and scholarships given to poor students by the government.

Quality of Provision

Current systems of financing education have a significant impact of the quality of education available. In 1985 only 2.7 per cent, and in 1988 2.3 per cent of GNP was allocated to education by the government. Local government, and communities (including factories and other enterprises) finance a significant proportion of the cost of education. As a result, there are considerable regional differences in the provision and quality of educational facilities. Indeed, the future impact of the current economic restructuring of enterprises on the financing of education could be quite dramatic, potentially leading to a fall in the supply of school places and/or to even greater geographical inequities in provision.

Although these factors will affect both males and females, the inadequate provision of facilities and equipment is likely to interact with demand factors to strengthen the bias against female participation within the education system. Within the primary sector many schools have been reported as overcrowded; little budgetary allocation is made for textbooks and other equipment and thus access to provisions depends to a large extent on supply by parents and even teachers; teaching methods and curricula tend to be both dull and rigid.

There is even evidence that the current system of financing education has negatively affected the provision of schools. For example, in Shaanxi Province between 1982 and 1986 the number of rural primary schools fell by 288, thereby effectively disenfranchising over half a million students from access to education. Both the numbers of female teachers and quality of teaching provided are important factors influencing the access of females to education.

Student/teacher ratios in primary schools tend to be quite low (i.e. average of 23:1 in 1985) compared to other low-income countries, although there are great rural/urban variations. In 1988 women comprised 42 per cent of primary teaching staff and 31 per cent of teaching staff at secondary level. Women have even less representation within the tertiary sector. In 1985 only 26.69 per cent of university teaching staff were female, a distribution reflective of the proportion of female students within the university system.

Bibliography

Barnes, J.A. (1961). "Physical and Social Kinship". *Philosophy of Science* **28** (3): 296–299.

Boon, James A.; Schneider, David M. (October 1974). "Kinship vis-a-vis Myth Contrasts in Levi-Strauss' Approaches to Cross-Cultural Comparison Kinship vis-a-vis Myth Contrasts in Levi-Strauss' Approaches to Cross-Cultural Comparison". *American Anthropolgist* **76** (4): 799–817

Broch-Due, Vigdis, Ingrid Rudie, and Tony Bleie, eds. (1993). *Carved Flesh/Cast Selves: Gendered Symbols and Social Practices.* Oxford: BERG.

Butler, Judith. (1993). *Bodies that Matter: On the Discursive Limits of "Sex."* New York: Routledge.

Butler, Judith.(1990). *Gender Trouble. Feminism and the Subversion of Identity.* New York: Routledge.

Carsten, Janet, and Stephen Hugh-Jones, eds. (1995). *About the House: Lévi-Strauss and Beyond.* New York: Cambridge University Press.

Carsten, Janet. (2004). *After Kinship.* New York: Cambridge University Press.

Carsten, Janet. (2004). *Cultures of Relatedness.* New York: Cambridge University Press.

Collier, Jane F., and Sylvia J. Yanagisako, eds. (1987). *Gender and Kinship: Essays Towards a Unified Analysis.* Stanford, Calif.: Stanford University Press.

Comaroff, John L. *The Meaning of Marriage Payments.* New York: Academic. Cooper, Frederick, and Ann Laura Stoler, eds. *Tensions of Empire: Colonial Cultures in a Bourgeois World.* Berkeley: University of California Press, 1997.

De Jorio, Rosa. (2001). "Women's Organizations, the Ideology of Kinship, and the State in Postindependence Mali." In *New Directions in Anthropological Kinship,* edited by Linda Stone. Lanham, Md.: Rowman and Littlefield.

Evans-Pritchard, Edward E. (1940). *The Nuer: A Description of the Modes of Livelihood and Political Institutions of a Nilotic People.* Oxford: Clarendon.

Feinberg, Richard, and Martin Ottenheimer. (2001). *The Cultural Analysis of Kinship: The Legacy of David M. Schneider.* Urbana: University of Illinois Press.

Fortes, Meyer, and E. E. Evans-Pritchard, eds.(1940) *African Political Systems.* London: Oxford University Press.

Fortes, Meyer, ed. (1962). *Marriage in Tribal Societies.* Cambridge, U.K.: Cambridge University Press.

Fortes, Meyer. (1949). *The Web of Kinship among the Tallensi.* London: Oxford University Press.

Fox, Robin (1977). *Kinship and Marriage: An Anthropological Perspective.* Harmondsworth: Penguin.

Franklin, Sarah, and Susan McKinnon, eds. (2001) *Relative Values: Reconfiguring Kinship Studies.* Durham, N.C.: Duke University Press.

Ginsburg, Faye D., and Rayna Rapp, eds. (1995). *Conceiving the New World Order: The Global Politics of Reproduction.* Berkeley: University of California Press.

Goody, Esther. (1962). "Conjugal Separation and Divorce Among the Gonja of Northern Ghana." In *Marriage in Tribal Societies,* edited by Meyer Fortes. Cambridge, U.K.: Cambridge University Press.

Goody, Jack. (1983). *The Development of the Family and Marriage in Europe.* Cambridge, U.K.: Cambridge University Press.

Goody, Jack. (1990) *The Oriental, the Ancient, and the Primitive: Systems of Marriage and the Family in the Pre-Industrial Societies of Eurasia.* New York: Cambridge University Press.

Goody, Jack., ed. (1958). *The Developmental Cycle in Domestic Groups.* Cambridge, U.K.: Cambridge University Press.

Gottlieb, Alma. (2004) *The Afterlife Is Where We Come from: The Culture of Infancy in West Africa.* Chicago: University of Chicago Press.

Haraway, Donna. (1991). *Simians, Cyborgs, and Women: The Reinvention of Nature.* New York: Routledge.

Haraway, Donna. (1989). *Primate Visions: Gender, Race, and Nature in the World of Modern Science.* New York: Routledge.

Houseman, Michael; White, Douglas R. (1998a). "Network mediation of exchange structures: Ambilateral sidedness and property flows in Pul Eliya". in Thomas Schweizer and Douglas R. White. *Kinship, Networks and Exchange.* Cambridge University Press. pp. 59-89.

Houseman, Michael; White, Douglas R. (1998b). "Taking Sides: Marriage Networks and Dravidian Kinship in Lowland South America". in Maurice Godelier, Thomas Trautmann and F.Tjon Sie Fat.. *Transformations of Kinship.* Smithsonian Institution Press. pp. 214-243.

Hutchinson, Sharon Elaine. (2000). "Identity and Substance: The Broadening Base of Relatedness Among the Nuer of Southern Sudan." In *Cultures of Relatedness,* edited by Janet Carsten. Cambridge, U.K.: Cambridge University Press.

Jayawardena, Chandra (1977). "Women and Kinship in Aceh Besar, Northern Sumatra." *Ethnology* 16:21-38.

Malinowski, Bronislaw (1929). *The Sexual Life of Savages in North Western Melanesia.* London: Routledge and Kegan Paul.

Read, Dwight W. (2001). "Anthropological Theory Formal analysis of kinship terminologies and its relationship to what constitutes kinship". *Anthropological Theory* 1 (2): 239-267.

Reid, Anthony (1979). *The Blood of the People: Revolution and the End of Traditional Rule in Northern Sumatra.* Kuala Lumpur: Oxford University Press.

Siegel, James T. (1979). *Shadow and Sound: The Historical Thought of a Sumatran People.* Chicago: University of Chicago Press.

Trautmann, Thomas R. (2008). *Lewis Henry Morgan and the Invention of Kinship, New Edition.*

Wallace, Anthony F.; Atkins, John (1960). ""The Meaning of Kinship Terms." The Meaning of Kinship Terms". *American Anthropologist* 62 (1): 58–80.

White, Douglas R.; Ulla C. Johansen (2005). *Network Analysis and Ethnographic Problems: Process Models of a Turkish Nomad Clan.* New York: Rowman and Littlefield.

INDEX

T

V

W